FREE TO STAND
FOR TRUTH AND JUSTICE

Laurent Gbagbo
with
François Mattei

FREE TO STAND
FOR TRUTH AND JUSTICE

Max Milo
ESSAIS-DOCUMENTS

Max Milo, Paris, 2023
www.maxmilo.com
ISBN : 978-2-315-01260-2

THE SCENT OF FREEDOM

At night, for all these years, his cell has always remained lit until dawn. True to form, Laurent Gbagbo reads or watches television at night until he falls asleep.

This Saturday, October 13, 2018, he donned the African shirt that his son Michel had worn to him from Abidjan, a few days earlier, in the visiting room of Scheveningen prison. A first visit and reunion between the eldest son and father, who hadn't seen each other for seven years: arrested, detained for many months, then banned from leaving Ivorian territory, Michel was finally able to travel to the Netherlands for a visit to the International Criminal Court penitentiary.

When I see him again, we pick up the thread of our conversation, begun in 2005 and never interrupted. At the back of the room, Charles Blé Goudé, ex-leader of the Patriotes, receives visitors from Belgium. He sometimes prepares African dishes, which he shares with his famous fellow prisoner and his visitors.

The latest developments in the trial do not seem to be upsetting Gbagbo too much - he has always said he was serene - even if this time they have given him renewed hope of a favorable outcome. As the deadline approaches in The Hague, he looks back on this violent episode in his political life:

- What brought me here," he says, "was the old debate about emancipation from the old framework imposed on Africa by the French Constitution of 1958. In fact, the battle for real independence… Taking over Article 8 of the Constitution of the Fourth Republic, Article 12 of the Constitution of the Fifth gave France's former colonies a status of false independence, where Foreign Affairs, Defense, the Mint as well as Higher Education remained in the hands of Paris. This is how our status, not to say our destiny, is engraved in the marble of the French Constitution! As far as higher education was concerned, it was decided one day to set up universities in Africa to limit immigration to France, by keeping the students there… The 1962 agreements finished sewing the straitjacket that kept us in infantilism and dependence, by giving France priority access to the riches of our countries' subsoil. It must be said that Houphouët-Boigny believed that the duty of Africans was to work for the greatness of France…

- Haven't things changed all the same?

- The texts and the spirit are still there, but the time of the killers has passed. Thomas Sankara in Burkina, Modibo Keita in Mali, Sylvanus Olympio in Togo, assassinated by soldiers taking orders, it's no longer possible… Today, there is public opinion in Africa. In Burkina Faso, Blaise Compaoré was ousted by his people… The time has come to finally build our independence in French-speaking Africa. I'm not talking here about Cameroon, which has its own particular history, and which is following its own path… My training as a historian and political activist prepared me for this task. It has occupied me all my life, and that's what's been going on here, at the ICC, since the start of my trial. I've never experienced it as a judicial matter, but as a special situation in the political battle I've been waging for my country, for Africa, since I entered politics. Even locked up in the fifteen square meters of my cell… I didn't go round in circles… I kept looking and walking in the same direction. Yes, Africa is changing: there are now African countries that dare to ask the Russians for advice on their Defense, and even Ouattara, who is French-born, knows the way to Beijing… For my part, I'd like us to really get out of this Article 12 and take care of our own Defense and our own currency.

- Are you still thinking about the terrible 2010 election?

- Of course, because that's where the trap was set to get me here. This was the first point I raised at the first court hearing, on December 5, 2011. I told the prosecutor that it was essential to know who had won the 2010 elections in Côte d'Ivoire. Without an answer to this question, how could we determine who was primarily responsible for the unrest and crimes that followed? I've been told that's not the question, but it is the fundamental one. In truth, in October 2010, I knew from the very first round that Ouattara had come third, and that he would therefore not be able to take part in the second round. People from Henri Konan Bédié's PDCI party - which came second - came to see me and passed on messages. I called Bernard Ehni, a close friend of Bédié, who has since become ambassador to Ghana. There had been a lot of fraud and irregularities. Ehni told me: "I was with Bédié all evening, we worked together. I'll call you tomorrow." Of course, there was talk of Bédié officially contesting the election. In the end, he didn't do so until the fifth day. Too late, the claim was no longer admissible. Bédié is not only an economist, he's also a lawyer. He knew what he was doing. He gave in to pressure from France, and to his wallet… Afterwards, it was all a staged event to justify my violent ousting. I had asked for a recount under international supervision, but the electoral material had been destroyed to make verification impossible. In any case, Barack Obama sent Raila Odinga, the Prime Minister of Kenya, who is of the same ethnic group as Obama's father, to Abidjan. The message was to ask me to step down… There was never any other intention than that: to oust me.

- At the end of this trial, what are your plans?

- My ambition is to return home to Côte d'Ivoire. I've reserved a house to welcome me. *I'm going back home!* I've already had mattresses bought to replace those stolen from my little village home. They've also taken all the sheets, and a tiny fridge that sits next to my bed. I'm not complaining: so many Ivorians have lost everything! I only mention this to emphasize that the rebels **were**, for many of them, just poor, manipulated, starving people: the theft of my mattresses is a case in point.

- And become president again in 2020?

- You don't have to be president to be involved in politics and be useful. Côte d'Ivoire, Africa, is my life, and I will always be concerned by their destiny. Are they prepared to resort to illegality to prevent me from returning home?

- What should our relations with France be like?

- Since the 1990s, France no longer has the financial and military means to manage Africa, or to play Zorro on the continent. It needs to reconsider its relationship with its former colonies. Africa's needs are growing fast, and France is no longer in a position to meet them. On the other hand, people in Paris should understand, and be wary: the new generations don't look like mine, taught from kindergarten to baccalauréat by French people, and white people at that. When I wasn't president yet, and didn't even have the means to help them, my grown-up daughters went to the United States, to Atlanta, to study. They no longer had the exclusive fascination with France. Young Africans know that they're not welcome there. It's no longer a dream for them. As a result, they are less well disposed towards France and the French than we are, and completely impervious to the arguments used to justify their power over our affairs… There's always the same underlying accusation: we're not capable of governing ourselves, and we don't know what democracy is…
When I hear, for example, French criticism of Kagame's power in Rwanda, judged to be too authoritarian, I say to myself that, yes, Parisian elites do have short memories, and are easily arrogant: Habib Bourguiba, in Tunisia, in agreement with Paris, reformed his country based on the iron power of his single party… Léopold Senghor created three parties in Senegal by decree, to please the West, in an imitation of false democracy… Amani Diori, in Niger, also came to power at the head of his single party, the only one authorized by Paris, which had banned a multi-party

system… He was opportunely ousted by a coup d'état sponsored by Paris, when he had the unfortunate idea of trying to negotiate uranium, the country's main resource, with Canada, which offered him a much higher price than France. If I add, for the sake of argument, that Madame Chirac was once invalidated in a local election because there were more voters than electors, I think we should stop taking lessons. I fought to establish a multi-party system in Côte d'Ivoire against Houphouët's one-party system, validated by Paris, and then to build institutions in my country. I disturbed them because I was popular. That's the profile they don't like, and it's a mistake in the medium and long term. With us, we'll have to develop partnerships, giving us complete freedom of choice, and everything will be better.

Today, I'm looking to the future, and I've never stopped doing so. You don't invest all your strength and all your life in the service of the Ivorian people, and of certain ideas, paying the price, only to give up at the whim of circumstances, even prison.

- Do you think Côte d'Ivoire can now live in peace?

- Everyone knows that Ivorians are peaceful. Being violent is not their nature. Everyone knows that violence has been imported into Côte d'Ivoire. Ivorians will come together to live the best life, together, if we give them back what they aspire to: truth, justice and dignity.

FOREWORD

Doors are the only thing in Scheveningen. I went there in all seasons for six years to continue chatting with Laurent Gbagbo. An ongoing conversation, started in 2005, often interrupted, never broken off. I found him again behind the walls of the *Inrichting Haaglanden Penitentiary*, at 32 Pompstationsweg, a terminus in principle dedicated to genocidaires, bloodthirsty tyrants and other dictators responsible for bloodbaths. The time has undoubtedly come for a less one-sided vision than that dispensed at the hottest moments of political and military combat, when the media artillery thundered. The war is over, the media fog has dissipated, the living are demanding to know why mass graves dug all over the country contain so many dead.

For ten years, Gbagbo and his family have been showered with an uninterrupted stream of accusations. It's hard to imagine what more could be added. We know in detail the black book of what he is accused of. Listening to him, and at the same time recounting a certain number of facts that are often concealed, can only contribute to a more complete vision of history. Laurent Gbagbo was for a long time alone in the dock at the International Criminal Court. Charles Blé Goudé, leader of the Young Patriots, joined him there, probably escaping death in Ouattara's prisons, only to survive in The Hague. Gbagbo's lawyers may well have persuaded the International Criminal Court to extend its investigations upstream of the post-electoral crisis, in 2002, to the roots of the crisis and the war, but they still haven't seen the judges tackle the exactions perpetrated by the rebels, and their leaders, in a finally global approach to the Ivorian affair.

A revealing chronology of causes and effects would pinpoint real responsibilities. Even if no one deserves to be given the good Lord without confession. If the Court persists, despite its promises of fair justice and the fight against impunity, in refusing to investigate the crimes of the ex-rebellion and its leaders, now in power, if it is content to judge only the defeated, then it will confirm to the world that it has allowed itself to be instrumentalized by certain countries and certain interests. Amnesty International, in a report published on February 26, 2013, castigates under the title *La Loi des vainqueurs* a one-eyed justice system, in Côte d'Ivoire and at The Hague. On its online newspaper the same day, RFI quotes this comment from Stephan Oberreit, director of Amnesty International France: "*From the moment when everyone reco-gnizes that there have been exactions on both sides, but that there have only been prosecutions on one side - at the level of the International Criminal Court, with Laurent Gbagbo and his wife, as well as at the level of Ivorian national justice, where only former members of the government or those close to Laurent Gbagbo are being prosecuted -, this creates a feeling of imba-lance and biased justice, which is detrimental to national reconciliation.*" Guillaume Soro, the current President of the National Assembly, doesn't care. As he shamelessly declared in an interview recorded by Cameroon's STV television: "*Where have you seen that justice for the vanquished has ever existed?*" Common sense, according to Soro, who unfortunately has a point. It would therefore be logical, according to this writing of history, to send a raped woman who has gouged out her attacker's eye to court alone, under the rapist's mocking eye… Here, then, is a counter-field, a multi-faceted version of a few moments in the Ivorian crisis, through a gallery of mirrors recomposing a more conformist reality. A reality that the young institution of the International Criminal Court has not seen fit to examine in all its complexity. It only took into consideration the defeated side in a civil war in which the aggressors, who came from abroad, armed and supported first covertly, then openly by France, committed every crime to carry out a bloody coup d'état, long premeditated. Fortunately, the wide world is not only populated by deaf, blind and mute monkeys.

1.

"I KNOW THAT TRUTH
WILL TRIUMPH IN THE END"

After all, it was only an electoral dispute: you don't go to war if you've won the elections, as Laurent Gbagbo has been saying for the past eight years.

Back to the facts:

Abidjan, April 11, 2011, late morning. When a French Sagaie tank blows up the gate and perimeter wall of the residence of the President of the Republic of Côte d'Ivoire, the tank's crew asks no questions. The last links in the military chain of command held by the Elysée Palace, the men of the 12th cuirassier regiment finish the job. Louis Ferdinand Destouches, better known by his pen name, Céline, who served as a brigadier, then Maréchal des Logis, during the 14-18 war, described in Voyage au bout de la Nuit, and Casse Pipe, the deeds of their cavalry ancestors, with sleeves emblazoned with the "Dauphin".

Surrounding the tankers was the 4th regiment of chasseurs from Bitche, who climbed to the target with them. The President of the French Republic, head of the armed forces, ordered them to open the door to the rebels, renamed Forces Nouvelles, then Forces républicaines de Côte d'Ivoire, to hand over Laurent Gbagbo, and install their leader in power, Alassane Ouattara. Ouattara declared himself elected with

54.10% of the vote in the second round of the presidential election held on November 28, 2010, according to the count by the Chairman of the Independent Electoral Commission, who spoke alone without consulting the members of his Commission. This figure will not be endorsed by the Constitutional Council, the only court empowered to rule on the validity of an election and proclaim the winner. Youssouf Bakayoko, Chairman of the Independent Electoral Commission, which is made up of a majority of Gbagbo's political opponents, announced the results under astonishing conditions. The results were announced on the evening of December 2, after the legal deadline of three days stipulated by the Constitution had passed. What's more, they were announced by the sole Chairman of the Electoral Commission from Ouattara's campaign headquarters, the Hôtel du Golf. At the same time, all the other members of the Commission were waiting in vain for their chairman, who had arranged to meet them elsewhere while he was taking part in a staged event organized by the French and American ambassadors. Both were present alongside the Commission Chairman. The French ambassador, Jean-Marc Simon, who told me with the utmost seriousness: *"I was passing by the hotel to see Soro, I don't remember why, he told me that Bakayoko was in a room"*, and the US ambassador, Philip Carter III. The cameras of France 24, the French public channel, are there, although the Ivorian press has not been invited. All journalists are awaiting the results, as expected, at the Electoral Commission headquarters.

Barack Obama and the UN's special representative in Côte d'Ivoire, Young-jin Choi, validated this incredible modus operandi and result, which Nicolas Sarkozy activated with a letter to the President of the Electoral Commission. Exiled by helicopter, Youssouf Bakayoko took refuge in Neuilly-sur-Seine, France, immediately after the announcement, aware and no doubt frightened by the illegality of his proclamation.

Nowhere else could such a spectacle have been staged as in Africa. Eighty coups d'état in the former French colonies over fifty years of independence show that elections there are often no more than a puppet show, with the strings being pulled behind the scenes.

What was the point of Laurent Gbagbo and Alassane Ouattara signing a proclamation addressed to all Ivorian citizens on November 27, 2010, in which they called for calm and pledged to respect constitutional rules, which stipulate that the Electoral Commission must calculate the results achieved by each candidate within three days, before the Constitutional Council verifies and validates them, and then proclaims the winner of the elections?

On December 2, with the blessing of Sarkozy and the United Nations, Youssouf Bakayoko pulled Alassane Ouattara's name out of the hat, in violation of the Ivorian constitution.

The following day, December 3, 2010, Côte d'Ivoire's Constitutional Council declared President Gbagbo elected with 51.45% of the vote. In so doing, it acknowledged the massive fraud that had taken place in the rebel-controlled northern part of the country.

The Constitutional Council has made up its mind: it is the highest legal body in the country and the only one empowered to designate the winner of the presidential elections. On December 3, it gave its name: Laurent Gbagbo.

Thus began the post-electoral drama in Côte d'Ivoire, when these elections were supposed to resolve the politico-military crisis that began in 2002. Albert Bourgi (not to be confused with his brother, lawyer-affairist Robert Bourgi), professor of Political Science at Reims, old friend of Laurent Gbagbo, who also knows Alassane Ouattara and the political life of the continent very well, declared on June 8, 2012 on African TV, TVM: "[…] *I don't know of many elections whose results were proclaimed under conditions comparable to what happened in Côte d'Ivoire* […]. *In addition to the Ivorian institutions, there was of course the United Nations* […], *which was supposed to provide certification. This notion of certification had never been applied by the United Nations in other peacekeeping operations in Africa. A completely vague notion, then. As vague as the official election results. Nobody knows them in detail. We don't know the results from the polling stations. Neither you, nor I, nor any other observer or researcher wanting to work on these elections knows them in detail. We don't know the results poll by poll. The abstention rate is a mystery* […]."

It wasn't until the fall of Gbagbo on April 11, 2011, that Paul Yao N'Dré's Constitutional Council proclaimed Alassane Ouattara President, although it did not formally reverse its December 3, 2010 decision. To establish the legitimacy of the new President, the Council relied on the decisions of the UN and African institutions. Thanks to the force of the international community's bayonets, the Ivorian Constitutional Council is suddenly respectable again in the West! At the end of March 2013, Vladimir Putin announced that the heads of the BRICS (Brazil, Russia, India, China, South Africa), emerging countries that see themselves as a counterweight to Europe and America, and are in favor of a multipolar world order, would no longer tolerate the use of force against sovereign states. For them, it's a question of drawing lessons from the military operations carried out in Libya and Côte d'Ivoire.

In Côte d'Ivoire, since the death of Houphouët-Boigny, the country's first president, there has never been a peaceful transfer of power. Henri Konan Bédié, President of the National Assembly, succeeded Houphouët in 1993, after the latter's death, in accordance with constitutional provisions. He went on to win the 1995 presidential election without glory, the united opposition having boycotted the ballot due to the introduction of a new Electoral Code he had inspired, requiring candidates to be born of an Ivorian father and mother. He fled to France when General Robert Guéï overthrew him in a coup d'état on December 24, 1999. Laurent Gbagbo subsequently defeated General Guéï in the presidential elections on October 22, 2000. Guéï withdrew to the provinces after attempting to contest the result with a military coup. A sarabande that ushered in the post-Houphouët era and the beginnings of a very long crisis.

In 2010, the crisis is at its height, following a presidential election that all parties had hoped for. On December 4, 2010, Gbagbo and Ouattara each took the oath of office. While President Gbagbo did so in compliance with constitutional rules, his opponent engaged in a sham at his campaign headquarters, applauded by the international community. The election ten years in the making produces two presidents. Only the naive are surprised. This is because the other players, including France, had prepared for it. Some had, it is said, imagined it, or even organized it: a great muddle that allows for all kinds of maneuvers. The outgoing president was sworn in on Saturday at the presidential palace by the president of the Constitutional Council. The challenger proclaimed himself president in a letter dated the same day, addressed to the President of the Constitutional Council, whose authority he thus implicitly - and paradoxically - recognized, even though he did not respect his decision to declare Laurent Gbagbo the winner of the election... The members of the Constitutional Council rejected Ouattara's action as unconstitutional. Ouattara camped out in a hotel, the Hôtel du Golf, for months with his French advisors, his warlords and his soldiers. Despite the Constitutional Council's refusal, he appointed a counter-government. The Electoral Commission, the UN Special Representative and finally the Constitutional Council gave three different results, points out Thabo Mbeki, the second President of the Republic of South Africa after Nelson Mandela. He knows the issue well, having mediated in the Ivorian crisis in 2004. He came to Abidjan with the idea that Gbagbo was wrong, but left convinced of the opposite.

On New Year's Eve 2011, in his televised greetings to the nation, Gbagbo proposed that the votes be recounted, in a general audit of the elections, under international supervision: "*We must understand how, announced as the year of elections, the year of the end of the crisis, 2010 is ending in perplexity. While Ivorians are suffering the violence of an armed rebellion at home, they have been the object of international hostility abroad, since the proclamation of the results of the presidential election on November 28, 2010. This is unfair. We are wondering about the reasons for the international community's attitude towards us; an attitude that has not been observed anywhere else before in a political crisis internal to a state... This is why I am proposing an evaluation committee designed to find out the facts and establish the truth about the conduct of the elections in Côte d'Ivoire. I am confident that the truth will triumph in the end. We have the law and the truth on our side.*"

Rejected by Young-jin Choi, the UN Secretary-General's Special Representative in Côte d'Ivoire, who claimed to have counted three times already, the recount was also rejected by Ouattara, France and the United States. Shortly afterwards, on the orders of the UNOCI, all ballot papers and documents relating to the election were destroyed, leaving no possibility of a peaceful outcome, let alone a recount... Laurent Gbagbo's fate was sealed. All his speeches and appeals will henceforth be considered derisory and illegal. They will be preferred to a military attack against

Gbagbo, whereas a new vote count under international supervision would have ended the debate without a single death, according to observers. *"If the final result had been a Gbagbo victory, the rebels would have taken up arms against him anyway,"* Jean-Marc Simon, the former French ambassador to Abidjan, told me. This linchpin of the operation thus dispels any regrets about a negotiated solution. A final strike by the French Licorne military contingent, after ten days of bombardment of the presidential residence by Puma and Gazelle helicopters, relayed by those of the UNOCI, brings to a close on April 11 not only this post-electoral crisis, but also Côte d'Ivoire's most troubled decade.

"I WANTED TO GIVE MEANING TO THE WORD 'INDEPENDENCE'"

At no time since his first election to the presidency in October 2000 has the Élysée under Chirac, then Sarkozy, accepted Laurent Gbagbo. Anchored historically and economically by the French presence in Africa, Côte d'Ivoire is the locomotive of West Africa, accounting for 40% of the country's gross domestic product. It has always attracted the jealous attention of the Élysée Palace, and all manner of covetousness. France has Côte d'Ivoire under its skin. With its cocoa, coffee, bananas, palm oil, deposits of oil, gas, uranium, diamonds, manganese, rare metals, construction sites, transport, communication networks and ports, this land of milk and honey represents exceptional financial and economic stakes… Major French groups - Areva, Castel, Total, Bouygues, Bolloré, Orange, Véolia - Anglo-Saxon groups - Armajaro, the cocoa empire run until 2013 in Africa by Loïc Folloroux, son of Dominique Ouattara - and other chocolate giants - Nestlé, Cargill, etc. - have expanded there without competition, monopolizing all the key sectors and making the fortunes of many. Not to mention Air France, whose long-held monopoly on major African destinations, with prohibitively high ticket prices, has bolstered its coffers. A privileged position, an advantage acquired through colonization and perpetuated by the Françafrique system. Even if, since François Mitterrand's La Baule speech on June 20, 1990, it has been fashionable to pretend that this is ancient history: *"The wind of freedom that has blown in the East must inevitably blow one day in the direction of the South* [...] *There is no development without democracy, and there is no democracy without development"*, declared the President, through the pen of Erik Orsenna.

Twenty-four years later, France still sees itself as the master of the game, as it demonstrated in Côte d'Ivoire, a veritable chasse gardée and keystone of the edifice. Until the last few years, the constant imperative was to control this country, without which the entire French system in Africa would collapse. But Gbagbo is not the man Jacques Chirac wanted. The French head of state knows that he will refuse the legacy of total submission to Paris, initiated by Félix Houphouët-Boigny, one of the founding fathers of Françafrique. When he fought against him in opposition, Gbagbo called Houphouët a dictator, criticizing his blind allegiance to France... Through Gbagbo, it was France that felt targeted. In the 80s, Gbagbo became the historic opponent of the "Father of the Nation" and his policy of French assimilation. First Jacques Chirac, then Nicolas Sarkozy, fought him in a succession of high-tension episodes interspersed with short-lived lulls. Against this opponent of its Ivorian political allies, France has always favored its more understanding, docile and assimilated friends. Chirac adored Houphouët-Boigny, raised in the seraglio and a French minister under the Fourth and Fifth Republics, as did his successor, Henri Konan Bédié, whom he personally supported with the RPR as far back as the 1990s.

Félix Houphouët-Boigny is the product of French nostalgia: the ideal African leader. But the mold from which he emerged was broken. He was a member of parliament, then a minister of the French Republic, before becoming his country's first president. His personal links with the men in power in France - today we would say his networks - earned him their unfailing support. Around him, at every level of his administration and government, were devoted French civil servants who served Paris before thinking of Abidjan. His manifest desire to freeze his capital in the status of a prefecture of a French province embodied what he envisioned for his country and for Africa. From his real name Dia Houphouët, he adopted the first name Félix in 1915, then added Boigny (Bélier) to his patronymic in 1945, as a skilful sculptor of his own destiny, of his own statue. A politician with two faces.

Abroad, Boigny knew how to distill messages of peace and humanism. In Africa, he supported French interests, and acted without hesitation against all socialist regimes, and against some of his African brothers, without reluctance to collaborate in coups d'état, civil wars, or at the very least, to carry out propaganda missions. He was convinced, and convincing. A black crusader for the white cause, an African who was more French than the French. In 1946, he initiated the law that definitively abolished the forced labor that white settlers had generalized in Africa. France's beloved dictator, his wildest whims were accepted and satisfied by the protecting power: the Basilica of Yamoussoukro, "bigger than the Basilica of Saint Peter in Rome" as he had dreamed, was naturally built in the middle of the bush by French companies. In one of the stained-glass windows of the Notre-Dame-de-la-Paix cathedral, his effigy appears as Jesus. **But everyone forgave Houphouët everything in those days,** comments Gbagbo. **In the 60s, he was sent to the United Nations to defend France's civilizing action in Africa, against American and Russian criticism...**

This is the landscape in which Laurent Gbagbo appeared from the outset, as an impediment to going round in circles. He was accused of everything, including being a xenophobic nationalist, because he didn't want to see his country - the honey of all neighboring countries - swamped by armed invaders, and because he believed it was up to Ivorians to write the history of Côte d'Ivoire.

A real culture shock. A break with the Houphouët model that was too brutal and unmanageable for a political France that was struggling, both outside and inside its borders, to renew its relationship with the world, and to project itself towards its "new frontier": Europe. This was undoubtedly because it was having difficulty changing itself, due to a political class more accustomed to managing the achievements of the past than imagining a future.

The days of France's "pretty colonies" are long gone. No sooner had it granted independence to Côte d'Ivoire than France took back with one hand what it had given with the other, and installed Félix Houphouët-Boigny, its worthy representative, in a sham presidential election in which he was the only candidate.

"The Old Sage", this was the flattering nickname he was given in France until his death in 1993, at a time when nobody in the West thought of discussing the value of elections won with 100% of the votes cast - without a single invalid or blank vote - in a single-party system, as in 1965 or 1985.

Nor were the methods of such a zealous servant criticized when he mercilessly suppressed regional secessionist unrest or student demonstrations, at the cost of thousands of deaths.

It's easy to understand why the opposition in Côte d'Ivoire was non-existent, or clandestine. Apart from a few pioneers of anti-colonialism, most of them Communists, no one took offense. During the Cold War, it was obviously Houphouët, the friend of the West, the bulwark against Marxist contamination in Africa, who was supported unreservedly.

The fault of Laurent Gbagbo, the historic opponent, surrounded by a few militants from a new underground party, the Front patriotique ivoirien, lies in having disturbed the French political class by breaking the comfortable consensus in which it would have long continued to live happily ever after. The multiparty system, agreed by Houphouët under the constraint of the opposition led by Laurent Gbagbo's FPL, and the emancipation of the Soviet Union's satellite countries after the fall of the Berlin Wall, should have signalled the liberation of Côte d'Ivoire from Franco-African ties.

Yet in 2000, when Gbagbo was elected, Charles Josselin, the Socialist Secretary of State for Cooperation, openly contested the *artificial elimination* of the *most serious candidates*" - by which he meant France's first choices - Bédié and Ouattara. The Élysée Palace was furious to see an intruder sneak in between the two Paris favorites, and win the day.

Laurent Gbagbo remark:

The Élysée has always had these two irons in the fire: "Bédié and Ouattara". The problem in Côte d'Ivoire arose from their rivalry after Houphouët's death, which went as far as Bédié's exclusion of Ouattara, accusing him of dubious nationality. He even issued an international arrest warrant against him for falsifying administrative

documents, which I lifted when I had the power to do so. Today, they are united against me. I wouldn't like to be in the privacy of their conscience...

In Parisian political circles, we're all too familiar with this history "teacher" whose critical analysis disturbs, who gives lessons and writes books on democracy. In Africa, he upsets his fellow presidents, who fear for their rents and situation, and take shelter under the protective wing of France to last. In 2010, Sarkozy naturally preferred his friend of twenty years, Alassane Ouattara, former Prime Minister of Houphouët, senior official at the IMF, familiar with financial and business networks and *persona grata* in Washington. These assets make him the undisputed champion of the new France-USA African tandem. France ensures political stability for its American ally, who does not seek to get involved beyond its economic interests. An American diplomat told me: *"No doubt we would have settled for any other relationship with Côte d'Ivoire, but we're pragmatic, and since France provides the service..."*

As for Laurent Gbagbo, who claims to be a Francophile and Francophone, and intends to free his country from the post-colonial shackles, he has everything to displease. Not only does he not follow the usual policy of reverence towards Paris, but above all, he came to power without any help from France. His long political experience makes him difficult to manipulate. His path is similar to that of many Africans from modest families who have made a career for themselves. Yet he is one of those who do not fall into line, who dream of emancipation and progress. He obtained his baccalaureate in philosophy, followed by a degree in history. A teacher at Abidjan's Lycée Classique, he became a researcher at the Institut d'Histoire, d'Art et d'Archéologie Africaine (IHAAA) in the 1970s. He holds a master's degree in history from the Sorbonne, and in 1979 defended a doctoral thesis entitled *Les Ressorts socio-économiques de la politique ivoirienne: 1940-1960*. In the early 70s, he entered politics, opposing Houphouët, notably to demand a multi-party system. He was imprisoned from March 1971 to January 1973 following major demonstrations by Ivorians, particularly students, demanding democracy. Gbagbo, the democracy fighter, became the undisputed leader of the demonstrators. In 1982, he founded the FPI, which campaigned for an end to the one-party system and the establishment of true democracy in Côte d'Ivoire. To escape the repression of democrats, he was exiled to France for three years in 1985. Back in Abidjan, he was appointed director of the IHAAA, and campaigned for a multi-party system. In October 1990, he stood before the statue of the Commander in the first free presidential elections. He won the status of opposition leader. Gbagbo was elected deputy for the Ouaraghio region in the November legislative elections the same year. In February 1992, as leader of the opposition, he was arrested after student demonstrations calling for democracy. He was sentenced to two years' imprisonment. "Ado", as he was already known, had President Houphouët-Boigny sign an anti-casser law on the eve of Gbagbo's arrest, so that he could put the troublemaker in jail.

Ouattara, a former senior IMF official, was appointed Prime Minister under pressure from France to devalue the CFA franc and restructure the Ivorian economy by privatizing it.

Definitely, the terms of the problem are set. Gbagbo was not chosen, not by Houphouët, not by France, not by international institutions. He owes nothing. And yet, **in ten years, I've been to France three times and to China once, by invitation. What's wrong with that?**

He answers his own question, that of original sin: **I just wanted to give meaning to the word "independence".**

Since 1960, and the reign of Houphouët-Boigny, inventor of the term "Françafrique", this system of financial, economic and political control - born under a façade of decolonization - has continued to operate, without saying its name. Despite regular announcements of its imminent demise, more than fifty years after the French-speaking countries of Black Africa gained independence.

In 1991, it was still the time of Houphouët, France's strongman in Africa since independence in 1960 - as Laurent Gbagbo analyzed in *Agir pour les libertés: "In Côte d'Ivoire, the highest State authorities have little confidence in Ivorians. All responsibilities, the real ones, are entrusted to Frenchmen, with Ivorians having only the titles of facade responsibilities, second-rate responsibilities. Every minister has at least one Frenchman in his cabinet (and I'm not being generous; the vital ministries (Economy, Finance, Planning, etc.) are practically swamped. The French army is lurking between the airport and the canal leading to the port, heavy and hardly reassuring [...] when one of those who truly hold the wheels of our country's economy and politics in their hands breaks the complicit silence that surrounds Côte d'Ivoire to bring to the world's face even a tiny aspect of the political practices of the one who reigns and governs, there is a sign, a symbol: the king is naked."*

To explain, or even justify, this overabundance of French executives in his administration, Houphouët always invoked the lack of competent Ivorian executives. In 2014, nothing has fundamentally changed in Côte d'Ivoire, or in most other French-speaking African countries. While the spy networks of the 60s and 80s have disappeared, the three main founding principles of Françafrique remain: a president chosen or at least accepted by France, a military presence in territories that have been independent in principle for fifty years and, above all, a currency managed in Paris, for states that live their sovereignty on credit, under the authority of the Banque de France. The close collaboration between the French authorities and Alassane Ouattara's camp during the Ivorian crisis of 2010 has given rise to a series of backhanded dealings - and lucrative "pantouflages" - that are reminiscent of Houphouët's heyday.

As La Lettre du Continent explains, "Alongside the theaters of operation, the number of military personnel recycling their skills in African palaces after retirement has not diminished. Experts in crisis management, they act as invaluable informal relays for Paris. General Bruno Clément-Bollée, head of the Licorne force from 2007 to 2008, has activated his Ivorian networks in recent months to lead the inextricable restructuring of the Forces républicaines de Côte d'Ivoire (FRCI). He has landed a contract as special advisor to Alassane Ouattara. He works in tandem with Claude Réglat, another general who has been housed at the Abidjan presidency since his appointment in 2011 by Nicolas Sarkozy. [...] Other senior French officers have preferred to join a structure of their own. With a second hat as a diplomat, General Emmanuel Beth, brother of Frédéric Beth, former head of the French Special Operations Command [...] has been recruited by ESL & Network. Head of the Licorne force from 2002 to 2003, he is to develop the African roots of this business intelligence firm founded by Alexandre Medvedowsky."

On the economic front, French companies own and largely manage the country's ports, telephones, water, electricity and automobile fuel distribution, banks, air and rail transport - in other words, over 30% of the overall economy. Behind this blue-white-red screen, the Anglo-Saxons gradually increased their stake in the Ivorian economy. Alongside Switzerland's Barry Callebaut and the Netherlands' Continaf, they already dominated most of the cocoa trade, of which Côte d'Ivoire is the world's leading producer with 40%. "Africa belongs to Europe," the Franco-Beninese banker and economist Lionel Zinsou once said in one of his lectures. With Cargill and ADM, the Americans are in a strong position. They have won back most of the oil exploitation contracts for the most recent fields.

It was through Ghana that the Americans entered our oil markets. I saw John Atta-Mills, the Ghanaian president, to get us to agree on a 50/50 split, because it's the same slick.

There's also oil in the town of San Pedro, on the border with Liberia, which is our second major port. The first oil company in Côte d'Ivoire was an American-Canadian company. We sold "squares" for exploration, then for exploitation. At the exploration stage, I never saw any French people. One day, Pierre Fakhoury, who had bought some squares, came to see me, very happy, to tell me that Total wanted to buy him out. I realized that there was a lot of oil, and I sold the remaining squares for three times the initial price.

Is this just a coincidence? Since the brutal ousting of Laurent Gbagbo in 2011, Total has been announcing the existence of new deepwater deposits, in May 2014 off the port of San Pedro, and a year earlier on the border with Ghana. As for Bouygues, we learned in March 2014 that it was moving into gas exploitation. Where? Côte d'Ivoire. As for British company Armajaro, world leader in cocoa, it was introduced to the Ivorian market thanks to the intervention of Alassane Ouattara, then deputy director of the IMF. Loïc Folloroux, son of Dominique Ouattara's first wife, becomes Armajaro's Africa Director.

In recent years, all you had to do to know whether a coup d'état was imminent in Côte d'Ivoire was to keep an eye on the cocoa price!

Speculative operations, in the form of massive purchases and stockpiling (in technical terms, this is called "agiotage") designed to boost cocoa prices, curiously enough, took place one month before the attempted military putsch against Laurent Gbagbo in 2002, as well as three months before the 2010 presidential elections. In August 2002, the man now known as "Chocolate Finger", whose name, Anthony Ward, appears at the very top of the Armajaro hierarchy, decreed the sudden purchase of 200,000 tonnes of cocoa. The war triggered by the rebel attack sent prices soaring. Armajaro pocketed a profit of almost 70 million euros.

At the same time as the rebels were occupying more than half the country's territory, neighboring Burkina Faso, a safe haven for the rebels, was becoming an exporter of cocoa (stolen from Côte d'Ivoire), even though it didn't grow any. In July 2010, as the first round of the long-awaited presidential election loomed, the British trader bought 240,000 tonnes of cocoa beans on the London commodities exchange: 7% of world production, 15% of world stocks, plus 700 million euros to buy, an exorbitant profit. Prices soared to an extravagant 3,264 euros per tonne, the highest since 1977. Criticism came from all sides. The competition smelled insider trading, and NGO economic observers saw this infernal game of roulette being played on the backs of Ivorian growers. Never mind, thanks to Ouattara and his son-in-law Loïc Folloroux, Armajaro has made its money. And its chocolate. The anomaly had obviously been spotted by the official services at the time:

In 2007, I launched a major investigation into the cocoa industry, resulting in numerous arrests, a clean-up operation, a serious judicial investigation and a series of trials. All this led to flagrant abuse and fraud on the part of most exporters, to the detriment of the State and planters, and with the self-serving complicity of certain ministers. I know some of them who turned their backs during the last elections to move over to the other side of the political divide, and stay dry...

There were strong suspicions that the cocoa industry was being financed by the rebels, with part of the profits diverted to them by Armajaro, in liaison with Alassane Ouattara and his followers. Cocoa is the gold and blood of Côte d'Ivoire. It has long been used to fuel speculation by foreign companies - Houphouët was confronted with this in his day - slush funds, illicit exports and arms purchases. On April 16, 2004, French-Canadian journalist Guy-André Kieffer disappeared forever while investigating this grey economy where money flows freely. Accusations against the Gbagbo clan, in this case Simone Gbagbo's brother-in-law, came to nothing. A former minister under Laurent Gbagbo, Ahoua Don Mello told me that the journalist had revealed in an article published under a pseudonym in 2002 the imminence of a military attack against Côte d'Ivoire, financed by cocoa industrialists. This other lead has never been explored. Which is astonishing, given the Ouattara family's involvement, through Loïc Folloroux, in the cocoa industry and its secret meanderings at the highest global level. In 2004 and 2005, Adama Bictogo, a close associate of Ouattara, was busy exporting huge quantities of cocoa diverted from Côte d'Ivoire. He passed through the port of Lomé, Togo, using a commercial base in Burkina Faso, Luxembourg and a French bank. We won't know what Kieffer discovered, but it's certain that his investigations threatened many specific business interests. The rebel zone in the north of the country allowed all kinds of trade, with no customs or tax duties, and no controls. A rebel and a businessman, Bictogo subsequently took an interest in everything that glitters: gold trafficking, capturing compensation bonuses for victims of the toxic waste dumped in Abidjan in August 2006 by the cargo ship Probo Koala and the Trafigura company, biometric passports... Promoted to Minister of African Integration by Ouattara, he was dismissed in May 2012, without being prosecuted, for having created other profitable schemes from which he would have profited alone.

During the post-election crisis on January 24, 2011, Guillaume Soro's call for a halt to exports was naturally the first step in Laurent

Gbagbo's economic asphyxiation. Anglo-Saxon operators obey their friend at the IMF with their fingertips. Armajaro chose this precise moment to unblock and sell the 240,000 tonnes purchased seven months earlier at full price, due to the artificially created shortage. The operation did not escape the scrutiny and criticism of the Anglo-Saxon business press.

"MY FATHER LANDED IN FRANCE, IN JANUARY 1940"

When Algeria gained independence in 1962, amidst the convulsions of a long and bloody war (more than a million people are thought to have died), and the exodus of more than a million Europeans, metropolitan France lost its gas and oil at the same time. De Gaulle found the magic potion, thanks to Africa, its raw materials and the allegiance of its heads of state chosen by the Élysée Palace, to maintain France's position as a great power between the two blocs of East and West. Françafrique is not an ideology, but the product of pragmatism and raison d'État. The dogma is France's best interests. The challenge is to maintain France's position among the great powers, and save it from decline. The means: a triple lock, political, military and financial. A Head of State who takes his orders from the secret services, the presence of a permanent military contingent, justified by defense agreements, and, nec plus ultra, like an invisible net, the CFA Franc (Franc des Colonies Françaises d'Afrique), a currency issued in France since 1945, guaranteed by reserves stored at the Banque de France. A real straitjacket.

To understand the Franco-Ivorian crisis, you need to know the main principles of Françafrique, and their current ramifications.

After the humiliation of the German occupation, the end of the Second World War and the weakening of the Republic in the face of its Anglo-Saxon allies, General De Gaulle's idea of France's energy, military and therefore political independence led him to build Françafrique as a model of imperialism. A true French cultural exception. An undertaking to subjugate African states in total contradiction with Gaullist rhetoric glorifying the right of peoples to self-determination. In an organized political schizophrenia, the aim was to safeguard the appearance of a Republic preaching universal values, while at the same time exploiting subservient peoples without a second thought. A devious form of dictatorship, betraying the principles of Liberty, Equality and Fraternity every morning. This adage was not conceived for African children who, for generations, were made to recite *Nos Ancêtres les Gaulois (Our Ancestors the Gauls)*. Embodied today by the debate on the France CFA, the last colonial currency, this intellectually difficult hiatus encourages us to maintain the utmost discretion on this shameful reality, which would discredit France in its international actions in defense of democracy if it were to be broken with too much fanfare.

The advent of a submissive African political class, plucked from the cradle of embryonic institutions and inculcated with the parameters of its own survival and petty interests, has helped the system to flourish. In Franco-African palaces, nothing is decided without a phone call or a trip to Paris. Most of the time, the personal security of heads of state is entrusted to French gendarmes or military personnel. Those who fail to assimilate the rules pay dearly. Even today, the Élysée Palace is a must for ambitious French-speaking African politicians. The "papal" anointment at the Élysée is indispensable, both for African presidents and for their opponents, who come to assure the republican pontiff that they will not preach the heresy of dissent if they come to power. Since the Second World War, France has remained one of the five powers making up the United Nations Security Council. It therefore still holds a share of the world's political power. Under De Gaulle, the small African countries aligned with France represented a portfolio of some fourteen votes that established our country as the "voice of Africa" at the UN, and in the world… The compass set to the antenna of the Eiffel Tower is therefore the most notable, and the only technological innovation of the presidents of French-speaking Africa. In France, as in Africa, a hundred years of absolute domination by Paris have created a set of reflexes, habits and customs, and consensual, complicit relations in the subconscious of French leaders and their African counterparts alike.

In the collective memory of African heads of state, the ghosts of those who didn't agree still lurk: Thomas Sankara, abandoned by France, and assassinated in Burkina Faso in 1987 by the men of Blaise Compaoré, the country's current president; Patrice Lumumba, in 1961, in the former Zaire; Sylvanus Olympio in Togo: elected president of the Republic in April 1960, he announced that one of his first objectives was for Togo to leave the franc zone in favor of the British currency. The agreements establishing the break between the Banque de France and the Banque du Togo were to be signed on January 15, 1963. Coincidence? He was assassinated by his successor, Gnassingbé Eyadema, two days before, on January 13. Eyadema took power, created a single party and was re-elected five times, until his death in 2005, with France's blessing. His son, Faure Gnassingbé, who succeeded him, is still in power in Lomé. By chance in Franco-African history, there was also the caricature of Emperor Jean-Bedel Bokassa, overthrown by France in the Central African Republic after it had pampered him, and the assassination of Félix Moumié, the Cameroonian independence leader poisoned in Geneva by William Bechtel, a fake journalist and agent of the French *Sdece*, on November 3, 1960 (tried twenty years later, the secret service man was acquitted by French justice). A dissident Cameroonian militant for total and immediate independence within the UPC, liquidated among many others in the 60s during a long and merciless military expedition, declared: "*Under the direction of the French army, Cameroonian troops razed the town of Yogandima to the ground, massacring nearly 8,000 unarmed civilians. For ten years, the colonial administration had faced opposition from the Union populaire du Cameroun (UPC). French High Commissioner Pierre Messmer organized the assassination of many UPC leaders, as well as punitive expeditions. At independence on January 1, 1960, Jacques Foccart installed a puppet government, presided over by his friend Ahmadou Ahidjo. The same day, the young state signed a military assistance agreement with France. Charles De Gaulle dispatched 5 battalions, commanded by General Max Briand. Between February and March, 156 Bamiléké villages are burned and razed to the ground. Tens of thousands of people were massacred.*" The

French press, muzzled and blinded by the Algerian crisis, said nothing of this terrible repression (apart from *L'Humanité* and *La Croix*). Finally, on October 2, UPC leader Félix Moumié was assassinated in Geneva. The collective work *Kamerun!*[1] offers different estimates of the death toll, depending on the source: never less than several tens of thousands of victims.

The memory of Baré Maïnassara, the president of Niger assassinated by his own guard in 1999 when he seemed to be distancing himself from his Western allies, and the recent images of the fall of Laurent Gbagbo (or those of the death of Gaddafi) call for caution, to say the least. Jacques Foccart, the great architect of the Franco-African edifice, who commanded a number of destabilization operations well beyond the Gaullist period, made no secret of the fact that all coups d'état carried out in Africa by his services always received the approval of the Élysée Palace's occupant (at the time General De Gaulle), who did not want to know the details of their execution. It also happened that the French army was called in - or not! - in the name of cooperation and defense agreements, to rescue a president from a rebellion, as was the case with Abbé Fulbert Youlou. An eccentric priest who had broken his ties with the Church and his vow of chastity, he ordered his cassocks from Dior, and De Gaulle didn't like him. In 1964, in the face of military subversion, he was overthrown[2]. After the 1947 insurrection in Madagascar, when thousands of Malagasy were killed, perhaps tens of thousands, in a relentless punitive war, after the bloody wars of independence in Indochina and Algeria, when, in the 1950s, the colonial Empire began to crumble, Paris organized to perpetuate its interference in the southern Sahel, to save everything that could be saved from our resources and position.

Taking part in the Biafran civil war between 1967 and 1970, France supplied arms and munitions to the secessionist province against Nigeria, which did not want to see this oil-rich region become independent and escape its control. All the Françafrique barons of the time, from

---

1. Thomas Deltombe, Manuel Domergue, Jacob Tatsitsa, *Kamerun! Une guerre cachée aux origines de la Françafrique, 1948-1971*, La Découverte, 2011
2. *Foccart, l'homme qui dirigeait l'Afrique*, documentary by Cédric Tourbe, 2010

Houphouët-Boigny to Omar Bongo, took part in supporting the Biafran rebels, under the direction of the French SDECE. Air-Gabon planes, flown by French pilots, clandestinely delivered arms to the Biafrans right up to the end. De Gaulle expected a Biafran victory to broaden France's oil base on the Gulf of Guinea, as the Biafrans would show their gratitude to those who had helped them under the radar. Pierre Messmer, De Gaulle's Minister of Defense, admitted forty years later that there was also a desire for revenge in this French intervention against Nigeria: *"I didn't forgive* [Nigeria] *for its attitude after our nuclear firing at Reggane. It allowed* [support for Biafra] *to make him pay! He had been both provocative and ridiculous. Provocative, in trying to rouse African governments against the French nuclear firings; and ridiculous, in saying: 'We Nigeria, will have the atomic bomb.' They are grotesques. I haven't forgiven them[3]."* Huge budgets were allocated to a major press campaign in Europe, through a Geneva-based agency, Mark Press, which secured the publication of over 500 articles. Because of the Nigerian blockade on Biafra, the theme was genocide by hunger. Maurice Robert, who led the operation for the French secret services, later revealed that the term "genocide" had been chosen by the SDECE and instilled into the daily *Le Monde*, where it appeared on the front page. All the other newspapers followed suit. In the end, 2 million people died in Biafra, and France quickly withdrew its marbles, leaving the defeated, their dying and their mountains of corpses to their sad fate. The *French doctors* of "Médecins Sans Frontières" (Doctors Without Borders), who had come all the way from Paris to dispense medicine and care to the survivors, were the final *French touch* to this sad story. This image replaced the clandestine one of the catastrophic intervention. To all appearances, honor was safe. Omar Bongo is said to have repatriated the remaining funds from this inglorious adventure to France, to finance the repression of the May 68 demonstrations in Paris.

These past episodes in France's "roman noir" on the African continent are just a few illustrations of the hundreds of well-known and lesser-known cases and episodes that have paradoxically forged a strong bond

---

3. Jean Guisnel (dir.), Roger Faligot (dir.), *Histoire secrète de la Ve République*, La Découverte, 2007.

between France and its former colonies: the famous "shared history", whose darkest pages are not easily recounted.

Because of the policy of linguistic, cultural and administrative assimilation of Africans before 1960 - which was never more apparent than when they joined the fight to liberate France - Africans always felt divided between the two homelands they thought they had. They later realized that this was an illusion. At home, they were not at home, and at home, they were still a little at home. But too late. Sub-Saharan Africa had provided its share of fighters, who in turn passed on their Francophile spirit to their sons.

My father was born the year the French first entered our region, in 1912. We were the only region not yet colonized. My grandfather died, we don't know how, but there had been resistance and clashes with the colonial army. My grandmother left, she was pregnant. She gave birth to my father, Koudou Paul, in a village that became the town of Gagnoa. In 1924, the priests arrived. They founded a church. My father went to school with them. My grandmother's second husband sent him there because he wasn't her real son: in those days, people were suspicious of white schools. My father became a Catholic. He was sent to Dabou, near Abidjan. There he met priests who later held important positions: Abbé Daniel, Abbé Noël, Cardinal Yago. In 1932, at the age of twenty, he was in his second year of elementary school. He could read and write.

He went to Tabou, near the Nigerian border, and worked on the ships as a cacatois. He supervised accounts, loading and unloading, stewardship... The ships were engaged in cabotage. He went as far as Matadi, in the Congo. When he came back, he quit his job and volunteered for military service, which lasted two or three years. Traditional military service was reserved for Europeans. For Africans, you had to volunteer, like my father. He was drafted into the 5th Battalion of Senegalese Tirailleurs. He did part of his service in Côte d'Ivoire, part in Dakar. He was a signaller, tirailleur 2nd class. He finished his service in 1939. Thanks to his ability to read and write, he was quickly promoted. He became corporal, then sergeant. He was discharged,

retired to the village of Babré, then recalled almost immediately, to go to war in France, in Normandy. He landed in France in January 1940, with the rank of sergeant. He was assigned to the 44th Colonial Infantry Regiment. In June, he was seriously wounded in the left arm at Douarnenez. He was taken prisoner by the Germans and managed to escape. Hospitalized for a time at Fréjus, he was demobilized and returned home. For years, he refused to eat meat, because it reminded him of the smell of burning human flesh… Nor would he want to hear any more about the war. In May 2003, he received a medal from the French authorities in recognition of his services, at the 43rd Bima French military camp in Abidjan, in front of our whole family. He was very moved. So were we. If I'm called Laurent, it's in homage to Captain Laurent, his leader, who was killed before his eyes in 1940.

On the 90th anniversary of the First World War, Jacques Chirac acknowledged the contribution made by Africans in the fight for France's sovereignty. The President paid tribute to the 72,000 recruits who died in combat: 7,000 of the 16,000 who fought on the Chemin des Dames in 1917. As for the mobilization of 179,000 Africans in 1940, 40,000 came to fight in metropolitan France, and 17,000 were killed - including 1,300 of the 1,800 members of the 25th Rifle Regiment, who fought in front of Lyon on June 19, 1940, according to Ministry of Defense figures. This commitment was punished by a monstrous lack of gratitude. The freezing of veterans' retirement pensions at the time of independence in 1960, which only came to an end in 2006, with most of the beneficiaries having disappeared. And let's not forget the famous and shameful 1944 massacre at the Thiaroye camp of 70 Senegalese infantrymen who, having been demobilized, demanded payment of their allowances and pensions a little too loudly.

Thirty years later, official France still saw Africa only in terms of its economic contribution, having somewhat forgotten the sacrifice imposed on its peoples. Thus, after the French military intervention in Kolwezi, a town in the south of the Democratic Republic of Congo, in 1978, Valery Giscard d'Estaing, then President of the Republic, explained on television the very next day: *France is acting in Africa on its own behalf. [...] Africa is a continent that has traditionally provided us with a certain number of our resources and raw materials. A change in the situation in Africa, a general situation of insecurity or subversion* [in the Democratic Republic of Congo] *would have consequences for France and Europe."*

Giscard also knew personally how to appreciate the charms of this vital need for French roots in Africa. As soon as he was elected President of the Republic in 1974, it was not to Washington, London, Bonn or Moscow that he reserved the honor of his first official trip, but to Bangui, capital of the Central African Republic, where Jean-Bedel Bokassa, future emperor, and the all-too-pretty Catherine, his empress, reigned... As we know, he subsequently made many pleasure trips to his friend Jean Bedel, until a miserable story about diamonds in *Le Canard Enchaîné* interrupted his honeymoon with Africa.

Democracy is best seen in Africa.

Thirty years on, the April 2012 report by the French Ministry of Defense, *Horizons Stratégiques,* says no different than Giscard d'Estaing. Against a backdrop of unbridled global economic competition for African resources, France is worried and reaffirms the need to control this area so close to us, from which we are separated only by the 14.4 kilometers of the Strait of Gibraltar. As we can see, the state of mind has not changed in the circles where French-style geopolitics is thought out: "[...] *nationalist or pan-African sentiments could develop, at times, to the detriment of Western interests".* Quoted by political observer Théophile Kouamouo in the Ivorian newspaper *Le Nouveau Courrier* on October 10, 2012, this report enables him to analyze the minds of its editors, such as Adrien Hart of *Slate Afrique: "Everyone keeps in mind the violent anti-French calls by pro-Gbagbo political leaders during the post-election crisis in Côte d'Ivoire. Will Africa's future see a proliferation of clones of populist leaders like Charles Blé Goudé or Julius Malema?* [South African nationalist leader]. *We don't hope so."*

Théophile Kouamouo comments: *"As soon as we are convinced that the main threat identified by Hexagon's official strategists is the awakening [...] of 'dignified Africa', it becomes obvious that an alliance with forces representing tribal feudalism [...] can be envisaged against African sovereignists. Civil wars and secessions become [...] 'problems' [...] that legitimize a military presence, thus strategic and virtuously presented as a matter of saving Africa from itself 'by preventing massacres'."* This dialectic, often used to dress up institutionalized interference in candid probity and white linen, has enabled France to consolidate its position in Africa.

"DO THEY WANT CÔTE D'IVOIRE TO DIE?"

"We colonized Africa," the English used to say, and left the Gallic cockerel to rub his dewclaws in the desert sands… Indeed, between Mauritania, Morocco, Algeria, Chad, Mali, Niger and Burkina Faso (formerly the Upper Volta), the continent had an accumulation of desert spaces. The phenomenon is set to worsen with global warming and the expansion of desert areas.

This is Côte d'Ivoire's first problem: it's the only island combining forest and wealth - apart from neighboring Ghana.

The people of the Sahel have always migrated there to find better living conditions. Then the colonial power recruited its workforce in these regions, and Houphouët-Boigny amplified this movement. There has long been an open route from the Sahel to Côte d'Ivoire. Houphouët used the workers, and France always encouraged this, because every additional immigrant entering Côte d'Ivoire meant one less immigrant in France.

Côte d'Ivoire has absorbed so many immigrants from all over the sub-region, including Nigeria, Guinea, Togo and Burkina Faso, that it now counts over 30% foreigners in its population. A record number. The administrative management of these populations has long been lax, giving free rein to land and electoral problems. Who owns the land? An Ivorian joke: "**In Guinea, there are Guineans; in Senegal, Senegalese; in Burkina, Burkinabe, etc. And in Côte d'Ivoire? There are Guineans, Senegalese, Burkinabés, Ivorians, etc.**"

Disputes are fuelled by conflicts between indigenous communities, who rely on unwritten customary law, and new arrivals (who may have settled there for several generations) who use written law to their advantage: for example, they claim that they occupy and use land, and then legally claim ownership of it. The land issue is so sensitive that it doesn't take much to inflame the situation and set the inhabitants against each other. Since the early 2000s, the rebels have been constantly rubbing salt into these wounds to justify their actions and legitimize their presence in the face of such tensions.

They tried to create a community of "peoples of the North" whose rights were not sufficiently recognized.

I've always refused to distinguish between Ivorians. We are all sons of the same soil. We have the same aspirations and the same rights. If everyone is to live as well as possible, whether they come from the North, South, East or West, whether they are Christians, Muslims or Animists, the rules must be respected. There are rules for acquiring land, and there are rules for acquiring Ivorian nationality. It's because the rules are respected that an individual's status has meaning, and that rights and obligations can be attached to it. Without respect for rules, there is anarchy.

The Burkinabés have nothing in their country except a little gold. They couldn't provide much other than mutton. We used to charter trains and trucks to fetch them at Tabaski [Aïd el-Kebir] to supply the Muslims. Whereas back home, not to mention the mineral resources, there are around 150,000 km2 (of our country's 320,000 surface area) to cultivate: coffee, rubber, cocoa, you name it, we can grow it.

Initially, the wealth was wood - mahogany for short. Then came coffee and, thanks to Houphouët, who foresaw the market, cocoa. Finally came rubber. The Burkinabés learned to cultivate.

In 1998, the Bédié law on land ownership made it compulsory to be Ivorian to own land. Foreigners could not own land. Today, it seems

that 700,000 stateless people have been identified - I wonder how? - who would be entitled to naturalization on simple request. They will ipso facto become the owners of the land they occupy: the Burkinabés are being paid in advance for their votes in the next presidential election. The problem of nationality and the problem of land are one and the same.

In a country where census-taking is all the more difficult because civil registers and administrative archives are often lacking, drawing up lists of voters eligible for democratic debate in elections poses a problem.

Being naturalized according to the rules poses no problem; becoming a landowner according to the rules poses no problem. But selling off Ivorian nationality to allow foreigners to monopolize land already belonging to indigenous communities is unacceptable. It is tantamount to depriving Ivorians, whatever their origin or religion, of their rights. It also means denying any meaning to the legal status of national or property owner, and thus denying the existence of legal rights.

The PDCI, if it continues to support Ouattara's policies, will have a big responsibility: changing the population to make Côte d'Ivoire soluble in Burkina Faso. In the west of the country, I know that they are bringing in truckloads of Burkinabés to this region, and that they are driving out the natives, whose plantations are being taken away. Who cares about the suffering of our people? Do they want Côte d'Ivoire to die so that Burkina Faso can live?

The other problem is France. It has never wanted to relinquish its stranglehold on our country. It clings on wherever it can, and even if it has rendered services, it is not at home to the point of allowing itself blind and unconscious support, and the distribution of arms to any rebel.

The problem of Mali, where you saw the crisis develop until the French intervention, is not a new one. I learned about it from Edgar Pisani, who came there in 1992. The problem should have been solved twenty years ago, especially since the presence of oil and uranium deposits was well known. In all these years, neither CDEAO, the African Union nor France have bothered to bring people together to find a real solution to a real problem. In Mali, the Tuaregs - the white people - have long been voicing their demands: when Pisani came, they already wanted to create an independent state over northern Mali, northern Niger, eastern Mauritania and a fraction of southern Libya. In the countries of the region, such as Sudan and Mauritania, blacks are frustrated by the Arabs, who rule over them.

Today, the question of Mali may seem settled. But it will come up again. What's more, the problem will resurface in Niger, Nigeria and Chad. Because, as the Westerners are perhaps unaware, they lost a lot with the disappearance of Gaddafi, who stabilized the region. He intervened a lot with the Tuaregs. We can't count on the Algerians to do that. They've turned in on themselves, and are no longer involved in anything in Africa, except a little in the Sahara, to push Morocco around and create a zone of intervention in northern Mali and Niger. They sometimes encourage the creation of hotbeds of tension among their neighbors by supporting this or that Arab or Tuareg group, but always from a distance. And then they phone neighboring countries and say, "It stinks where you live.

In any case, the international community, i.e. France, Great Britain and the United States, has methods of intervention that don't solve problems, and don't bring lasting solutions to conflicts. In Syria, a conference should have been held much earlier. While the French government was ready to mount a military expedition! The West is surprised that the Chinese and Russians are now opposing their interventions, even if they are covered by the UN. But this is simply because they have seen how they exceed their rights, and go beyond the mandates entrusted to them. The UN never asked them to kill Gaddafi, and to come and arrest me in my own home. In Côte d'Ivoire, there was an electoral dispute, which had to be treated as such, and without arms.

"The UN, you know, it's a figment of the imagination, it doesn't exist", Jean-Marc Simon told me, illustrating both the freedom of the great powers to act as they please within their mandates, and De Gaulle's famous definition of the United Nations *"contraption"*.

5.

"VILLEPIN AND BOURGI ASKED ME TO SPILL THE BEANS IN 2002"

Even today, the former colonial power's control of African countries' currencies reveals the reality of the close bond of dependence between them. It enabled the fourteen countries of the "franc zone" to be kept on a tight leash. This "French cultural exception" is the source of Africa's political and social underdevelopment. We don't like to talk about it in Paris. This currency brings us face to face with our responsibility, shared with the African heads of state who have allowed themselves to be persuaded not to break the consensus, and to endorse our stranglehold in exchange for benevolent protection. Some of them - but wasn't that what they were put in place for? - are the first to defend the status quo, especially when it comes to their monetary dependence. Alassane Ouattara is one of them.

The CFA franc[4] deprives the countries on which it was imposed in 1945 of the right to mint their own currency: banknotes are printed in Chamalières, in the Puy-de-Dôme region of France, depriving the countries of French-speaking Africa of the hallmark of their sovereignty. Right from the start, these young states were condemned to remain captive, under-age, and subject to the goodwill of their financial backers - first and foremost, of course, France. This obviously delayed their gradual accession

---

4. The "Franc des colonies françaises d'Afrique" became the franc of the African financial community.

to real political awareness, independence and dignity. The financial infantilism and irresponsibility in which they are still held have given rise to chronically assisted peoples. Their heads of state have become beggars and thieves, practicing on the one hand a policy of reverence towards the foreign power that protects them and holds their purse, and on the other, despoiling their populations. Without going into the technical details of a complex system, it's important to know that the quantity of currency delivered to each of the African countries in the franc zone is subject to a quota, and that, in absolute terms, France can reduce or stop its banknote deliveries at any time. It can also decide to devalue the currency. This is what it did in 1994 with the IMF and the United States, with very harsh consequences for African states and populations. In addition, as a guarantee, France is authorized to store and manage 50% of the foreign currency generated by exports of franc zone countries in "operating accounts" in Paris. Until 1973, France withdrew the entire amount, and the equivalent of 65% until 2005. The foreign exchange earnings from cocoa, coffee, rubber, oil, cotton, uranium, gold, diamonds, manganese, rare metals, etc., sold around the world, therefore largely flow into the Banque de France, and not into the African franc zone countries that generated the exports. A flow of dollars, pounds sterling, yen and euros which the French Treasury holds in safekeeping and places on the international financial markets for its own benefit. The CFA franc system constantly oxygenates the French economy, thanks to the direct and indirect profits and interest it generates. Nicolas Agbohou, a professor of economics at the Sorbonne in Côte d'Ivoire, estimates that 17 billion euros worth of franc zone currencies are blocked in France, when they should be working in the Central Banks of West African States (BCEAO) and Central African States (BCEA) of the franc zone, as well as in the countries they serve. Following in the footsteps of many others, three African intellectuals have launched a desperate petition against a historic colonial anachronism that is plaguing the fourteen countries of the franc zone. To the point of prohibiting these countries from creating a single market or currency, since the CFA franc of one country is not used in neighboring countries. The icing on the cake is that there are two different CFA francs, non-convertible between them. Just like the different gauges of the rails in neighbouring countries, such as Cameroon, Gabon and Congo, the epitome of "colonial genius" aimed at preventing circulation between these countries, and maintaining division, a Cameroonian cannot use his francs in Senegal or Côte d'Ivoire, and vice versa… The Central African franc and the West African franc coexist, ignoring each other. How can we fail to see this as an obstacle to the economic development of trade between the countries and zones concerned? The call for a "free franc zone" by Makhily Gassama, professor of literature, former Minister of Culture and former Senegalese ambassador, Martial Ze Belinga, economist and sociologist, and Bamba Sakho, Doctor of Science with a degree in economics, demonstrates denial. This scandal has been part of the Franco-African landscape from the outset, to the point where it is no longer visible:

"In the name of an alleged 'convertibility guarantee' for the currency used in 14 countries, more than 3,000 billion CFA francs [4 million euros] *from the BCEAO issuing zone were deposited with the French Treasury at the end of 2011, i.e. almost twice the wealth created in Togo in 2010, and more than four times the total wages and salaries paid by the Ivorian state in 2011! For the BCEAC issuing zone, the reserves held in the 'Compte d'opérations' of the Treasury of the former colonial power exceeded 6,100 billion CFA francs, equivalent to ten times the salaries paid by the Cameroonian civil service!*

"In 2011, the two issuing zones of BCEAO and BCEAC totaled almost 14,000 billion CFA francs in foreign exchange reserves unavailable for the needs of African economies. For the BCEAO, these idle holdings represent a currency issue coverage rate of 109%, compared with the required 20% and 98.7% for the BEAC. It should be noted that these sums exceed what is officially referred to as 'official development assistance' from France to the major African recipients, namely Côte d'Ivoire, Cameroon, Senegal, Congo, Mali and Burkina Faso combined! Enough to raise many questions…

"To appreciate the exorbitant cost of the constraints imposed by the CFA franc, and to illustrate this massive destruction of wealth in terms of infrastructure financing - a matter of almost absolute urgency - we need to bear in mind, for example, the estimated 40 billion CFA francs cost of the road project to open up the Sahel, the 300 billion CFA francs needed to clean up the water-threatened city of Cotonou, or the nearly 50 billion CFA francs required to build the bridge linking Kinshasa to Brazzaville.

"The confiscation of African reserves taken from the financing of development and local activities therefore borders on a form of economic crime. [...] This is an opportunity to point out that few leading African politicians, whether leaders or opponents, have directly raised the issue of foreign exchange reserves and, more generally, the scandalous monetary management of the franc zone. This shows how little these leaders and elites care about the well-being of the African people. While the mechanisms of the franc zone have an obvious neo-colonial bias, the excess of reserves over the required ratios is largely attributable to African decisions that are incomprehensible in the light of the stakes involved in economic and social development. [...]

"The franc zone and its central banks, now fifty years old, are a veritable historical and economic anachronism. Here we have a monetary zone born as a colonial variant of the French franc, which outlives the latter, now merged into the euro [...] at a time when all the emerging countries have total monetary sovereignty, China with the yuan, South Africa with the rand, Brazil with the real, South Korea with the won and India with the rupee. What incoherence and misery this generates!"

Another very advantageous confiscation for France: the deposit of African gold in our vaults, which serves to guarantee the currency, means that, with reserves of 2,435 tonnes, we rank among the Western states with the highest gold reserves, after the United States (8,400 tonnes), Germany (3,400 tonnes), the IMF (3,200 tonnes) and ahead of Italy (2,400 tonnes). A not inconsiderable advantage in times of crisis. A good way, for example, to reassure rating agencies and the markets from which France borrows to balance its budget.

Last but not least, the CFA franc is first and foremost a political lever, enabling direct interference in a country's affairs. It was enough for Sarkozy's government to turn off the taps at the Central Bank of West Africa, and close the banks - subsidiaries of French banks - in Côte d'Ivoire, to put Laurent Gbagbo in a difficult position.

France has representatives on the CFA franc's board of directors. And the Banque de France holds the funds. The operating accounts, each linked to one of the African central banks, which are nothing more than subsidiaries of the Banque de France, receive our coun-

tries' exports in the Banque de France. When France comes to the aid of one of our deficit countries - it's always the same ones, the poorest - it does so with the surpluses and profits generated in the other countries of the franc zone. France then appears as a very generous country, when in fact it only lends Africans other Africans' money! Money from the credit account of another is paid into the deficit account of one, and that's it!

Obviously, given its economic volume, Côte d'Ivoire is the indispensable stumbling block in the edifice of West Africa. That's why it's always better to have someone at the helm who won't question anything.

All credit operations granted to indebted countries generate interest - always on our own money, but for the benefit of the lender, i.e. the Banque de France - at rates set unilaterally by the latter. They further indebt poor countries, pushing them deeper into underdevelopment. For France, the gains are not negligible, and contribute to your budget, but the funds blocked in Paris on the very opaque "operating accounts" at the Banque de France, would be better used in investments for the development of Africa. And let's not forget that it's the Banque de France that holds the banknotes and manufactures our currency in proportion to the credit we create for ourselves through our export surpluses. In this franc zone, there are us, the countries of West Africa, and then there are other countries, such as Gabon, Chad, the Central African Republic, Cameroon and Equatorial Guinea. As I said, there are French people on the board of the CFA franc. During the post-electoral crisis, this enabled them to forbid the BCEAO to allow me access to my own country's revenues. Is that independence? This direct control over eight West African countries, those of the UE-MOA [the West African Economic and Monetary Union includes Côte d'Ivoire, Burkina Faso, Mali, Togo, Senegal, Guinea-Bissau, Benin and Niger] has always astonished English-speaking African heads of state. They used to say to me: "Why does France still have its hands in all your affairs? The English themselves changed after American independence. Only in India, in 1947, were they surprised and overwhelmed

by the Gandhi phenomenon. Otherwise, they were able to achieve true decolonization."

Moreover, their former African colonies, such as Ghana, Kenya, Nigeria, India and Pakistan, have national currencies. Algeria, Tunisia and Morocco are not as dependent on the Banque de France as we are.

"We prefer trade to domination", they said in essence. That's my credo too. It's not France's, which has continued to milk its African cow, instead of moving towards a form of cooperation worthy of our times, and certainly more profitable for all concerned. There was a tremendous card to play. I am not and never have been anti-French. Is it my fault that it was France that didn't want to settle the colonial pact, and look to the future to envisage other relations? We were ready, I was ready. They didn't want to. That's the crux of the problem.

The problem has never been our relationship with French companies, nor with the French themselves, but with the State, with the Élysée Palace. In 2007, Sarkozy had a field day when he said in his Dakar speech: "L'homme africain n'est pas assez entré dans l'histoire" ("The African man has not made enough history"). Without going back to the slave trade and colonization - that's in the past - he pretended to ignore the role still played by French tutelage as a brake on our emancipation and nation-building. Is this really ignorance? It would be incompetence. Out of Christian charity, I prefer to opt for bad faith.

In 1960, Jean Boissonnat, an economic journalist and member of the Banque de France's Monetary Committee, described other significant advantages of this currency: "[…] *The franc zone enabled France to purchase certain raw materials [...] without spending foreign currency. It has been calculated that* [in 1960] *it represented an annual saving of $250 million in foreign currency... It has been estimated that 500,000 French people in mainland France derived their livelihood from the franc zone economy as a whole[5]."* We can only imagine what these savings must be today, since the CFA franc has been attached to the euro zone. Figures concerning

---

5. Jean Boissonnat, "La Zone franc, survivance du passé ou promesse d'avenir", *La Croix*, February 17, 1960.

the CFA franc are a "state secret" and do not appear, for example, in the balance sheets published by the Banque de France.

In economics professor Nicolas Agbohou's book *Le Franc CFA et l'euro contre l'Afrique*[6], the perverse financial mechanisms that are fatal to Africa's development are perfectly analyzed. François Mitterrand's terrible words on what he considered to be the swindle of the century are quoted. Arguments taken from Laure Adler's book of interviews, *L'Année des adieux*[7]: "*It is an immense deception to make people believe [...] that De Gaulle enabled the decolonization of Africa. When I hear the hymn of Gaullist decolonization, my heart sinks. The Brazzaville conference was not the great act of emancipation for black Africa. De Gaulle had failed in Dakar. He had to win over a certain number of Africans. The abolition of forced labor he spoke of in his Brazzaville speech was not carried out by him. He therefore ruled out any possibility of Africans taking over the running of their own country. At the same time, the British accepted the total emancipation of such important colonies as Hindustan and Pakistan, and the Dutch accelerated the independence of Indonesia in 1941. All these countries became free and sovereign [...]. De Gaulle, on the other hand, never thought about self-government. He had no historical vision of Africa. [...] De Gaulle asked us to submit. For him, you joined the community if you refused sovereignty*".

François Mitterrand himself, who acted no differently when he came to power, was scandalized that anyone could say De Gaulle had decolonized Africa.

The mysteries of the dichotomy between thought and deed, the quintessence of politics: during his fourteen years at the Élysée, Mitterrand kept the Gaullist system in place, even appointing his son Jean-Christophe to head the Élysée's opaque African unit. Third-worldist and humanist, perhaps, until someone explained to him the hole in the coffers that would result from the loss of Africa?

---

6. Nicolas Agbohou, *Le Franc CFA et l'euro contre l'Afrique, Pour une monnaie africaine et la coopération Sud-Sud*, Solidarité Mondiale, 2000.
7. Laure Adler, *L'Année des adieux*, Flammarion, 1995.

In *Africaphonie*, a 2008 documentary by Michaël Gosselin, Jacques Chirac told the truth in his own way, even after he had retired from business. The former President reveals the truth with his trademark false bonhomie: "[…] *Some, not all, but a lot of the money in our wallets comes from centuries of exploitation of Africa. We need to have a little common sense, I'm not saying generosity, and justice, to give back to the Africans what we have taken from them, especially as this is necessary if we want to avoid the worst convulsions or difficulties with the political consequences that this entails."*

Speaking of the French people's wallets, the former President forgot about those of political parties, including his own, and of politicians: lawyer Robert Bourgi, one of his shadowy African advisors who went on to work for Nicolas Sarkozy, recounted in *Le Journal du Dimanche* on September 11, 2011, how suitcases of cash circulated between African capitals and Jacques Chirac's Élysée Palace. The aim was to fuel elections in France, particularly the one in 2002: *"Through me, five African heads of state - Abdoulaye Wade (Senegal), Blaise Compaoré (Burkina Faso), Laurent Gbagbo (Côte d'Ivoire), Denis Sassou-Nguesso (Congo-Brazzaville) and, of course, Omar Bongo (Gabon) - paid around $10 million for the 2002 campaign,"* the lawyer accuses. For several days, he let loose in interviews in which he said he *"saw Chirac and Villepin counting the money"*.

Pierre Péan's book *La République des mallettes (The Republic of Briefcases)*[8], published at the same time, would fuel similar revelations. Laurent Gbagbo implied that the practices denounced by Pierre Péan were commonplace.

He told me that in 2001, Villepin and Bourgi had asked him to finance Jacques Chirac's election campaign for the 2002 presidential elections. He knew that the protagonists of the Black Mercedes coup had taken refuge in Burkina and could make another attempt at any time if they knew they were backed by powerful interests. Above all, it's difficult to say no to representatives of the French authorities when they are the military bosses on the ground. When there is such an imbalance between the powerful and the weak, what room for manoeuvre is left for the weak? That's what Françafrique's supporters are counting on.

---

8. Pierre Péan, *La République des mallettes*, Fayard, 2011.

It was 2001, I think. Villepin and Robert Bourgi asked me to spill the beans for the 2002 elections in France. We were in a lounge of the restaurant La Pérouse, on the Quai Voltaire, near the Documentation française. It was the price of peace in Françafrique. I had a meeting with Chirac, which went very well. He saw me off, was very friendly, and tapped me on the shoulder on the stoop: "I'm not an ingrate." I'm not proud of this episode, but I thought it would give me the leeway I needed to move forward towards our objectives. I was criticized for it, saying that it was proof of my double standards, that I was relying on neo-colonialism to criticize it. As if we could always respond to such powerful partners without using cunning and diplomacy. Right from the start, I was put in a situation of permanent crisis and urgency. At least they never came back at me. I wouldn't have agreed. They knew that. That didn't improve our relationship.

Later, Chirac said he'd "missed" me, but I didn't understand why. He claimed that I had leaked the information.

More than a bonus for our economy, more than a state secret, Africa's wealth is the stock-in-trade and family secret that De Gaulle's successors have been passing down for the past fifty years. Not to mention the fact that the debts we are partly responsible for in these countries under our control are regularly transformed into juicy profits for our major corporations. Public opinion is often irritated by announcements of "debt cancellation" for this or that African country. Another gift, they think. In reality, the debt owed by the African state in question to the French state is never cancelled, but "privatized". It will eventually be paid, up to the amount due, to French companies, which will carry out public works in the country concerned. The choice of these sites and companies is made not in Africa, but in France… Everything's good with pigs, and in Africa, everything's a source of money, even debts.

This is the common thread running through French policy on the continent: Africa may be a worry, but it's always a good deal. Better still, our position in Africa is an invaluable asset on the international stage, helping to establish us as a valuable and influential partner. As soon as we returned to NATO's integrated command, the United States found the ideal pilot fish to penetrate a continent they know little about, where for once they didn't need to commit themselves militarily in the open.

Those in French political circles, or in Africa, who have dared to take on this state within a state with a gun to their head, have not made a career of it. All they had to do was move a match, and the house fell on their heads.

Jean-Pierre Cot, short-lived Minister of Cooperation, resigned in 1982, the day he confronted his ethics with the reality of France's African neo-colonialism. Later, under Nicolas Sarkozy, the bad manners of Jean-Marie Bockel, one of Cot's successors at Cooperation, who had the unfortunate idea of publicly calling for an end to Françafrique, led him to leave his post quickly under pressure from two barons whom he had upset, and who feared for their rents: Denis Sassou-Nguesso and Omar Bongo. Omar Bongo telephoned Robert Bourgi, who was a skilled tam-tam between African presidents and the Élysée Palace, to pass on the message: Bockel out! Wish granted! Jean-Marie Bockel was reassigned in the Fillon government, to the Secretary of State for Defense and Veterans. He is now working on a project for the government to reorganize relations between France and Africa. His ideas have, it seems, been better received by François Hollande, without resulting in the death certificate of Françafrique. As a senator, Bockel co-signed with Jeanny Lorgeoux, a former soldier in Mittérand's Françafrique, in 2013, the famous senatorial report entitled "Africa is our future", which is much more inspired by the interests of France than those of Africa. Like others before him, Senator Bockel has been purged of his anti-Françafrican revolt...

The joint Obama-Hollande communiqué on February 10, 2014, prior to the President's trip to the United States, opened up a different perspective: *"Africa is the most visible theater of the new partnership between France and the United States,"* they asserted in chorus in an op-ed published by *Le Monde* and the *Washington Post*. France has always been able to make its military know-how and knowledge of Africa valuable to the Americans, who let it manage this other part of the world until the 1970s. The covetousness aroused by Africa's riches, including oil, and its strategic security stakes, convinced the United States to become more directly involved in the 1980s. And to play their part. They created Africom, the military command for Africa, in 2006-2008. Based in Stuttgart, Germany, and Djibouti, this unit brings together the various African departments formerly responsible for the continent in Washington. It oversees Uncle Sam's security, strategic and economic interests in Africa. But on the ground, French soldiers are still running around in Côte d'Ivoire, Mali and the Central African Republic, with diplomatic and sometimes logistical support from the Americans. Is "Françafrique" dead? Long live "Atlanticafrique"! Since France joined NATO's integrated command in 2009, at the instigation of Nicolas Sarkozy, its army has been defending more than just our national interests. "*You have become the West's Senegalese riflemen*", African humorists joke. A French communicant with extensive contacts in Africa sums up the current reality: "*From now on, the Americans do the cooking, and the French do the washing up.*" He was referring to the first USA-Africa summit, scheduled for August 5 and 6, 2014. Barack Obama has invited 47 African heads of state to Washington. According to the White House, the aim is to strengthen ties between the two continents. For the first time, the usual channel will be dispensed with: the French intermediary. On the agenda for this major event are "*trade and investment in Africa*", *as* well as "*security and democratic development*". Promising young talents are also invited to this mega-summit. For whom is the bell tolling? we wonder in Paris. The great Américafrique rave will make traditional summits between France and its old colonies a thing of the past. America is striking a blow and breaking the exclusive tête-à-tête with the former colonial power. And if African heads of state see this as an opportunity to change the balance of power with France, thanks to their new mentor… What if the Washington summit heralded the end of the oft-heralded Françafrique? A global reversal of alliances, with France pushed out of its own backyard by its American friend? Didn't the Ivorian affair accelerate this process, dealing a fatal blow to the "family" relationship between France and its ex-colonies? In May 2014, Africom organized a training symposium in Germany for press attachés and journalists from French-speaking Africa. The second Europe-Africa summit held in Brussels on

April 2-3 was no doubt aimed, among other issues, at counterbalancing America's rise to power on the continent. France is playing on both sides of the Atlantic, and also has its butt between two chairs. A fine challenge for the French authorities, who must make up for the mistakes of the previous administration. Other players are laying siege to the citadel of ex-French feudalism, and have even invested in it, to the extent of their own means: Mohammed VI, already dubbed the new King of Africa, is constantly traveling to sub-Saharan Africa to forge cooperation agreements in Mali, Gabon and Côte d'Ivoire. He proposes an original partnership, with the attractions of a model not imported, and above all, not imposed by ex-colonial powers. *"Africa is a great continent,"* he explains, *"in terms of its vital forces, resources and potential. It has to take charge of itself; it's no longer a colonized continent. That's why Africa has to trust Africa. It needs less assistance… it's human and social development projects that our continent needs most. Africa must not remain hostage to its past, nor to its current political, economic and social problems[9]…"*

The Ivorian Treasury Department commissioned BMCE (Banque du Maroc pour le Commerce Extérieur) to raise $500 million in borrowings on Euronext in July 2014. Today, Moroccan investment in Côte d'Ivoire has surpassed French investment.

Unusual intermediaries are also appearing in the approach to the disputes to be resolved: the Tuareg independence fighters of the MNLA - Mouvement national de libération de l'Azawad - went to consult in Moscow during the second week of March 2014, where Boubacar Keita, the president elected in Mali in 2013, had already visited. While there are historic links between Mali and Russia, it seems that Paris is no longer the only destination. And what about South Africa, a member of BRICS alongside Brazil, Russia, India and China? Its people skills and technical expertise make it a serious new competitor for France and Europe, with the advantage of not appearing as an invader: like Morocco, it is an African nation.

As for the Chinese giant, it is playing its cards close to its chest through the Ministry of Commerce and the Ministry of Foreign Affairs,

---

9. abidjan.net, February 24, 2014.

via the China Development Bank and China EximBank. According to *La Lettre de l'Expansion*, the latter *"is now the biggest lender on the black continent. Its loans systematically exceed 2.5 million euros […]"*. *It already accounts for 92% of financial investment in African infrastructure. The* "diplomacy of the checkbook" founded the "Chinafrique" *"which saw Sino-African trade exceed the symbolic $200 billion mark for the first time in 2013"*.

Jealous of its Asian neighbor and competitor, Japan released 7.7 billion euros to finance infrastructure in Africa over a five-year period in 2013.

6

"WE ARE FREE IN APPEARANCE ONLY—INSIDE THE CAGE WHERE WE HAVE BEEN PUT"

We can't go from one dependency to another. Independence and partnership are the only way forward.

A meeting of West African experts from the CDEAO met in Yamoussoukro, capital of Côte d'Ivoire, in early March 2014, to discuss around the single currency project. Those who already have their own currency, such as Cape Verde (escudo), Nigeria (naira), Ghana (cedi), Guinea-Conakry (Guinean franc) would like to organize a convergence towards those who still have the CFA franc. Too little political will, no progress… On October 12, 2012, during a visit to Dakar, François Hollande dared to raise the issue. With words that were unprecedented for a President of the French Republic: "[…] *I am convinced that the countries of the franc zone must be able to actively manage their currencies and mobilize more of their reserves for growth and employment.*"

For the moment, it's all talk. As long as the pillars remain in place: the presence of the French army, the CFA franc, and the choice of presidents, the sovereignty of African countries will be nothing but a delusion, and Françafrique will be the reality. It's an anachronism, a scandal so enormous, this dependence, that it was really necessary to organize a large-scale lie to try to conceal it…

Seriously, it's time the French understood why their leaders, whether right or left, have been so attached to Africa for decades! Why they maintain garrisons there, and send expensive military expeditions, even though they say they've run out of money. They've even gone so far as to pretend that we're expensive for them...

I was right too soon. It's time for others in Africa to take up the fight against Françafrique. It's worth it, both for Africa and for France. The end of this system would usher in an era of shared progress and dignity. We need you, because we are underdeveloped, and you need us, because we have what you need, because you are in crisis.

We need our sovereignty, we're entitled to it, and not letting us conquer it will only lead to constant frustration and tragedy among new generations. Without it, how can we be expected to build our democracies? Gaddafi once said to me: "Laurent, why are you bothering with the North? Cut the country in two. Keep the South and leave the North to them, and you'll have peace." Gaddafi was like a loudspeaker: he would repeat to me what he had heard, or what someone had suggested to him. I thought this partition was a plan. It made me smile. I've always defended the integrity of the national territory, and I've never accepted that it's been infringed. This is an idea that came from elsewhere: it had already appeared in the 90s, when Ouattara was Houphouët's Prime Minister, with the story of the "Charter of the North". This document was circulating everywhere, advocating the dismemberment of the country. Houphouët was irritated.

African leaders need to take charge of their own lives. When you look at international conferences in Africa - the ones on the Ivorian crisis were a flagrant example - whether at the African Union or the CDEAO, there are sometimes more Westerners and Whites in the corridors, donors or representatives of the powers that be, to bring pressure to bear. That's why I don't judge my colleagues, even when they sometimes fail me. There's one who you all take for a Françafricain, because he doesn't make any noise, and who isn't, and that's Paul Biya, in Cameroon. One day, at the UN in New York, he took me in his arms after a speech from the podium, and said: "You are our pride". After

the Syria affair, he went to Russia to discuss defense agreements. As he once said, "Cameroon is Cameroon".

It's not easy to get things moving, to oppose diktat, and what's happening to me is a case in point. We are free only in appearance, inside the cage in which we have been placed, our finances and economy under trusteeship, with no real weight at international level, threatened with being fined if we don't obey. This is untenable. One day, together, we'll get out of it.

Côte d'Ivoire had the means to leave this dependence on the franc zone, even on its own, and I was about to do so, which is why they wanted to prevent me from continuing my journey. Without us, and what we represent economically, the CFA franc collapses, and with it the whole Franco-African edifice. And what a bad example for neighboring countries... Now that we've joined the euro zone, it's easier to understand why France was able to drag the European Community and the United States into the Ivorian adventure. It was in nobody's interest to see us leave the CFA. A president from the IMF, who understood their interests, was preferable to Laurent Koudou Gbagbo.

France has painted its post-colonial relationship in the hypocritical colors of a long friendship stemming from its pompous "shared history" with Africa. While it cannot be denied that individual sentimental ties have been forged, it is no less true that France defends what it considers to be its historical achievements. Without it, it would be like Spain, or Italy, limited to its strict borders, economically dependent on its own resources. "Without the CFA franc", a former director of an African central bank told me, "France would be an economic dwarf in Europe". *A state doesn't have friends, it has interests"*. After currency, the other keystone of the Françafrique cathedral is the defense agreements signed with former colonies, guaranteeing the intervention of the French army in the event of external attack. The secret economic clauses they contain, in return for French protection, give France privileged access to the country's subsoil riches. These agreements justify not only intervention on request, but also the presence of French troops on the continent. A guarantee of security for the militarily under-equipped African governments, but also a means of subliminal pressure for Paris. An institutionalized interference of sorts, which Laurent Gbagbo no longer wanted. And that's what lost him. *"There isn't a square meter where you set foot that doesn't belong to France"*, an Ivorian army officer confided to me in Abidjan in 2005. This title deed is the consequence of the presence of a French military contingent, the third pillar of Françafrique.

Like everything else that grows on the Ivorian soil, the subsoil abounds in high value-added resources, not even counting oil. Indeed, Africa has often been referred to as a "geological scandal".

In the 60s, a French company [Mokta] mined manganese in Grand-Lahou. It left one day, we don't know why. It had left tons of ore on the port of Abidjan. In 2001, the Chinese bought up everything abandoned on the docks. They did some research, and discovered previously unknown reserves. But there's also a lot of gas, bauxite, gold and diamonds. French geologists have mapped the subsoil, and have long been aware of all the riches to be found there.

After France's refusal to assist us in 2002 against the rebels who had attacked us, I no longer wanted these defense agreements, which had proved useless and even harmful. What's more, since they give France all our strategic raw materials in return for this non-existent military aid, I decided to put an end to this fool's bargain. I made it clear that I intended to put an end to it. This was to happen after the 2010 elections. We were going to restructure and strengthen our own army. Sarkozy knew it. He must not have liked it. To appease me, in 2009, a French delegation came to our country to renegotiate these agreements, without success.

Félix Houphouët-Boigny feared military coups. A number of his colleagues had been overthrown in neighboring countries. The President was therefore quick not to invest in a national army. He relied entirely on France for his security. The perfect, even caricatural, illustration of the Franco-African spirit can be seen in the construction of his private residence, "his bunker". The two buildings are linked by a tunnel, enabling the "Father of the Nation" to take refuge on French territory in the event of an emergency. The whole Françafrique mentality, nurtured on connivance, submission and protection, can be seen in this armored tunnel. With defense agreements - in other words, dependency agreements - signed as early as 1961. Mamadou Koulibaly[10] *"We should say 'agreements for the administrative, commercial and monetary protection of our countries by France'. These are protectionist agreements."*

These agreements were renegotiated and signed in Paris on January 26, 2012 by Alassane Ouattara and Nicolas Sarkozy.

My decision to leave the CFA franc was irrevocable. We had contacts for the purchase of paper and machinery. But you don't make such fundamental reforms - it's practically a revolution - in troubled times. First of all, we had to maintain the State.

This must be done within the framework of the West African Monetary Union [8 French-speaking countries: Côte d'Ivoire, Burkina Faso, Mali, Guinea-Bissau, Senegal, Togo, Benin, Niger]. To achieve this, each head of state must have the courage to defy the tutelage of France. And to turn, together, to the Central Bank of West Africa, instead of the Bank of France.

Or else, Côte d'Ivoire goes it alone: Cape Verde has done it, and has a currency that holds its own. We in Côte d'Ivoire account for 40% of the WAEMU's GDP, and 62% of its exports. But you don't make such fundamental reforms in a period troubled by war. As I said, the first thing to do was to maintain the State. This is a burning obligation everywhere, and even more so in Africa, where everything still needs to be done...

Africa, like Asia and South America, hasn't found its way. It's about time we got on with it, and made it possible for us to be treated in Dakar, Abidjan, Lomé and elsewhere. In the past, you could go to Kinshasa. Nowadays, people go to Europe or Cape Town, South Africa: that's the failure of black Africa.

In the days of Françafrique, special advisors appointed to heads of state, ambassadors like Maurice Robert or Maurice Delauney *("Politics*

---

10. Mamadou Koulibaly was President of the National Assembly under Laurent Gbagbo.

takes precedence over morality in the exercise of my official mission", he once said), mercenaries thrown into hot spots like Bob Denard, all kept a watchful eye on things. The entire state apparatus of French-speaking countries was in the hands of French officials and agents. The maintenance of presidents like Léon Mba in Gabon, restored to the throne by French military intervention after a coup d'état, and then, on his death, his replacement by Albert-Bernard Bongo, through the invention of a hand-sewn vice-presidential post for the occasion, are well-known examples among many other twisted coups, rigged elections, targeted assassinations and so on.

Behind all these actions, a single name: Jacques Foccart. The most powerful man in France after the President of the Republic, Foccart didn't pay much for his private export business. He held no official position, and never agreed to be paid by the State. Which is an understatement when you consider that, in charge of African and Madagascan affairs, he ran a formidable money machine through the networks that bear his name. No one had any problem with the secretive, mafia-like nature of his operations. In the context of the Cold War, it was supposed to contribute to the fight against Communist influence. Ideology often disguises, or accommodates, the most materialistic motivations. Foccart's African cell, based at 2, rue de l'Élysée, had a staff of over a hundred, and decided everything to do with Africa in the greatest secrecy, without any democratic control, far from parliamentary debate or the press. A black cabinet to run the empire underhand. Foccart reported only to the President. He was the only man allowed to see De Gaulle every day, in the late afternoon, during his two mandates… Unlimited financial resources - thanks to the slush fund of ELF, the oil company created and managed by Pierre Guillaumat to exploit Gabon's oil - control over special services such as the Sdece, and the recruitment of men from the Gaullist secret services - the BCRA - created during the war, enabled Jacques Foccart to carry out for thirty years, under several presidents of the Fifth Republic, the mission assigned to him by De Gaulle: to keep Africa for France. After his departure, General De Gaulle never saw Foccart, his daily evening visitor, even though they had never missed a single daily meeting. Chroniclers still wonder about this attitude, which resembles the disavowal that men of dirty deeds incur. From SAC to Françafrique, Foccart's two creations, necessity was the law. The end justified the means. One can have ideas of grandeur, and, in certain periods, govern by holding one's nose.

By this time, Paris had become accustomed to seeing African policy as a mere extension of French policy. Côte d'Ivoire was treated as an extraterritorial dependency, and the leaders of its pré carré, the former colonies, as obligations. The latter, for the most part, have understood this so well that they have been eager to get involved, more out of self-interest than conviction. At times, they have even become the best defenders of a system of alienation that Gbagbo has always criticized. So it's natural that the right-wing French presidents from 1995 to 2012 saw Gbagbo as nothing more than an adversary. Firstly, he is a socialist by atavism - his father had joined the SFIO in 1947 - and was for a time vice-president of the Socialist International. Secondly, what has always bothered Parisian circles, on the right and left, is that apart from his membership of the Socialist Party, of which he has never been a godillot, he belongs to no coterie, no freemasonry, no underground network. There's nothing to identify him, assimilate him, co-opt him or put pressure on him. His fellow heads of state in French-speaking Africa love the secret initiation ceremonies of the Masonic rites, and all the other paraphernalia they believe will enable them to enter the world of the powerful, the universe of the Whites.

Alassane Ouattara's connections with international finance, thanks to his position at the IMF, combined with his wife Dominique's media and social networks, mean that he hasn't needed to rely on his "brothers in light" to achieve his ends. He may need them to restore the image of him portrayed by *The Economist* in 2013: that of a President surrounded by militia leaders and criminals, of whom he would be a prisoner. On December 31, 2012, an article in the *Huffington Post* was more radical. Under the pen of Philip N. Howard, a professor at Princeton University, Alassane Ouattara was included in a list of sixteen aging dictators, whose eventual demise augurs unrest and "surprises" in the countries where they rule. The problem with this American ranking is undoubtedly that Alassane Ouattara appears in it after having been chosen by the international community.

7.

"LET THEM CHECK THE FACTS!"

"Why in France do you prefer Alassane Ouattara?" I once asked a famous Parisian journalist. He replied: "Because he looks like us!"

Gbagbo often tells this anecdote because it amuses him, and seems to reveal the root of his problems.

Henri Emmanuelli, former President of the French National Assembly, friend and "astral twin brother" of Gbagbo[11], sums up this antagonism as follows: "*Laurent Gbagbo had one concern from the outset: to make Côte d'Ivoire an independent country. That's what he hasn't been forgiven for.*" Then he recounts the attempt to overthrow him at the start of his presidential term: "*In 2002, the Ivorian president warned that an insurrection was in the offing. France replied that it knew nothing about it.*"

Referring to the massive military attack from neighboring Burkina Faso to occupy half the country, which definitively deprived him of any influence over most of the territory, Laurent Gbagbo recalls this response from the French authorities. **Of course they didn't warn me. Because they were in on it.**

Michèle Alliot-Marie was then Minister of Defense in the Chirac government. When asked about France's passivity in the face of these events, to officially justify its failure to comply with the defense agreements signed in 1961 between the two countries, which obliged France

---

11. They were born on the same day of the same year: May 31, 1945.

to provide military assistance to the legal authorities in the event of external aggression, she replied, with the utmost bad faith: *"This is an Ivorian-Ivorian affair. Of course, there's no question of France interfering in its affairs."*

As far as she was concerned, these agreements were null and void. That's what she told me when I asked her to intervene in the defense agreements. She's the kind of person who talks first, then tries to justify what she's saying. It's often grotesque.

This is what Laurent Gbagbo, who survived the military coup, the non-assistance of his "historic ally", and then, for twelve years, the occupation of 60% of Ivorian territory, tells me.

In 2000, when I was elected, a smear campaign flourished in France. Because they wouldn't accept my election. Again in 2010, they refused to accept my election. Because the crux of the debate during the post-election crisis in 2010 was who won the election? We didn't want that debate. They evacuated it by trying to delegitimize me once again. Instead of recounting the votes and examining the PVs from the polling stations, they let the rebels launch violent attacks against the forces of law and order, and then accused me of being behind the violence. They didn't want to see the facts. When you deny the facts, when you want to ignore them, it's because you're acting in bad faith, it's because you're lying. I'll say the facts, under any circumstances, without necessarily trying to convince, but so that people can check the facts. That's where the truth lies. But thanks to the proceedings before the ICC, the truth that we tried to hide is emerging. My defense team has shown that the accusations against me were politically motivated: the accusation of having suppressed a peaceful demonstration on December 16, 2010 doesn't hold water for a second, because in fact the peaceful demonstration was an attack led by groups of well-armed, well-equipped, well-trained professional mercenaries, obeying a strategy put in place by Ouattara and his warlords with the aim of seizing power by force; all the evidence is there, including footage shot at

the rebels' headquarters. Nobody wanted to see this evidence, because the idea at the time was to use this alleged repression of a supposedly peaceful march to convince the international community of the moral illegitimacy of my presence in power. The accusation of having fired on a women's march in March 2011? It doesn't hold water either, as my Defense team demonstrated in February 2013. You will note that my lawyers proved that one of the favorite modus operandi of the Ouattara camp, advised apparently by the French, was to organize pseudo "peaceful marches", placing women and children in the front row and concealing fighters armed not only with weapons of war like Kalashnikovs but also heavier weapons like RPGs, in the midst of the demonstrators whom they used as human shields. Here again, the reality of the facts was irrelevant: all it took was for the accusations to be made to be picked up, without investigation, by the French media. What was the point? To put an end to the mediation attempts we had initiated. The accusation that government forces bombed a district of Abidjan in March 2011? My lawyers did justice to that. They laid bare the basis of this allegation: vague, contradictory testimonies, each one more incoherent than the last, many obtained by hearsay. Once again, the French media have made themselves the objective allies of the Ouattara camp. Why these accusations? A few days later, France lobbied the United Nations Security Council to adopt a resolution permitting the use of force against us. French diplomats - and journalists - drew parallels between the bombing of the Abobo market and the bombing of the Sarajevo market. The aim was to speak to Western consciences and convince them to let the French launch a military offensive. As soon as the 1975 resolution was passed, the French army launched rebel groups from the north of the country towards the south, having organized their route and ensured their logistics. They committed abominable crimes as they advanced, before attacking civilian populations in Abidjan. As in 2000 and 2002, in 2010 it was we who were attacked, and if there were deaths - too many deaths - it was because a war had been launched from abroad, resulting in an invasion of mercenaries recruited from neighbouring countries, supported by French forces. The aim was to topple the government of a sovereign country and seize its institutions. Do you want to list the victims of rebel attacks in 2000, 2001, 2002, 2010 and 2011? I'm not afraid of the truth; I've always asked for it. The truth appears in the documents exchanged before the ICC, in particular in the summaries my lawyers produced in response to the Prosecutor's accusations. My opponents, on the other hand, are running away from the truth, always refusing the means to bring it to light. They pushed for a confrontation between Ivorians, and they know why. They tried to blame me for the fighting. They went even further, talking of exactions allegedly committed by government forces. But as I said, accusations don't stand up to scrutiny. No matter who the accuser is, particularly the prosecutor, he or she never manages to attribute a large number of victims to the FDS. Yet there were many victims during the post-electoral crisis in 2010 and 2011. So who is responsible? The armed rebel groups who infiltrated Abidjan before the elections; the Invisible Commando, who preyed on the population and killed in the heart of Abidjan; the French forces, who carried out numerous attacks against government forces and caused a great deal of "collateral damage"; the rebel forces who invaded the south of the country in March 2011, leaving behind them a trail of horror and bloodshed. How many innocent victims? No one seems to care. Yet thousands of civilians have been killed.

After the attack on the country in September 2002, the invasion and occupation of the territory by rebels from Burkina Faso, Wade and Chirac asked me to grant an amnesty for all their crimes. Over three hundred people had been killed in 24 hours in Abidjan, including army officers, my Interior Minister and childhood friend Émile Boga Doudou, all of whom were murdered by surprise, and General Robert Guéï - whose murder was blamed on men from my camp. I declared a general amnesty so as not to cut ties with our aggressors, even if they were wrong, even if they had put the country to fire and blood. I wanted to leave a chance for future peace. And now I'm being called to account? All those who followed the line of appeasement and reconciliation I advocated are today persecuted, hunted down and imprisoned by the new authorities. They are said to be criminals to justify their treatment in the eyes of the world. It's a rather heavy-handed line, but it allows for all kinds of excesses in terms of repression and confiscation of rights and property. How many people have we imprisoned for no reason? How many have been driven from their homes? Their homes have been stolen, and are now occupied by rebels, or by foreigners who have come to seek their fortune thanks to the war and the invasion of our territory.

When François Hollande went to Dakar and Kinshasa in October 2012, I listened to his speeches, and he talked about Northern Mali, the North Kivu province of Congo, the aggression of rebellions from outside, and France's support for aggressed states. I was deeply distressed. I didn't hear this when I was attacked in 2002. Those who should have reacted - France and the international community - did nothing. Why didn't they? Because they were in on it! From then on, I had to react, to see who could help me, since those who were supposed to do so were working against me. I was born in a country under French domination, and I became President of the Republic in a country where, before me, care had been taken not to build an army, and where we had these defense agreements. It wasn't my choice; I had to make do with what existed. In politics, you can't overestimate your abilities, and you have to take realities into account to help them evolve.

Barely three months after my election on October 22, 2000, in January 2001, a first putsch attempt against me by people close to Ouattara failed. It was the so-called "black Mercedes" affair, the car of IB, the leader of the mutineers and former bodyguard of Alassane Ouattara. Those who carried out this operation remained close to Alassane Ouattara.

In September 2002, I was visiting Italy when another coup d'état took place. The one that led to the partition of the country, and opened the politico-military crisis that was to last ten years.

I remember that we had just passed the health insurance law, and the attack took place shortly afterwards. I saw a cause-and-effect relationship: this particular project had to be broken. If we'd managed to implement it, with two funds - one for farmers, one for all other workers - the lives of Ivorians would have been changed. For the farmers, it was easy to finance, with cocoa, coffee and rubber. For the other fund, it was more difficult, but we had planned to finance it through levies on the mines: gold, diamonds, etc. We had already bought the building that was to house the fund. We had already bought the building that would house the offices of this health insurance scheme.

We had begun decentralization, with the creation of general councils that are still in operation today. High schools, dispensaries and roads were built by these councils. But we weren't allowed to go all the way: regional taxation, with the creation of ten large regions and departments, would ensure development. We provided free access to primary and secondary schools right from the start, and if not the whole country benefited, it was because of the war and the division of the country into two parts.

In Paris, this policy frightened them. They realized that Côte d'Ivoire had the means to do it all on its own: in the end, in ten years, I electrified more villages than had been done in forty years. We didn't have the time to do what we'd planned with solar power. We've lost our momentum.

We were self-sufficient, and continued to be so after the 2002 attack, even though we no longer controlled more than 40% of the national territory: the salaries of government employees have always been paid, and only twice have we had difficulties with repayments: once 100 million to the ADB, another time to the World Bank. But we've managed. Economically, despite the huge debts left to us by the previous Bédié government, we always managed to be self-sufficient, and finally, through very prudent management, to meet the HIPC [Heavily Indebted Poor Countries] criteria. We were in a position to ask for Côte d'Ivoire's debt to be cancelled, and I initiated the negotiations. But you have to know what "debt cancellation" means, which many French people don't know, because they think they're giving "gifts" to Africans. No one gives gifts to anyone in this world: the government debts that are announced as being "cancelled" are in fact privatized: in other words, the sums owed are ultimately paid to private companies in the creditor countries, to carry out work in our countries. It's a golden windfall for Western companies, French in particular. The poverty of some makes many others richer. That's the system.

On September 18 and 19, 2002, I was on an official trip to Rome. As soon as I arrived, who did I see at the hotel? Robert Bourgi. Of course, I found the coincidence curious, and to be honest, it couldn't have been. We had dinner together.

I met the President of the Republic, then I met Silvio Berlusconi, who was then President of the Council. We talked politics and projects: he gave me a brilliant talk on "E-government", proposing his country's collaboration in computerizing our administration. He told me that he had lost a lot of money in France. He walked me back to the car, holding my arm, and when we were alone and he was sure no one would hear him, he said: "I like you. If I can give you one piece of advice: watch out for Chirac. He's very nice like that, but he's a backstabber."

After that, I saw the mayor of Rome, and was due to see the Pope the next day. I went back to the hotel. At around 3 or 4 a.m. - it was 2 a.m. in Abidjan - I received a phone call informing me of the massive military attack launched throughout the country. I decided to return home immediately. Robert Bourgi appeared at that moment and insisted: "Go to Paris to see your big brother [Chirac]". At the time, I thought of all those heads of state in Africa who had gone on a trip and had never been able to return... I didn't see the Pope, I didn't go to Paris to see Chirac. I went back to Abidjan.

There was a problem with the flight plan, as the pilots had not been warned early enough. I couldn't leave Rome the same day. I returned on September 20. The Minister of Defense and the Prime Minister were waiting for me at the airport. It was they who informed me of the death of Émile Boga Doudou, the Minister of the Interior, who was assassinated as he tried to flee his home, alone and unarmed.

I spoke on Ivorian television the very day I arrived. I called for unity in the face of the coup. I reiterated our progress objectives. I pointed out that, from the day I was sworn in on October 26, 2000, we had gone from a negative growth rate of minus 2.3% to minus 0.9% by the end of 2001, and that we were heading for 5-6%, according to expert forecasts. Our place in international institutions was restored. There was no question of stealing the fruits of our efforts and jeopardizing the country's future for the sole benefit of a few. I obviously condemned the action of the putschists.

Chirac phoned to reproach me for having been too harsh in my remarks: "You called them terrorists!" "But finally," I said, "if you wake up and are told that rebels have just attacked the capital, what do you say?" He said, "You have to negotiate with them." I suspected that the rebels had been trained at the Pô camp in Burkina. There had been rumors. But the day I mentioned it to Villepin, some time before the coup, he replied: "Blaise [Compaoré, the President of Burkina Faso] wouldn't do that!"

The coup failed, leaving hundreds dead on the ground. The rebels occupied more than half the country. France sent in a peacekeeping force and set up a "zone of confidence". I decreed a general amnesty as a message of peace.

8.

"A WHITE-GLOVE COUP D'ÉTAT"

Dominique Galouzeau, better known as Dominique de Villepin, Chirac's Minister of Foreign Affairs, set up the Linas-Marcoussis Round Table in France in January 2003. This conference was presented as a French initiative to restore peace, achieve disarmament and organize cohabitation with the rebels. I wasn't invited, in other words, the Ivorian state wasn't invited to a discussion on the future of Côte d'Ivoire! I've only been invited to the subsequent meeting on Avenue Kléber, where the agreements are to be signed. I don't take part, I don't have a say, but I'm asked to come and sign... That's the great thing about Galouzeau de Villepin, who always seemed so sure of himself! Around the table were all the Ivorian political parties, some of which, having emerged from the rebellion, were thus recognized by the French authorities as valid interlocutors, placed on an equal footing with the parliamentary and democratic parties. Between the three rebel parties, and those of the opposition, who marched together, the government parties found themselves, from the outset, in the minority. At first, I thought that France wanted to curb the rebellion. But I was wrong.

I've always chosen to talk to everyone... To find a way out of the crisis, there were meetings in Lomé, Togo, in Accra, Ghana, on three occasions, in Pretoria, South Africa, in Marcoussis, France, then in Ouagadougou, Burkina Faso... Not to mention all the meetings in Abidjan, the 2001 Reconciliation Forum, the regional elections I orga-

nized despite the obstacles, and the informal meetings devoted to the search for peaceful, negotiated solutions.

As a historian, I've never in history seen a "dictator" negotiate with his adversaries, and better still, make so many concessions to them.

In my own camp, not everyone has always understood that I would go so far in dialogue, after the war they waged against us in 2002. Is this the mark of a dictatorship? Well, at Marcoussis, France built me an armed opposition… with which I was asked to govern. Dominique de Villepin and Pierre Mazeaud even tried to give the Interior and Defense Ministries to the rebels! Even though they had just carried out a military putsch against the elected President, killing hundreds of Ivorians! They had lost the game, and France put them back on the same footing as the legitimate authorities… Villepin called it "diplomatie de mouvement", but I see it more as a coup d'état in white gloves.

This levelling of responsibilities in the Ivorian conflict, with aggressors and aggressed placed back to back, was indeed officially initiated in 2003, at Linas-Marcoussis, during the "Round Table" organized by France, keeping out the incumbent president Laurent Gbagbo. The aim was to organize a government of national unity bringing together the political parties and the rebels, as Mamadou Koulibaly recounts in his book *La guerre de la France contre la Côte d'Ivoire*[12]: "*[…] After the failure of the coup d'état (of September 2002) and its transformation into a rebellion supported and organized by France, it became imperative to make everyone admit that there were no military solutions. Having failed, France did not give the Ivorian state the right to retaliate, but forced it to negotiate with the rebels… […] I still remember the scene where* [Pierre] *Mazeaud, his arms open like banners, proclaimed from the top of his perch that there were no rebels in Côte d'Ivoire, and that there were none around the Round Table either. From that moment on, everything becomes possible, since there is no longer an aggressor, no longer a victim, and therefore no longer a guilty party…*" Mamadou Koulibaly was so shocked by what he saw as a hostage-taking of his country's future, and a denial of its sovereignty, that he slammed the door and returned home.

---

12. Mamadou Koulibaly, *La Guerre de la France contre la Côte d'Ivoire*, L'Harmattan, 2003.

But the reversal of history is well underway. The coup d'état machine, having abandoned its failed "military software", is now operating in "political mode". The cursor has been placed on the same objective as Gbagbo: the organization of elections. A high-risk convergence of minds.

The Marcoussis Round Table therefore took place without me, bringing together a majority of opposition and rebel parties, since there were seven of them, and a minority (two parties) representing the government, with my Prime Minister Pascal Affi N'Guessan for the FPI. I hesitated before coming to the Avenue Kléber conference. People around me were telling me either to go, so as not to leave my chair empty, or to refuse, so as not to enter an endless tunnel. It's true that it looked like a trap, but in the end I decided to go, to see, to listen, and to keep my hand in. I couldn't let things develop out of control. I soon realized that it was going to be a tough game. I arrived on Thursday January 23, 2003, on a scheduled Air France flight: I was afraid my presidential plane would be shot at. Anything is possible. I was due to meet Chirac at the Élysée Palace at 4 p.m. the next day. On the morning of that famous Friday, the text of the Marcoussis agreements was slipped under the door of my room at the Hotel Meurice. Bongo was staying at the same hotel, to work on my body. He was a friend of Ouattara's, and France's most loyal ally since the death of Houphouët. I left for the Élysée Palace at 11 a.m. Le Monde had already been published. I read it in the car, and discovered that on page 2, it already listed the name of the future Prime Minister, Henriette Diabaté, a close friend of Ouattara's and a member of his party, the RDR.

When Chirac, Galouzeau and I were together, Chirac told me that he wanted Henriette Diabaté to be Prime Minister. Thank you, I'd already read that in the paper! That's exactly what Françafrique is all about. I refused to sign. Chirac asked me why. I explained that, for the Ivorians, it would appear as a bonus given to the rebels, because Ouattara was notoriously considered the organizer and perpetrator of the September 2002 aggression against Côte d'Ivoire. Chirac admitted as much. I asked them to come up with another name. I too suggested several. Chirac asked Villepin to accept my proposals at the next mee-

ting. Galouzeau told me we'd meet again at 7pm, at the Quai d'Orsay: "You'll be received with the honors due to your rank, through the front door", he said.

At 5 p.m., when I enter the meeting room, Ouattara and Bédié are already there, settled in. Soro is not there. Villepin telephones him. When he finally arrived, he was ushered in through the main door. Like the other two before me, of course. Villepin made it clear how little respect he had for me and my position.

Villepin, Soro and Ouattara took up Henriette Diabaté's mantra in chorus. It was like a choir that had rehearsed its concert together. I said to Villepin: "Aren't you even listening to your president?" He seemed to think he was a bit like Jacques Foccart, a bit like Jacques Chirac, and I wonder if he didn't think he was superior to both, by thinking he was Dominique de Villepin. He also wanted to avenge the tumultuous welcome he had received from a few hundred Ivorians a few weeks earlier in Abidjan, who had tried to prevent him from reaching the French Embassy residence, adjoining that of the Presidency, where I had just received him. His expressions of sympathy for the rebels, and his handshake with their leader Guillaume Soro during his visit to their stronghold of Bouaké on January 4, had earned him the wrath of Abidjan's Ivorians, still traumatized by the coup attempt of the previous September 19. France has never been a mere arbiter in Africa. It has always found every reason to remain a highly directive player in the internal life of the countries it controls.

"In so doing," writes Guy Labertit[13], *"France, officially committed to the rule of law, has legitimized an armed rebellion supported by neighboring countries, and delivered a tremendous slap in the face to the elected president, Laurent Gbagbo, for whom the town of Bouaké and half the country have become a no-go zone."*

---

13. Guy Labertit, *Adieu, Abidjan-sur-Seine! Behind the scenes of the Ivorian conflict*, Autres Temps Éditions, 2008.

Villepin told me that if I didn't accept Henriette Diabaté, he would give the Interior and Defense ministries to the rebels. I refused everything and left the Quai d'Orsay very angry.

On leaving this nerve-wracking meeting, where the objective alliance between Ouattara, Villepin, Bédié and the three rebel parties was obvious, Gbagbo remembers exclaiming to his friend Guy Labertit: *"The HQ of the rebellion is the Quai d'Orsay!"*

We met on Saturday January 25 at the Avenue Kléber conference center, and I had a restricted meeting with President Omar Bongo, UN Secretary General Kofi Annan and Villepin. We discussed the issue of the Prime Minister, which was still unresolved. The choice fell on Seydou Diarra, a former Prime Minister under Robert Guéï, who accompanied Pierre Mazeaud, the Marcoussis master of ceremonies. Villepin was very insistent; I know he said, referring to me: "You have to twist his arm."

We then shared out the ministries to form a government of national unity.

It was on that Saturday evening that Guillaume Soro set Abidjan ablaze, claiming on a French public radio station that the rebels had won the Interior and Defense ministries. Soro wanted to make people forget that he had not achieved his aims. It was a question of claiming victory, while at the same time stirring up unrest, since the Ivorians were certainly not going to admit that the rebels were so favored by the French. This unrest would then be blamed on me, and against me, by those who might have thought I'd betrayed them.

It's not a solution that was presented at Marcoussis. They just wanted, at best, to turn me into the "Queen of England", so that I no longer had any real political role. Emptying the Constitution, and my status, of their content, that's what Chirac wanted. And that's what I reproached him for. I didn't recognize his right to weaken the State. As for Villepin, he wanted to get rid of me.

In neighboring countries, still in 2003, Jacques Chirac was less careful about democratic orthodoxy. The President congratulated General

Eyadema even before his umpteenth re-election was proclaimed, a re-election of dubious regularity. In power since 1967, with two successive coups d'état - the first against Sylvanus Olympio, whom he and his accomplices assassinated in January 1963, then against his friend Nicolas Grunitzky, whom he overthrew in June 1967 - in 2003 he passed the milestone of thirty-six years of dictatorial power, with the massive support of France, for whom he played the role of regional policeman. This earned him the compassion of Jacques Chirac post mortem - in 2005 - when he spoke of the *"loss of a personal friend"*.

9

"THESE PEOPLE FEAR NO IGNOMINY"

At Marcoussis, according to Jean-Christophe Notin[14], author of *Le Crocodile et le Scorpion,* an "official-officer" of Sarkozy's military campaign in Cocody, Dominique de Villepin self-congratulated: *"I've pulled off a brilliant coup, I've given Defense and Interior to the rebels, who will now be forced to disarm themselves."* Isn't this simply contempt for Ivorian institutions? Is it not a refusal to recognize the existence of a government elected by the Ivorian people? Notin sees this as a step forward. But by claiming that this attempted coup de force was carried out with the acceptable intention of forcing the rebels to disarm, he is rewriting history. In fact, he is merely justifying *a posteriori* France's role in its bad manners against the president of a sovereign state. Jean-Christophe Notin, a historian of military affairs who has become a specialist in the Ivorian crisis as seen from the Élysée Palace, was *"encouraged"* to take an interest in the case, even though, according to him, he had no particular knowledge of, or interest in, the Ivorian affair. But his book has the answer to everything. He was given the files concocted by the French government and military authorities at the time: his acknowledgements page is edifying in this respect. From Claude Guéant to Jean-David Levitte, diplomatic advisor, André Parant, Africa advisor, General Benoît Puga, the President's private chief of staff, and all the members of the Quai d'Orsay, the Treasury, the army, etc., who took

---

14. Jean-Christophe Notin, *Le Crocodile et le Scorpion: la France et la Côte d'Ivoire (1999-2013),* Éditions du Rocher, 2013.

part in the anti-Gbagbo offensive. Signed at swordpoint, *"an 'S' standing for Sarkozy"* appears as a watermark behind the author's name. The French state is fully mobilized, as if it were the "Great War". In the exaltation of this epic tale, a Licorne officer even goes so far as to compare the courage of his soldiers during the assault on Gbagbo's residence to that of the poilus of 1914! An incongruous allusion, insulting to the million and a half French dead of the Great War, whose centenary we are celebrating in 2014. Our heroes all returned safely from their assault on Abidjan in 2010. *"Zero deaths"*, says an officer at the end of the operation. As part of a meticulous communications plan, this epic of the Ivorian crisis was obviously conceived in high places, with a view to Nicolas Sarkozy's victory in the 2012 presidential election. *A posteriori* justification of the French intervention, in particular the military intervention, explanation of the close ties forged on this occasion by French civilian and military officials with the new masters of Abidjan, a memoir in defense against possible prosecution, but above all the first real attempt to construct a global narrative designed to support the charges brought against President Gbagbo in The Hague. *Le Crocodile et le Scorpion* is all these things at once.

Abidjan once earned the nickname "Little Paris". The city stretches from boulevard Mitterrand to pont Charles-de-Gaulle, from boulevard Valéry Giscard d'Estaing, to boulevard Angoulvant (a French colonial administrator), to the commune of Port-Bouët (commandant Bouët-Villaumez was sent by the French king in 1837 to negotiate agreements with local authorities). The capital's toponymy is riddled with French names. They can be found everywhere, particularly in zone 4. It's easy to see why a Frenchman would feel at home here. During his ten years as president, Laurent Gbagbo never renamed a single street, square or bridge to replace it with an African name, as was done everywhere else after independence. Noting this in passing would no doubt have softened the anti-French character deliberately attributed to Gbagbo, the better to stigmatize him and make him hated. On the other hand, Notin's book does contain a number of "revelations" that are quite outrageous. Mamadou Koulibaly is said to have tried to bribe participants at the Marcoussis conference. Those who know and appreciate the former president of the National Assembly, as well as those who detest him, including those in

Laurent Gbagbo's entourage, share the same inextinguishable laughter. For if there's one flaw Gbagbo's ex-numéro 2 doesn't possess, it's a taste for *combinazione*. Mamadou Koulibaly, whom I know well, sees any compromise as a risk of compromise. In fact, he has often been criticized for his intransigence when it comes to republican values, which his detractors find too unpolitical for their liking.

The Hague prosecutor Fatou Bensouda, who will no doubt have read *Le Crocodile et le Scorpion*, will no doubt recognize her own calligraphy of the Ivorian drama. Jean-Christophe Notin pulls out all the stops to try and make people believe that Gbagbo was a dictator. As a result, the author pulls out all the stops. The problem is that he hasn't interviewed anyone who might have been able to show a reality other than that conveyed by French officials and the media. Since Gbagbo's fall, this version of history has been challenged by researchers, and above all by President Gbagbo's defense team, led by international lawyer Emmanuel Altit, in The Hague, before the International Criminal Court. To lend credibility to his thesis, Notin spares no detail: secret political meetings, comments by French officials, troop movements. The whole rhetoric is based on a wealth of details concerning action on the ground, from 1993 to 2011. How can we doubt a text in which the first and last names of every officer, the topography of locations, the identification of equipment used, the calendar of dates and the times of events are so precisely recorded? Information skilfully scattered throughout the book aims to legitimize French action, to answer objections point by point, and, as a bonus, to discredit Laurent Gbagbo once and for all. When it comes to portraiture, Jean-Christophe Notin gives up the keyboard and takes up spray-painting: "[…] *like Charlie Chaplin playing with a globe in* The Great Dictator, *the President himself activates a 'galaxy', a group of associations of idle young Ivorians, to whom his colonialist speeches have made them forget their misery*". But sometimes the discourse is flawed, and the truth shines through. For example, when Notin quotes the French ambassador to Abidjan, Renaud Vignal (2001-2002), who wrote in a report: *"With Gbagbo, we have one of the best heads of state this country can currently have"*. Go figure… Laurent Gbagbo remembers the ambassador's U-turn.

After Lionel Jospin's defeat in 2000, and Chirac's victory, followed by Dominique de Villepin's takeover of the Ivorian issue, everything changed, and Renaud Vignal was no longer the same vis-à-vis me.

Jean-Christophe Notin "polishes" his demonstration with a number of juicy revelations. After the President's arrest: "[…] *the French went to search Gbagbo's residence. They discovered all the 'classics' of a despot on a holiday: cigars and grands crus, hundreds of pairs of shoes and outfits, as well as a substantial stock of Viagra pills for Mr. and brown heroin for Mrs.*"

Simone Gbagbo has been so discredited in the French media that no limits are respected in her regard. Even if the author indicates, in a discreet footnote, that he doesn't know whether *"it's for her personal consumption or that of those close to her"*. Treated in turn as God's madwoman, a witch leading *"death squads"*, we finally discover her to be a drug addict, or at best, a drug dealer. Anyone who has come into contact with Simone Gbagbo, whether friend or foe, knows that this revelation is not credible. Drugs have never been part of Simone Gbagbo's world. If this had been the case, how could it have escaped the indulgence of those who have scrutinized her for ten years? While the Gbagbo bubble was infiltrated from all sides…

As for the Head of State's cellar, it contained nothing more, and rather less, than that of his counterparts, for invitations and receptions, namely wine cellar and cigars.

I stopped smoking a long time ago. Wine, champagne and cigars for receptions were certainly a hundred times less, perhaps a thousand times less, than at the Élysée Palace. Most of the time, it was my visitors who gave me cigars. And I, in turn, offered them to amateurs. As for me, I know only too well what this attack means. As for alcohol, look at Ouattara, who drinks scotch, or Bédié, who is more of a cognac drinker… On the other hand, the reference to the discovery of Viagra and heroin is the epitome of French political thought under Nicolas Sarkozy… These people fear no ignominy, and to see them at work in Africa only shows what they are capable of… Here, they've shown their true colors. What they should say, and what is true, is that I pro-

bably had the most beautiful library of classic French books in all of Africa, and they destroyed it all with their incendiary bombs.

As Notin's book sets out to demonstrate the legitimacy and effectiveness of army chief Nicolas Sarkozy's Abidjan military campaign, we learn, among other things, that Alassane Ouattara employed a DGSE officer to write his war speeches during the crisis. These were retransmitted by a satellite TV station entirely supplied, installed and paid for by Paris. As was the bill for the Hôtel du Golf, where Ouattara, Soro, their government and several hundred armed men stayed for over five months, supplied and transported by our helicopters and those of the UN. Not to mention the installation by French companies, at great expense, of a pro-Ouattara television and radio station. Jean-Christophe Notin, who likes to be precise and exhaustive, may have had access to the total cost of the shipment. In these times of crisis, this budgetary aspect would be of interest to many French people, and would no doubt shed light on the price Nicolas Sarkozy paid for the victory of his friend Alassane Ouattara in Côte d'Ivoire. Certainly much more than a simple recount. But this detail is nowhere to be found in this 441-page pamphlet. It should be noted that Jean-Michel Fourgous, the French National Assembly's defence budget rapporteur at the time, officially put the cost of the intervention in Côte d'Ivoire at 65 million euros. The annual cost of the French military presence in 2010 was estimated by some[15] at 150 million, and by others at 200 million euros. Unfortunately, the author is silent on the timing of the bill and the details of the special services involved.

Finally, Notin's account of a telephone conversation between Laurent Gbagbo and Robert Bourgi in Claude Guéant's office at the Élysée Palace, in the presence of the latter, leaves me perplexed. The Franco-African lawyer and intermediary confirmed the existence of this conversation. But unlike Notin, he does not say that Laurent Gbagbo adopted a threatening tone or language. Perhaps to lend credibility to his unvarnished portrait of Laurent Gbagbo, Notin attributes the following remarks to him: *"You*

---

15. *Le Monde diplomatique*, April 15, 2011.

tell Sarkozy that I'll be his Mugabe! I'll never leave Côte d'Ivoire to Ouattara, I'll bathe it in blood!"

After the alcohol, the drugs, the *"bloodbath"*. Robert Bourgi, an influential intermediary in relations between France and "his" Africa, received me in his office on rue Pierre-1er-de-Serbie, Paris, on November 29, 2012. Surrounded by drawings by his daughter Clarence, Laurent Gbagbo's goddaughter, Napoleonic relics that make his office look like an imperial museum, framed photos of Omar Bongo, De Gaulle, and one of him with Gbagbo in a white shirt, he tells me about that famous telephone conversation. He called Laurent Gbagbo in early December 2010, at Nicolas Sarkozy's request. A consummate actor, he reproduces the dialogue he had for a few seconds with Gbagbo, loudspeaker open, while he was at the Élysée Palace, with the President of the French Republic, and his Secretary General, Claude Guéant.

"'I beg you Laurent, leave the place. Five years goes by fast. You'll run again, and win hands down. You'll have head-of-state status, a teaching chair, you'll be able to come and go between Paris and Abidjan, and travel the world wherever you please. Listen to me, you know, we're the same age!' 'No, you're a month older than me,' Laurent Gbagbo replied, laughing. I argued and begged. He told me he wouldn't flinch. Finally, he hung up on me... I burst into tears. The President escorted me back to the grand staircase. 'Nicolas, you can't do that, you can't do that,' I said. 'If Bongo were still alive, you wouldn't dare!' I added in a tone full of innuendo. Nicolas looked at me and said, as we parted: 'It's a done deal, Robert, and I won't change the course of things'."

According to this testimony, Nicolas Sarkozy had already decided on his position on the Ivorian issue, and probably decided on military intervention, as early as December 2010. An analysis shared by an Ivorian politician from Abidjan, who often came to Paris. He still lives there, hence his anonymity: *"My friends at the Quai d'Orsay clearly told me, as early as the end of November 2010, that the Élysée's aim was to oust Gbagbo. The elections were just a pretext. The army staff and the entire French state machine were already preparing for action."*

I told Laurent Gbagbo what Robert Bourgi had said. He simply shrugged: **"When people ask me if I know Bourgi, I always reply that I know**

only one: Albert. University professor and political scientist, and brother of the other, Albert Bourgi has always been a selfless supporter of Laurent Gbagbo. Robert, clearly, no longer inspires confidence in a sulky Gbagbo, who imitates with a wavering hand the undulation of an elusive creature.

Jean-Christophe Notin's version is implausible: Laurent Gbagbo, even in the worst moments of his life, even under the bombs, even in prison, was never threatening or even discourteous. Robert Bourgi knows this better than anyone: his brother Albert, a university professor in Reims, would not have maintained thirty years of friendly, almost fraternal relations with a man who would eat such bread. To finish with this sample of lies set up like mortar rounds, Jean-Christophe Notin's account of Désiré Tagro's death will go down in history. A new definition of the term "beating". The assassination of Laurent Gbagbo's former Minister of the Interior, his jaw shattered by a point-blank shot as he surrendered to the rebels with a white flag to negotiate, bleeding to death as he was taken to the Hôtel du Golf, where he died, became for Notin an incident in a local police station: *"… having been beaten, he succumbed to his wounds the following day"*. A delicate euphemism. Yet Tagro had received assurances from the French special forces who were besieging and bombing the presidential residence. He was shot dead in front of the French soldiers.

Two confidences that Notin shared with me prove that he is not devoid of sensitivity. I asked him if he'd seen the photo of Simone Gbagbo kneeling during her arrest, held like an animal by a few henchmen posing as they do with game after the hunt. He tells me that he has seen many other, much more distressing photos in the files entrusted to him, which prove that Simone Gbagbo, like others, suffered unspeakable violence at the hands of the rebels after their capture. French army cameras filmed everything, before, during and after the attack on President Gbagbo's residence. Has Notin not seen the photos of Tagro's body? Did he not see the images of all those captured in the President's residence and murdered in the hours that followed? Some of the civilians who were about to be executed were, we might add, saved by French soldiers.

"THE BLUNDER WAS FRENCH"

After the attempted coup d'état in 2001, I asked the French ambassador, Francis Lott, to send me some technicians, because we'd had maintenance problems with our military equipment. The Ivorian army was a small army, not very numerous, not very well equipped. There was no need to have a big army, because the French were supposed to come to our rescue if we needed them. We only had a few planes, for example. Our planes either couldn't take off, or their equipment jammed. Two officers from the French air force landed at the Bouaké air base. They inspected the planes. They laughed: everything was seized up in there. So we tried to buy spare parts, but to my great surprise the French suppliers - since we had French equipment - refused to sell them to us. It was the aim of the French authorities to ensure that the Ivorian police, gendarmerie and army were disarmed in the face of rebels who had already made their presence felt on several occasions and were about to do so again. So, not only were the French refusing to honor their obligation under the defense agreement to provide assistance and protect us from repeated attacks by rebels regrouping and rearming in Burkina Faso, but they also wanted to make it impossible for the forces of law and order to do their job and protect the population from criminals. I couldn't leave the country at the mercy of highwaymen. It's important to understand that, in those days, rebel groups were akin to the great companies that devastated Europe in the

16th century. Later, in 2010 in particular, mercenaries were recruited en masse, trained in Burkina by foreign advisors, equipped with the latest gear and transferred to northern Côte d'Ivoire. In 2011, these mercenary units will be unleashed on the south of the country with the help and under the direction of French forces.

Returning to the beginnings of the rebellion, when the Minister of Defense was offered some equipment from Eastern Europe, he accepted to avoid leaving the country disarmed. Needless to say, this did not go down well with the French.

By 2004, the situation had changed: reconciliation was underway, and the central government was recognized by all, including some former rebels, as the legitimate government. In the rebel-occupied north of the country, the population was suffering more and more, victims of rackets, extortion, arbitrary confinement and murder. They regularly called on the authorities for help. So we thought it was time to put an end to these crimes, and then reunify the country. The general staff prepared a limited military operation, the echo of which was enough to make the rebels flee to Burkina Faso. The aim was to destroy the stockpiles of weapons that the rebels had amassed in Bouaké, in the center of the country. Allow me to remind you that, although I had done my part by integrating former rebels into the government, the rebels had never fulfilled their commitment to disarm. Quite the contrary, in fact. They had become rich through arms, and they didn't want to give that up. At that time, if the rebels had kept their promise, the country would have been reunited and all the armed groups disbanded. We were therefore doubly in the right, since on the one hand we had to uphold republican order, and on the other to prevent illegal armed groups engaged in criminal activities from doing any harm.

On November 6, 2004, I was told that nine French servicemen had died as a result of a bombing raid on Bouaké by our two aircraft. We were stunned. It later turned out to be a plot whose ultimate aim was to overthrow the legitimate government and oust me from power. For a long time, people didn't believe me. Today, the truth is beginning to emerge, thanks to the struggle of the families of the French servicemen killed, and also thanks to French army officers.

It's important to say today how it happened. I haven't spoken about it since 2010. I lived through this serious affair, understanding at every moment that I didn't have all the facts. I was on very good terms with the French ambassador at the time, Gildas Le Lidec, but he too was taken by surprise by the turn of events.

Contrary to what has been said, or written, based on confidences that I never made, and attributing to me remarks that I did not make, I was not opposed to an operation to destroy the rebel military infrastructure in Bouaké, which would then have enabled the reunification and pacification of the country. Some time earlier, I had to prevent officers from launching an offensive on Bouaké without orders from their superiors. The soldiers had arrived near Bouaké, a town that lies roughly in the middle of the country, on the median line between north and south, and were threatening to attack the rebels. I took a helicopter to talk to them and tell them that nothing had been decided and that they had to withdraw. This attempt by certain officers had sounded a warning: the army and the population wanted an end to the rebel exactions.

I knew that my chief of staff, Mathias Doué, was very close to the French, and to General Poncet in particular. Doué had studied at Saint-Cyr. I also knew that he had reservations about the planned operation in Bouaké. He didn't tell me anything about his misgivings, but I was aware of what he was saying on the outside. He wasn't being straightforward. I didn't understand what he had in mind.

I telephoned the French ambassador to tell him that the situation in the North was unbearable for the population, that the rebels' exactions had redoubled, that they were behaving, despite their commitments, on conquered ground and, given their persistent refusal to bow to republican legality and respect their written commitments, we had no choice but to launch a targeted military operation. We were close enough, and trusted each other enough, for me to understand that he wasn't against it, far from it… Two days later, on Tuesday November 2 I think it was, I received him and General Poncet.

Poncet tells me not to act, not to launch the attack. Le Lidec looked away, dreamily taking a drag on his cigarette. I listened to the general, but finally replied:

"I didn't call you to ask your opinion, but to inform you. France is a friendly country with troops on the ground. The aim is to destroy the rebels' military infrastructure in Bouaké."

On Wednesday November 3, the phone rings: it's Chirac. He shouts:

"Seydou Diarra (the Prime Minister I appointed following Marcoussis, who headed the national unity government including rebels) doesn't know! it's unbelievable!" Patin couffin.

I replied, "Seydou Diarra wasn't even elected town councillor. I'm the head of a republican state that functions in a republican, constitutional manner. Republican legality must apply, and the rebels must cease their exactions, not to mention the fact that they promised to disarm."

On Thursday 4th, we launched the operation. It was to last two days. UNOCI issued a statement that day to underline the professionalism of the operation, which had not caused any collateral damage. We had previously carried out a meticulous survey of rebel installations for this very purpose. I wouldn't have wanted to spoil this success for the world.

Our objectives had been achieved. I announced that I was going to make a statement on television: to announce the imminent end of the fighting, to say that our soldiers were in Bouaké, and to reach out to the adversaries to negotiate an end to hostilities, and plans for the future. This was the political translation of the military operation.

On Saturday 6th, I'm in my office writing the text of my speech, when Doué comes up to me and says: "Our planes dropped bombs on French soldiers, and one of them died." I asked him for an explanation. I never received one.

Barely an hour later, I received word that our two Sukhol aircraft had been destroyed in Yamoussoukro by French forces. In Abidjan, French soldiers were destroying all our helicopters and small planes on the airport tarmac with axes. By the end of the day, we had nothing left to fly.

The French and American ambassadors came to see me. They told me there were nine French dead, and one American. The US ambassador didn't say a word to me, apart from hello and goodbye. It was

Le Lidec who informed me of everything, and I was overwhelmed. I immediately asked the Minister of Defense to suspend the Chief of Staff pending an investigation. I summoned the relevant ministers and the military prosecutor and instructed them to shed light on these tragic events as quickly as possible. I insisted that the military prosecutor launch an on-site investigation. General Poncet denied the Ivorian magistrate access to Camp Descartes, where the bombing took place. He opposed our investigation. As far as I know, there was no investigation on the French side either.

As for the Americans, I've heard practically nothing about them. A woman came to see my Minister of Finance, but the American government didn't even send me a letter about their slain national.

For the first time, we were unable to pay tribute to the French soldiers who died on our soil before they were transported to France.

As soon as I was informed of these shocking events, I learned that a French column of armored vehicles was approaching Abidjan from the center of the country. In the middle of the night, this column surrounded the presidential residence where I was staying. Rumor has it that Doué was in one of the column's vehicles. Doué then disappeared and only reappeared after my fall, in Ouattara's luggage. We expected the worst. We called the Élysée to sound them out and warn them against any ill-considered attack. We also warned foreign diplomatic missions. Maybe that's what saved us. After a while, the French retreated a few hundred meters away, to the Hôtel Ivoire.

The French said afterwards that "they had made a mistake on the route". When you know Abidjan, that's impossible to believe. The plan was to put Doué in my place, "on an interim basis", but he chickened out. That's another reason why the deal fell through.

The destruction of our small air force and the threat of an attack on the presidential residence sent Ivorians into the streets. They demonstrated against the presence of Licorne. There were reactions and even looting of French property in town, because there are always thieves and looters ready to take advantage of this kind of situation. And also because tension and exasperation were at their height. The French army fired on the crowds as they crossed the lagoon from the

Charles-de-Gaulle bridge to the 43rd Bima's barracks on foot to demand its departure. They fired from helicopters, leaving dozens dead, hundreds wounded and disabled. Tension mounted around the Hôtel Ivoire. After a while, French troops were ordered to break ranks with the crowd surrounding the Hôtel. The military convoy made its bloody way through, leaving behind dozens, perhaps hundreds, of dead and wounded. All civilians. Then they fired again at civilians demonstrating around the Hôtel Ivoire, where Licorne had taken up residence. Here too, they killed and seriously wounded many unarmed civilians, because they were afraid of the crowd.

On Sunday, the day after the death of the French servicemen, Le Lidec told me that the French services had the pilots responsible for the bombing, Belarusians, and the maintenance crew for both planes. The French knew exactly who the pilots and maintenance crew were, and what they were doing at all times. Military security never let them out of their sight, day or night. They knew how many beers they drank, where they went out, at what time and with which girls they came home. French soldiers rubbed shoulders with them, in nightclubs and in the "maquis" of Abidjan. The two pilots had been filmed and photographed by the French on their return from their bombing mission. Now that they had been arrested, the truth was going to be known.

I was surprised to learn shortly afterwards that the pilots and the entire maintenance crew had been accompanied by the French to the Ghana border, from where they had flown to Togo. When we questioned the French authorities, they told us that no interrogation had taken place and that there was no record of it.

Togo's Minister of the Interior, François Boko, has them arrested. He kept them for ten days. He called the French Embassy, the Ministry of Foreign Affairs in Paris, the Ministry of Justice, to say: "We have them at your disposal". President Eyadema, who was very subservient to France, because he needed its help and that of Europe, was ready to do anything to please Chirac. Well, he was! France didn't want him! This proves that this was a French blunder, not an Ivorian one.

My explanation is that there was a parallel network working over the heads of the ambassador, and even Henri Poncet. A French jour-

nalist from Le Parisien once told me that, in his opinion, it was the French intelligence services that had used the Belarusian pilots, and that there had been a blunder that accidentally led to the death of the nine Frenchmen.

I have followed from afar the complaint lodged in France by the families of the French soldiers, and I have read what has been written about the obstacles placed in the way by the French authorities on the investigating judges who have succeeded one another in this case. I know that the lawyer for the families of the victims is convinced of my innocence, as are all those who, in French circles of power, have had to deal with this case.

On November 11, 2004, the day after these events, our ambassador to France and our military attaché at the time, General Camille Lohoues, were warmly welcomed by Jacques Chirac and their military counterparts to the anniversary ceremonies of the Armistice of the First World War in Paris: had they been convinced of our guilt, it's obvious that we wouldn't even have been invited. In France, there are people who know exactly what happened... A three-cushion billiard shot gone wrong... The blunder was French... That's why they've always found better things to do than investigate.

We've been deprived of our air superiority over the rebels, and unable to finally win the war and reunify the country: if that was the goal, it's been achieved.

No autopsy, no investigation. Bodies picked up from the ground, in their bloody clothes, with dust and stones, as if they had wanted to make everything disappear immediately. Later, thanks to the insistence of two families who wanted to see their missing boy one last time, and who had obtained an exhumation, it was discovered that two bodies had even been switched. Each had been buried under the identity of the other, in the state in which they had been found. As for those directly involved in the Bouaké raid, notably the two pilots, Yuri Sushkin and Barys Smahin, they had vanished into thin air. Some say they were killed. The mystery remains, since the judicial investigation has been declared secret. Jean Balan, the lawyer for the families of the thirty-eight French servicemen killed or wounded that day, declares that this is *"an affair of state"*. Throughout the investigation, which has now lasted almost ten years, despite the difficulties it has faced, and thanks to the courage of a few magistrates - such as Brigitte Raynaud, who complained about the obstacles placed in the way of her investigation, and Sabine Kheris, currently in charge of the case - Jean Balan has highlighted the inconsistencies in the explanations given by Michèle Alliot-Marie, Minister of Defense at the time. Without, however, succeeding in having her brought before the Court of Justice of the Republic. This was refused at the end of 2013. The highly suspicious attitude of the French authorities towards the Belorussian auxiliaries responsible for the bombing, who were helped to flee without being questioned, then refused to be recaptured even though they had been arrested in Togo, pushed even the then Minister of Defense, from cover-ups to dilatory answers, to the point of the most shameless lie. Michèle Alliot-Marie claimed before the examining magistrate that there was no legal basis for apprehending these individuals on suspicion of murder. This was not true. A year before the Bouaké affair, the Pelchat law of April 14, 2003, passed under Jacques Chirac, had enriched the legal arsenal precisely to enable the apprehension and prosecution of those guilty of criminal acts. The Minister of Defense could not have been unaware of this. Dominique de Villepin, Minister of Foreign Affairs, Minister of the Interior, then Prime Minister, was involved in the Ivorian issue as closely as possible. He practically made it his own. Today, he explains that he knew nothing about it, and played no role in the Bouaké affair. It is well known that he had taken the ascendancy over an already tired Chirac, on the eve of his stroke, and that he intervened at all levels of consultation and decision-making. On December 20, 2005, after the President's stroke, which had occurred three months earlier, Villepin confided to Bruno Le Maire: *"The President, you know, he fights for life, that's the only thing, life. Everything else, power, the government, elections, the party, doesn't interest him anymore."* How can we believe that, in 2004, the Minister was kept on the sidelines at a time of such acute crisis?

What is certain today, after the October 16 and 22, 2013 hearings of several French military officers, is that the Élysée has obviously not said everything. On October 31, under the pen of Philippe Brou, *Jeune*

Afrique reported in substance the revelations of three high-ranking officers who were perfectly aware of the events:

"In his interview with Judge Kheris, General Malaussène, deputy to General Henri Poncet at the time of the events - and therefore at the heart of the secret - exonerated Gbagbo, blamed the French authorities and quoted Alassane Ouattara."

Having had access to this same information, here is the exact sentence pronounced by the general on this subject, before the examining magistrate: *"I think there was a political project which was to put Ouattara in place and get rid of Gbagbo, who is an intelligent, cultured, fine man, who has been through many crises and who, deep down, loves France." "I'm convinced that Gbagbo didn't want to kill French soldiers, and that someone in his entourage took this decision without telling Gbagbo..." "I believe that the Gbagbo movement has fallen into a trap."*

I've always been convinced of this. Of a plan hatched by two or three people in Paris, in a small committee, and relayed by an accomplice in my army.

Contrary to constitutional rules, General Bentégeat, then Chief of Staff of the French Armed Forces, reveals that he did not take part in any restricted Defense Council at the Élysée Palace, before or during the operations of the Franco-Ivorian quasi-war that broke out in November 2004. This is an important clue in support of the conspiracy theory against Gbagbo.

As for the involvement of General Mathias Doué in what, according to these new elements, appears to be an attempted coup d'état, this is suggested by General Destremau. At the time, General Destremau explained the presence of French tanks in front of the Ivorian president's residence as a GPS error. Before Judge Kheris, he gave a different version: "... [He] *now refers to a mysterious 'guide',"* writes *Jeune Afrique*, *"who was in charge of taking them to the Ivory Coast - the hotel - (while Michèle Alliot-Marie refers to the French ambassador's residence) while he was in a helicopter above them. A 'guide' who committed 'a professional error' out of fear and incompetence".*

When the bosses of the Grande Muette open their mouths - a rare occurrence - politicians are in a quandary. It can happen that the military want to save their honor, when they feel manipulated. And some of their men have died as a result. Mamadou Koulibaly, who was involved from start to finish in Operation Dignity and its aftermath in Abidjan, said to me recently, with characteristic conciseness: *"The day will come when tongues will be loosened."* He wasn't wrong.

Perhaps all efforts to conceal responsibility for this tragic affair will ultimately fail. Jean Balan remembers that in 2005, on the very day the case was covered in a major article in *Le Monde*, the Firmin Mahé affair broke out in the media. A highwayman arrested by Poncet's soldiers, then suffocated with a plastic bag while being transported in an armored vehicle. Henri Poncet's case dismissed. Four-year suspended sentence for one of the murdering soldiers. One-year suspended sentence for his accomplice. According to Jean Balan, this case was *"a smokescreen thrown up by Michèle Alliot-Marie, who personally went to the front of the line to stifle the media coverage of the other case, that of Bouaké, which was beginning to emerge"*.

Laurent Gbagbo, too, was astonished by the sudden importance attached in France to the Firmin Mahé affair.

Don't get me wrong, I'm never insensitive to a man's death, but when, as in the case of Kieffer or Mahé, an unfortunate story is made into an issue, I tell myself that there are hidden reasons for doing so: in Côte d'Ivoire, those who give lessons pay little heed to the thousands of citizens who have been murdered or disappeared in the violence instigated by the rebels. We exploit people's deaths when we need to, to get our message across. At the same time, we are careful to ignore everything that could be credited to my government: the investigations launched to shed light on these tragedies; the willingness of the Ivorian authorities to help whenever possible. For example, in 2006, I gave instructions to the Minister for the Gendarmerie to seize Youssouf Fofana, the leader of the Gang of Barbarians, who had kidnapped and tortured to death young Ilan Halimi in Paris. We went beyond what the French judicial authorities asked of us. The examining magistrate, Madame

Goetzmann, only wanted information from us: Youssouf Fofana, of Ivorian origin, was hiding in Abidjan after having escaped from the French police. We had him tracked down, arrested on February 23, brought to trial as a matter of urgency, and I signed his deportation decree so that he could be brought before the French justice system. He left France under escort on March 5. The police, the judiciary and the President of the Republic of Côte d'Ivoire did their job, but they did it well. I don't recall anyone congratulating us on this seamless collaboration.

You didn't need to be a graduate of the École de Guerre to be able to sniff out, even in the heat of the moment, that something wasn't quite right with the official French version of the Bouaké tragedy. I remember that at France-Soir, where I was working at the time, and even though I had never yet set foot in Côte d'Ivoire, a quick investigation led us to headline the front page on November 8, 2004: "Comment la France a dérapé" ("How France went off the rails"). Without knowing all the facts, it seemed to us that too many pieces were missing from the puzzle, and that they had been scattered too quickly, obviously to avoid reconstruction. Since then, all manner of speculation has been allowed to run riot, without arriving at any judicial evidence, even if Jean Balan's factual reconstruction and the statements made by the protagonists before successive examining magistrates are convincing. What is still missing is the spark that will blow away the leaden blanket that protects those who lied in this affair, in which nine young French soldiers lost their lives. At the end of April 2014, Sabine Kheris travelled to Scheveningen to hear Laurent Gbagbo in prison. She was accompanied there by Jean Balan, the lawyer for the families of the French soldiers killed in Bouaké.

After the Bouaké affair, Le Lidec told me: "After that, you're in for twenty years!" He was referring to the many casualties the French army had caused, which, according to him, forbade the French from taking any further violent action to try and destabilize me. He was mistaken.

"I'M IN POLITICS, NOT BUSINESS"

On January 4, 2011, Nicolas Sarkozy reaffirmed France's peaceful intentions at the Saint-Dizier air base, during the ritual vœux aux armées. He added that the French army present in Côte d'Ivoire *"has no vocation to interfere in the internal affairs"* of the country.

Words contrary to reality, no doubt to lull the adversary to sleep. In fact, the 900-strong French Licorne force, which has been present in Côte d'Ivoire since 2004, and which does more than "arbitrate" the debate between the belligerents, will see its strength almost doubled in 2011.

Four UMP deputies, invited to Abidjan to meet Laurent Gbagbo, may have thought they could meddle behind the boss's back. A hilarious episode... They were to pay the price for Nicolas' nervous breakdown. On February 4, as they were packing their suitcases before sneaking off to Roissy 2 E airport to catch their 11:30 p.m. flight, they were ordered back into the doghouse. Their clandestine travel plans were leaked to the media, and Nicolas Sarkozy himself phoned Jean-François Mancel, the expedition's leader, to forbid him to travel.

Approached by the "kind organizer" of this "Gbagbo Tour", a Senegalese apprentice communicator, I agreed to join the small troop of these elected representatives to observe them at close quarters: what on earth could drive four deputies from the presidential majority to brave the wrath of the castle? I asked myself. The trip was initially designed to meet President Gbagbo alone, without seeing the other president, i.e.

Ouattara. So I found myself in the departure hall at Roissy on February 4, 2011, waiting for these three intrepid Musketeers. Or how I came close to meeting Jean-François Mancel, Cécile Dumoulin, Yves Censi and Jean-Michel Fourgous… I only met lawyer and academic Emmanuel Caullier. On the lookout for anyone who might remotely resemble the image of truant MPs, I approached him as he paced up and down the almost empty terminal at this late hour.

We share the last sandwich and the last two cans of cold drink from the kiosk opposite the departure lounge. Around midnight, alerted by a phone call from the Senegalese communicator, who was waiting for the delegation in Abidjan and had been warned that his UMP operation had been scuppered, we decide to head home.

Intrigued by this move, which risked making Nicolas Sarkozy lose face, I stayed sober. The film of the MPs playing truant in Africa promised much. One thing was certain: those who were presented in the French press as the inventors and promoters of this adventure, National Assembly President Mamadou Koulibaly and lawyer Marcel Ceccaldi, had nothing to do with it.

Thus, after the elections and in the final weeks of the crisis, there were more or less sincere guests on Paris/Abidjan flights. No doubt Laurent Gbagbo, in these difficult times, needed these visits to believe, and show, that he still had many supporters and friends.

Back in March 2010, and in a much calmer climate, he had already launched the media tom-tom. He was seen chatting with Jack Lang, accompanied by Jean-Marie Le Guen, Vice-President of the French National Assembly, at Queen's, footballer Didier Drogba's nightclub, one of the most exclusive on Rue Princesse, Abidjan's red-light district. While the former soberly claims only *the mission of re-establishing the bridge between the French socialists, President Gbagbo and the Ivory Coast*[16], our eternal Minister of Culture, intoxicated by the African night, is lyrical, dithyrambic, Dalinian: *"Gbagbo is a true man of the left, who has a sense of solidarity… With President Gbagbo, I feel in harmony, in connivance, in synchrony, in resonance. I like people like him who are both patriotic and*

---

16. *Fraternité-Matin,* March 29, 2010.

have a sense of state." Even if it meant begging him nine months later, live on RTL, on December 30, 2010: *"Laurent, you've got to go!"* Lang abandoned ship, citing a ballot-box result disputed by the two "Abidjan" winners. Laurent Gbagbo laughs:

Understandably, Jack was in a job-hunting phase at the time.

At the end of 2010 and in the first weeks of 2011, many others took up the baton. In Africa, it's customary for guests never to leave without a gift. The kind organizer of the Gbagbo Tour des députés UMP had prepared envelopes of 30,000 and 50,000 euros. For this last ball in Abidjan, the orchestra of egos plays while the ship sinks. Like violins on the deck of the Titanic. But the musicians will never be paid.

Personally, I've never paid anyone. Even the pre-election polls were paid for by supporters with more money than me. I've never confused the state budget with political expenses. I've never given a single euro to Fouks at RSCG. I always agree when it doesn't cost anything. The same goes for guests. Perhaps those who wanted to do me a favor were baiting them, but I never wanted to know. I'm in politics, not business.

"I WAS ARRESTED WHILE BEING BOMBED"

During all those years, I was like a fish that someone wanted to suffocate by constantly throwing it out of the water. But I always managed to dive back into my element, catch my breath, and carry on with the difficult mission for which the Ivorians had elected me. So, in the end, Sarkozy picked up a club.

Laurent Gbagbo was not overthrown in 2002 or 2004. If he fell in 2011, he did not die under the rubble in which he was buried by bombs, the treachery of some of those close to him, the vindictiveness of the Élysée Palace, the UN, the European Community, the Organization of African Unity, the International Criminal Court, the horrors of the French and international press...

On December 5, 2011, at his first appearance hearing at the International Criminal Court, he arrived before his judges like a breathless swimmer, but still possessed enough strength to declare, *"I was arrested under French bombs... It was France that did the work..."*

On February 28, 2013, in front of the ICC, in the same Nordic-designed setting of white wood, concrete and glass, modern and sober, populated by computers and screens, President Gbagbo stands up and speaks. This marks the end of the two-week confirmation of charges hearing. The judges will then have to decide whether to hold a trial. To do so, they will have to examine the weight of the prosecutor's case, in other words, whether the prosecutor's allegations are supported by sufficiently consistent and credible evidence. In the first few days, the prosecutor deployed a wealth of rhetoric to try and convince the judges. The court was told that he had never prepared a hearing with such care. But in the days that followed, everything changed: the defense took the floor, an efficient team that knew its case inside out. Led by Emmanuel Altit, the defense team meticulously destroyed, piece by piece, all the evidence relied on by the prosecutor. On the contrary, Emmanuel Altit's team has demonstrated that, contrary to the prosecutor's assertions, it was not President Gbagbo who plotted to stay in power regardless of the outcome of the elections, but rather the rebels, backed by the French authorities, who implemented a long-standing plan to seize power. Who conceived this plan to destabilize the country? At the end of the fifteen-day hearing, the answer is clear: the French authorities. But the prosecutor seems determined to "forget" their involvement.

President Gbagbo rose to his feet reassured and reassured, though still suffering from the after-effects of eight months' inhuman incarceration in Côte d'Ivoire. As an experienced tribune, he breaks free of the imposed framework, as he has always done in his speeches. In a few words, he introduces his own vision of the post-electoral crisis. Excerpt:

"Madam President, ladies and gentlemen of the court,

"I followed these debates, I heard a lot of things, sometimes I found myself in Côte d'Ivoire, but other times I found myself so far away from it. The questions we asked were so far removed from our own experience [...].

"I'd just like to say that Madame Procureure said something that shocked me a little.

"By saying that we're not here to see who won the elections and who didn't. But we can't talk, we can't debate the post-election crisis and not know how the elections went.

"Who won the elections? Because the one who didn't win was the one who caused trouble. I think that's the logic. So the question is: who won the elections? And so when I asked for the votes to be recounted, it wasn't just an empty phrase. You yourself have seen the documents in the prosecution's possession, on which voters' votes are listed. In Bouaké alone, 100,000 votes were added to my opponent's tally.

"That's the heart of the matter. [...]"

It was the culmination of fifteen landmark days of hearings. All the observers thought Gbagbo would lose, anticipating his inevitable conviction and going with what they thought was the wind. Now, having heard Emmanuel Altit, his associates and Laurent Gbagbo, and above all having listened to their arguments and analyzed the evidence they presented, most observers are convinced that a trial under these conditions would be disastrous for the International Criminal Court, and that Gbagbo will be freed.

So the hundreds of millions of euros spent on delegitimizing an elected president, organizing smear campaigns against him, building up an armed rebellion, imposing him on the international community, convincing the media, persuading the international community and the UN Security Council will have been for nothing. In the end, Gbagbo is likely to win again.

The violence of Alassane Ouattara's supporters, and the countless crimes they have committed, raise questions even for his closest supporters. An Ivorian president captured by French commandos; Burkinabe or Nigerian mercenaries in the rubble of his residence after repeated attacks that left dozens of civilians dead; his wife Simone paraded on her knees after her arrest by grizzled Dozos holding her by the hair; images of her son Michel, shirtless, arriving bloodied at the victor's HQ, and narrowly escaping lynching by Ouattara supporters. And the corpses of innocent victims all over Abidjan and southern Côte d'Ivoire...

Born in Lyon, Michel Gbagbo is Franco-Ivorian. Son of President Gbagbo's first marriage to Jacqueline Chamois, a French teacher who still supports him today. The only fault of this psychology professor at Abidjan's Faculty of Criminology is that he took refuge with his wife Viviane at his father's house. He never held any political office. Imprisoned for two years in disgraceful conditions, then released provisionally on August 5, 2013, along with thirteen other people close to Laurent Gbagbo, he was arrested again on February 14, 2014, on his way to Abidjan airport. He was on his way to Paris to answer a summons from the examining magistrate, Sabine Kheris, in charge of investigating his complaint against Guillaume Soro and the rebels for *"kidnapping, confinement and*

12. "I WAS ARRESTED WHILE BEING BOMBED"

degrading and inhuman treatment". Released three days later, he was told that he was not authorized to leave Ivorian territory. No one in Abidjan or Paris has any interest in opening this Pandora's box.

The fate of my son Michel raises real questions: he is being held hostage. Today, he is being denied access to justice, after what he has suffered. It's up to France to help him assert his rights as a French citizen. How else are we to interpret this obstruction of justice?

No sentimentality when you want to show the world what the bastards who defy Western democracies are up against. The more violent their downfall, the clearer the message. The arrest of Saddam Hussein, extracted shaggy from the hole where he was holed up, the furtive images of his hanging in a dark corner after his trial, the lynching of Gaddafi in the middle of the street, beaten, bled, then finished off and exposed on the floor of a hangar, set the stage for the mistreatment suffered by Gbagbo and his people in public opinion: the former president of the Ivory Coast would have been just another tyrant. It's all in the interpretation of the images. The amalgam is a deception that works at full speed. It takes what it takes: Western media society desacralizes the image, acting in the end like certain primitive peoples, who teach that you don't innocently capture a photograph of a man without taking his soul. It's even easier to do this with an African head of state who is the butt of many negative prejudices, and who doesn't have a media armada equivalent to that of his detractors. Are the most simplistic comparisons used to achieve this? Hillary Clinton, the US Secretary of State for Foreign Affairs, doesn't mince her words: *"The arrest of Laurent Gbagbo,"* **she says**, *"sends a signal to dictators everywhere that they cannot ignore the results of free and fair elections, and that there will be consequences for them if they cling to power.* The "on the Hill" version of *"let it be known, and notice to amateurs"*. The evidence against Laurent Gbagbo is overwhelming, we hear, from the first weeks of May 2011, in Parisian editorial offices. *Ite missa est.* Before justice, the media judged and condemned. Everything had been decided after Ouattara's self-enactment in December 2010. In a joint press release, Henri Emmanuelli and François Loncle accused *"the majority of* *the French media, relayed by a certain number of political leaders* […] *all lesson-givers* […] *of having undertaken a one-way campaign of suspicion and denigration against the Ivorian authorities*".

The sophisticated diplomatic mechanism perfected by Nicolas Sarkozy's advisor, Jean-David Levitte, in tandem with General Puga, and described by Jean-Christophe Notin in *Le Crocodile et le Scorpion* to avoid accusations of neo-colonialism, worked. The scenario, reproduced in Libya, gives the appearance of the respectability now necessary for any external military intervention. It's all about building an alibi beforehand and selling it to the international community. No difficulty for France, a member of the UN Security Council, where the recognition of its African expertise enables it to win its case: *"In fact,"* writes Notin, anxious to justify the French intervention, *"Gbagbo would not have stayed in office for six months after losing the elections, or at least after attracting the opprobrium of Paris"* (revealing slip of the tongue). (revealing slip of the tongue) *"Thanks to their multiple relays, in Abidjan with Ambassador Simon and General Palasset, in New York with French representative Gérard Araud, in all the French and international administrations involved, the Levitte-Puga duo made a major contribution to drawing up a new crisis management model that was reproduced in Libya* […] *and in Mali in January 2013: first, a call for help from the legal or legitimate government; an initial promise of help from the regional organization; then a UN mandate; and finally, and only finally, France's diplomatic, economic or military intervention."* *"Each of these four stages,"* emphasizes Jean-David Levitte, *"is indispensable"*. Contrary to what has been said in the past, we can hear here an admission of cold, meticulous preparation of the Abidjan operation, far from the humanitarian pretexts invoked at the time of the action to justify the French attack on Laurent Gbagbo's residence. *"I loved what you did,"* Nicolas Sarkozy told Lévitte and Puga, in the tone of the Emperor's *"Soldats, je suis content de vous"* after Austerlitz.

All that remained was to affix the stamp of international justice. A seal engraved in the finest wax had long been waiting to be dipped in indelible ink. It is interesting to note that the prosecutor at the International Criminal Court did not see fit to prosecute the rebels who had committed crimes against humanity and war crimes in Côte d'Ivoire in 2002 and 2003, even though these crimes had been referred to him. But the prosecutor rushed to accuse President Gbagbo. In this respect, how can we fail to note that this same prosecutor seems to have remained in constant contact with the Ouattara camp since the second round of the presidential elections in November 2010, but did not bother to contact representatives of the Ivorian government? His bias will become apparent on several occasions, as he goes so far as to threaten President Gbagbo with a *"bad ending"* in an interview given to the Kenyan channel K24 in early 2011. There are none so blind as those who refuse to see. The Prosecutor's indictment states that :

"Laurent Gbagbo would have incurred individual criminal liability, as an indirect co-perpetrator, for four counts of crimes against humanity:
(a) murder, (b) rape and other sexual violence, (c) acts of persecution and (d) other inhumane acts, allegedly perpetrated in the context of the post-election violence on the territory of Côte d'Ivoire between December 16, 2010 and April 12, 2011."

The final blow to President Gbagbo, the one that his opponents believe will lead to his definitive disappearance from the political scene and the correlative triumph of Alassane Ouattara. Until February 19, 2013, it is fashionable to consider that the trial before the International Criminal Court is a foregone conclusion, and that the holy condemnation of justice, the final stage in his banishment from history, in universal reprobation, will be no more than a formality. When he climbed onto what was to be his pyre on February 19, 2013, who was afraid of Laurent Gbagbo? At that moment, nobody.

13.
TOO BAD FOR THOSE WHO VOTED!

Between late November 2010 and early April 2011, Côte d'Ivoire was on the TV news agenda, often as the opening item. During France 2's *8 o'clock news,* Marie Drucker found the right accents to state what all her colleagues took for granted. She calls Laurent Gbagbo a *"self-proclaimed President".* Who can blame her? The official version is broadcast over and over again by the most powerful protagonists. France, the UN and the United States, co-authors of the tragedy, are at the same time the media's legitimate source of information. What's more, in opposition, the entire Socialist Party (PS), apart from Labertit and Emmanuelli, who have long been sidelined, agrees with the Elysée Palace. Only Jean-Luc Mélenchon and Marine Le Pen do not bark with the pack. Irreducible ideological and political adversaries, they are nonetheless equally suspicious of the international community's alliance against a single man, and the misuse of the UN's mandate to protect civilians, not to overthrow and arrest a head of state.

Antoine Glaser, former editor-in-chief of *La Lettre du Continent*, was called in by television channels as an "Africa specialist" to comment on the results of the Ivorian election, which he did not question at the time. Today, he admits that he had no certainty about the truth of the vote: *"I didn't investigate at the time, and since no recount took place, we'll never know who won,"* he told me in a telephone interview on July 3, 2013. He had, however, justified his decision by pointing to the discrepancy in the vote "in favor of Ouattara", and "Gbagbo's obligation to withdraw". Who could claim to have investigated the reality of voting and counting conditions, violence and fraud in Côte d'Ivoire, when no one has even done so in France, at the polling station around the corner?

In Lille, Toulouse, Strasbourg, Lyon and Bordeaux, as well as in Nice, Amiens, Arras and Valenciennes, the Ivorian diaspora voted in a calm and healthy cohabitation of supporters of the various candidates, but the electoral material sent by the Abidjan Electoral Commission (run by Ouattara's friends) arrived… The day after the first-round polling day in Marseille. In Toulouse, the material was strangely routed to the embassy on Avenue Poincaré in Paris. Thanks to an express return trip by Toulouse officials, it was recovered just in time.

In Paris, Gbagbo supporters were intimidated, threatened and physically assaulted. Videos of the violence on polling day can still be seen on the Internet, and records can be found in nearby police stations.

Of the twenty-eight polling stations open in the Île-de-France region, eight were closed outright because of raids by "loubards" who smashed tables and ballot boxes, stole registers, ballot papers, printed matter and ink stamps, and beat up pro-Gbagbo voters.

As a precautionary measure, some ballot boxes were transported under police escort to the headquarters of the Independent Electoral Commission, in an outbuilding of the embassy on boulevard Suchet. Here too, gangs opposed to candidate Gbagbo were waiting, and damaged the building's gate.

The representative of the opposition party loyal to candidate Alassane Ouattara arrived an hour late (10 a.m. instead of 9 a.m.). Voting having started without him, he removed the ballot boxes and refused to allow the vote to take place. As a result, only the eighteen ballots used before the arrival of this man more rigorous for others than for himself were counted.

And so much the worse for all those who got up early and froze to death all day on the Paris asphalt, hoping in vain to do their civic duty.

So much for the twenty Parisian polling stations where everything went smoothly, so much for Marseille which was unable to vote, so much for the 2,475 voters in Reims, Amiens, Bordeaux, Nice, Toulouse, Lille,

Arras, Valenciennes, Nice, Lens, Lyon, who voted without a hitch, in perfect transparency.

All those who managed to vote will have to resign themselves to hearing the IEC spokesman shamelessly declare on November 29, 2010, the day after the second round of voting, that *"in France we hardly voted at all"*. And that as a result, the vote of Ivorians in France will be globally, and totally, cancelled.

Is it presumptuous to consider that there may be a link between the composition of the IEC, with its large majority of members from parties opposed to the outgoing President, and the fact that the latter's victory in France (57.58% vs. Ouattara's 42.61%) was thus overlooked?

These facts and figures are verifiable, and have been validated by representatives of both parties. It all took place in France's biggest cities. Who noticed, or cared? Even if the partial electorate represented by the incontestable votes, which should have been taken into account, is greater than the total number of voters from the diaspora in Belgium (709), Germany (279) and Burkina Faso (1,400). Even if, in terms of the number of registered voters, this electorate comes in third place behind the United States (3,184) and Italy (2,611). *Le Monde* preferred to highlight *"Ouattara's victory abroad, with nearly 60% of the vote, against Gbagbo's 40%"*, in its December 2, 2010 issue, without going into the details of the election. However, the Ivorian diaspora worldwide represents 15,000 voters. The inclusion of the 2,475 votes cast in France would obviously have upset this result. What happened in Paris and Marseille augurs well for what may have happened in the savannahs of northern Côte d'Ivoire, where polling stations, surrounded by rebel Kalashnikovs, were generally controlled by political friends of candidate Ouattara.

Of course, it's not only in Côte d'Ivoire that voting incidents and dubious scores have disrupted elections, as Jean-Pierre Raffarin pointed out during the UMP crisis. In the United States, we still remember the ubiquitous recount of the "little holes" on the computerized ballot cards between George W. Bush and Al Gore in 2000: the operation lasted a few weeks, with, in the end, a result accepted by both candidates, but which remained rather opaque: In August 2009, Western democracies showed themselves to be less observant in Afghanistan: Hamid Karzai, their favorite, running for a second term against the former Foreign Minister Abdullah Abdullah, who came from the Northern Alliance. A third of Karzai's votes were invalidated for massive fraud after the first round, in which he came out on top. The second round, scheduled for November 7, never took place, due to Abdullah's withdrawal prior to the second round. Nevertheless, on November 2 he was declared the winner and was officially inaugurated for his second term on November 19. When the international community wants…

In Haiti, at the very moment of the Ivorian imbroglio in autumn 2010, the Organization of American States decided to recount the votes in the current presidential election, under pressure from the streets. Fraud and challenges to the results of the first round, announced by the Provisional Electoral Commission, threatened to degenerate into serious street clashes. Demonstrators demanded a recount, and finally succeeded in overcoming the relative inertia of representatives of the European Union and the United Nations. The Organization of American States, of which Haiti is a member, decided to review the results.

After a new evaluation, under the aegis of an international panel, the candidate who came third and was eliminated in the first round of voting, singer Michel Martelly, was re-qualified for the second round. He eventually won, with almost 68% of the vote. Eliminated in the first round, he was finally elected President of the Republic of Haiti.

In France, at the end of 2011, the UMP produced an Ivorian-style scenario: the similarities are uncanny. It's a case of "the irony of history", or "the kick in the ass", since it's Nicolas Sarkozy's party. Jean François Copé and François Fillon both declared themselves winners in the race for the party presidency. Insults, threats, accusations of ballot-box stuffing and suspicions of a mafia-style organization are the order of the day. A lamentable soap opera that reveals the ambitions and hatred that underlie relations between the party's caciques. A recount commission is set up, whose decision François Fillon refuses in advance, while he temporarily creates his own party… It has to be said that Copé is the president of the UMP - until his downfall in 2014, forced to resign by the discovery of false invoicing, and that having organized this disastrous election, he controls the apparatus. François Fillon has no confidence.

But in France, it's well known, everything ends in song. The two roosters meet, talk and make up for the photo…

We'll even go so far as to vote on whether to… vote again to elect the party president! Even in Africa, we laughed… So many precautions and good manners to settle a problem which, after all, only concerns one political party, i.e. at best a few tens of thousands of French people. What did Henri Guaino say on RMC on February 12, 2013, when Jean-Jacques Bourdin pointed out that a new UMP vote *will cost money*? *"Well yes,"* replies the former Élysée advisor, *"democracy sometimes costs a little, but when it's done well, it pays off a lot."* My cab driver, who by chance happened to be an Ivorian from Paris that day, *"addicted to RMC because of the sport"*, with whom I overhear this statement as we drive along the banks of the Seine, near the Maison de la Radio, laughs: *"You said it, Henri!"*

Henri Guaino forgot to whisper his words of wisdom to the right people when, a few months earlier, the fate of a country of 20 million inhabitants, and the lives and deaths of tens of thousands of Ivorians, depended on it. A recount, negotiations, a new vote? The author of Nicolas Sarkozy's famous Dakar speech didn't think of this at the time of the Ivorian post-electoral crisis. He didn't hear Gbagbo's request: because the African man *"who has not"*, according to him, *"gone down in history enough"* isn't *"worth it - well - enough?"* as a pastiche of a L'Oréal advert would say - well enough? Let's add the fact that, according to AFP, quoted by *Le Nouveau Courrier* on November 27, 2012, during his lunch with François Fillon, Nicolas Sarkozy had advised a new vote *"to avoid escalating the conflict"*. And that Jean-François Copé, straight, and even a little stiff in his boots, had decreed: *"The National Appeals Commission is like the Constitutional Council for us. Who could imagine appealing another ruling after the Constitutional Council's decision?"* The unfortunate thing for Ivorians is that these principles travel badly, especially in the tropics. As if to imply that these people are not yet capable of appreciating them. In Paris and Port-au-Prince, we count and recount; in Abidjan, we send in tanks and helicopter gunships.

Back to Africa, where we again find France, its loves, its troubles, its small and large arrangements with principles. The latest in a long line of chosen heads of state: Ali Bongo - whose father Omar Bongo was installed by France for over forty years at the head of our private oil emirate, Gabon - who never won the 2009 elections. In fact, it largely lost. Michel de Bonnecorse, Jacques Chirac's former Africa advisor, is categorical. In Patrick Benquet and Antoine Glaser's documentary *Françafrique, 50 ans sous le sceau du secret,* he asserts that the figures of 42% and 37% actually achieved by André Mba Obame and Ali Bongo were simply reversed to the detriment of the former. And to make the latter triumph. *"Even the local AFP knew about it,"* says Jacques Salles, former head of French intelligence in Gabon, in the same film: *"But nobody said anything [...] I was outraged."* So Ali succeeded Omar, perpetuating the lease in the name of our best interests, and forbidding anyone to go rummaging in the drawers where a thousand traces and over forty years of Franco-Gabonese corruption with a strong whiff of oil rest in peace. Nicolas Sarkozy was quick to congratulate President Ali Bongo on his victory in the rigged election. An equally self-serving tolerance allowed the very docile Eyadema Gnassingbé to rule Togo for thirty-six years, after a coup d'état, and then through rigged elections. His son, Faure Gnassingbé, shunned by Sarkozy but welcomed by Hollande, succeeded him thanks to the support of his army. The Franco-Togolese Kofi Yamgnane, Socialist MP for Finistère and Secretary of State for Integration under François Mitterrand, knows what this is all about, having attempted to run against the current President in his country's presidential elections in 2005, and again in 2010. He knows that in the 21st century, French-speaking African banana republics still exist.

14

A LONG-PREPARED TRAP

Back in November 2006, *L'Express* revealed the existence of a secret poll conducted by ONUCI between July 14 and 24 of that year. In it, Laurent Gbagbo appeared as the "most respected personality" in Côte d'Ivoire (39.3% favorable opinion), far ahead of Alassane Ouattara (9.4%) and Henri Konan Bédié (4.7%). As for Charles Konan Banny, then Prime Minister of the cohabitation, presented by the weekly as "the foal" of the international community, he garnered just 7%. The ball was already rolling, and the roulette wheel would continue to spin for a long time before settling on one name.

In October 2010, Claude Guéant came to visit me in Abidjan. He told me that the Élysée had no candidate. I listened politely. That very morning, I had received a note from the DGSE explaining that Ouattara was Sarkozy's candidate. The trap had been prepared from the start. I was constantly urged to go to the polls, and international pressure was very strong, even though one of the first conditions for guaranteeing a peaceful election - the disarmament of the rebels - was never met. In all our agreements, disarmament is a sine qua non condition for any settlement. In all eighteen United Nations resolutions, disarmament is mentioned. And yet, we're being pushed into the elections: because we wanted a brutal and definitive outcome. I spoke to people around me, including François Loncle, a Socialist member of parliament, about the fact that I knew they were planning fraud and mischief.

No one wanted to slow down the march towards war, or the inevitable violence that would be its consequence. Slate Afrique's May 28, 2011 article on the hidden UN report is revealing. The site reveals the existence of a pre-election report which explained why the conditions for holding the presidential election had not been met. But this report was kept hidden from the world for months, until the elections were held and its publication was no longer of consequence. This is another way of saying that in New York, at the headquarters of the United Nations, they knew long before the elections what the dramatic consequences would be. In Côte d'Ivoire, the chronicle of a foretold catastrophe was about to unfold, and was deliberately concealed.

"For seven months, a United Nations report that sheds new light on the recent crisis in Côte d'Ivoire lay dormant in drawers. [...] If it had been published before the presidential election, it would, if not have led to its postponement, at least seriously undermined the most optimistic forecasts for the outcome of the second round on November 28, 2010.

"On September 17, 2010, the five experts appointed to investigate possible violations of arms embargoes and raw materials trafficking sent an initial letter to Maria Luiza Ribeiro Viotti, the Chair of the UN Sanctions Committee for Côte d'Ivoire, set up by Security Council Resolution 1572 (in 2004). The letter preceded their report, which should have been published a few weeks later. In the end, it was not published until seven months later, accompanied by a letter dated April 20, 2011, signed by Maria Luiza Ribeiro Viotti, addressed to the President of the UN Security Council."

The report was published on April 20, 2011, a week after the fall of Laurent Gbagbo. A date whose choice raises a question that probably contains an answer. The evidence provided by this report of the rearmament of the two camps, and of the inevitability of a warlike outcome to the next election, shows that the UN has failed in its mission. Or that we chose not to let the organization stop the plan leading to the seizure of power by Ouattara and his French backers.

In my opinion, all the operations leading up to the elections - for example, the census, the issuing of voters' cards, the implementation of the electoral operations themselves - should be entrusted

to the National Institute of Statistics (INS), as was previously the practice.

However, without my knowledge, the French had a hand in all the preparatory operations for the elections, through Sagem, a Safran group company. I personally was never questioned, nor did I authorize any contract with this company. Charles Konan Banny, who had just become Prime Minister of a "national unity" government, did so behind my back. By the time I realized it, it was too late; Konan Banny had started paying. What was to be done? If I started a fight, people would say: Gbagbo is afraid to go to the polls… Sagem's subsidiary in Côte d'Ivoire was run by Sidi Kagnassi. He's Malian and Swiss. He's the one who set up the scam. He and his people went to Paris all the time. As a reward, he received a contract worth over 100 billion CFA francs [152 million euros] after their victory. As for the Electoral Commission, which included a majority of anti-Gbagbo members, in early 2010 it was caught red-handed transforming the electoral rolls: according to calculations, over 450,000 bogus voters' names had been added to the electoral files.

Sidi Kagnassi's career did indeed "soar" to the heights of business in Côte d'Ivoire, in sectors such as construction and public works, where he had no skills whatsoever. Thanks to some fabulous government contracts, as reported in *La Lettre du Continent*[17].

"Businessman Mohamed Sidi Kagnassi is in exclusive negotiations with Côte d'Ivoire's Minister of Education, Kandia Kamissoko Camara, for the construction of 10,000 classrooms across the country. Since Alassane Ouattara came to power in 2011, the former boss of the now-defunct L'Aiglon group and ex-representative of Sagem has enjoyed a steady stream of construction contracts. Although he did not own any companies in this sector [...] Mohamed Sidi Kagnassi won the contract (worth 160 billion CFA francs) to renovate and refurbish Côte d'Ivoire's public universities. Since then, he has founded SIMDCI (Société pour la modernisation et le développement des infrastructures en Côte d'Ivoire)."

------

17. 1. N° 677, February 26, 2014.

It has to be said that the rebels and the troops of the Licorne Force and UNOCI committed enormous damage during the events of 2011. Professor Jérôme Balou Bi Toto, General Secretary of the University of Cocody, who was arrested on April 19, tortured and then imprisoned in Bouna, testifies to this at[18]: *"Shells fell during the bombardments. [...] The university was attacked with heavy weapons. They destroyed student housing, killed students, and chased wounded students, finishing them off in the rooms of the university hospital. I saw UNOCI and Licorne convoys on campus. They took part in the atrocities. I understand why the university was rehabilitated so quickly. The bodies were painted over. [...] There has to be an investigation."*

He will never be summoned and heard by the prosecutor…

Fatou Bensouda in The Hague, who told *Jeune Afrique*[19], at the end of February 2013: *"our ambition is that all perpetrators of crimes, regardless of their side, should be prosecuted"*? As time goes by, and even if no one ever believed it, this seems increasingly unlikely. Contrary to Madame Bensouda's assertions, the ICC has never been concerned with neutrality. During the post-electoral crisis that gave rise to the unrest, there was not a single attempt by Luis Moreno Ocampo, then in charge, to make contact with Laurent Gbagbo or his government. The ICC prosecutor was therefore, from the outset, and *a priori*, all for the Ouattara camp. He had determined a camp of good, that which had been indicated to him by the great powers, first and foremost the French authorities, and a camp of evil, that of so-called narrow nationalism, even before investigating. Consequently, it seems logical that no investigation ever took place.

I was surrounded by compromises, treachery, mercantile alliances and duplicity. Of course, my entourage had been infiltrated… It was easy: those around me were betting on my downfall and my survival at the same time… This state of affairs was helped by the fact that the rebels had taken part in the government, since I had agreed, in the spirit of reconciliation, to include rebels in the government, at the head

---

18. In an interview broadcast on René Kimbassa's blog on August 27, 2013.
19. *Jeune Afrique*, n° 2720, February 2013.

of which I had, moreover, appointed their leader Guillaume Soro, in the hope of achieving definitive peace in the country. I couldn't turn my head to the right or left, or I'd be decapitated. So I looked straight ahead to the elections, the way out of the tunnel.

Here again, I didn't choose to clash. It was therefore necessary to play politics, to discuss, and to move forward as best we could and as peacefully as possible towards a way out of the crisis. It's in my character to try to find compromises, and it was in the country's interest to reach a solution based on a democratic verdict. This was what I aspired to and what I had been trying to put in place for years, always prevented by the rebels, backed by their French sponsors, who refused to disarm and put an end to the constant atrocities they were committing against the population in the north of the country.

A political junkie, Laurent Gbagbo likes tight games. He feels more at home in them than in routine. His past as an opponent, and the electoral crisis that began as soon as he came to power, have prepared and trained him for this.

In a geographically divided country, whose northern part was under the control of gang leaders, and faced with certain groups or political parties whose leaders were throwing oil on the fire to set Ivorians against each other, it was necessary to act with caution, so as to be able to extinguish, through discussion, negotiation, listening to others and compromise, the fires that the blowers were trying to ignite.

In the most difficult situations, it is important for a head of state to appear as a credible recourse, a father to all his children, to show no preference, to let all those who wish to speak speak and listen. That's why I felt it was so important to guarantee the exercise of civic and individual freedoms. It was the condition for a peaceful debate. In my view, there was no other way forward than to establish a democratic debate and to give a place to all opponents if we were to achieve a true restoration of the republican state throughout the country, and if all populations were to benefit from safety, security, education, healthcare, work - all things to which they were entitled, and which they absolutely had to be given. That was my goal. That was my ambition. I thought that pledging to the opposition and allowing them to establish strongholds would reassure their leaders and the international community. I was wrong. The rebel leader headed the government, and the rebel units had been integrated into the government forces in a common structure. Leaving the Electoral Commission in the hands of would-be opponents proved to be a mistake: it allowed them to manipulate the election results and, on that basis, to organize maneuvers that I suspect the French were behind. What I had underestimated was Nicolas Sarkozy's irrevocable determination to do everything in his power to bring his close friend Alassane Ouattara to power. I had more than a few doubts about the sincerity of the French when I learned that they had appointed Emmanuel Beth, a military man, a former boss of Licorne, who was said to be anti-Gbagbo, and whose brother ran the COS, in charge of "special operations", as ambassador to Ouagadougou, Burkina, a few weeks before the first round of our election. It never happens that a French general is appointed ambassador. And here, three months before the presidential elections, a general close to Sarkozy, brother of the man who organized the French services' dirty tricks, is appointed ambassador at the very moment when mercenaries from Burkina Faso and neighboring countries are being recruited, trained and armed in Burkina Faso's army camps, before being transferred to the north of Côte d'Ivoire. Some of them infiltrated Abidjan even before the elections, while others were organized under the orders of rebel leaders, ready to swarm the south of the country; which they did in March 2011, thanks to the logistical and operational support of the French special services. When I mentioned this to Compaoré, he replied: "Ah? I didn't even know Beth was there!" In fact, they were setting up the rear base for the Special Forces intervention.

But we had to get out. I didn't trust Soro, Compaoré or Ouattara. I knew that their aim was to seize power by whatever means necessary. For them, it was a matter of making Côte d'Ivoire disappear into a larger whole, including Burkina Faso, ruled by them. It's important to understand that southern Côte d'Ivoire is the cash cow of the entire sub-region. They come from arid regions, producing little wealth. To have real wealth, to have real power at home and abroad, you have to get your hands on the south of Côte d'Ivoire. Their aim was to draw on some of the many immigrants from the north of the country, from Burkina, Niger and Guinea. Today, they are encouraging the immigration of tens of thousands of foreigners and offering them voting cards, so as to "drown" the native population in numbers. I don't know how France would manage something like this, when it has never succeeded in integrating its 10% Muslim French population. Côte d'Ivoire's problem isn't foreigners - they've always been welcomed here - it's the fact that Compaoré and Ouattara want to merge Côte d'Ivoire into Burkina. It seems that both of them have revenge to take on Côte d'Ivoire...

Personally, I wanted a peaceful country and harmony among its citizens. I didn't care where anyone came from. In my close circle, many of my friends were from the North, as were my relatives. In Côte d'Ivoire, marriages between members of different ethnic groups are common. It was this balance that had to be preserved, to avoid one group attacking another. It was in everyone's interest to preserve a status that had made Côte d'Ivoire a prosperous country, rich also in its multiplicity. Why do you think I was supported by the people? Because Ivorians, of all origins, refused violence, because they knew that my approach to appeasement was the right one. Because they wanted to preserve their gains, whether collective (health, education, etc.) or individual (higher living standards, etc.). My supporters were to be found in all strata of the population, in all groups. The Sofres polls, of which there were eight in the months leading up to the 2010 elections, always showed me as the winner. I know they reflect reality. Jean-Marc Simon, the French ambassador, claims that they had been arranged by their authors to numb my vigilance and prevent me from seeing the manoeuvres underway. In any case, they put Ouattara in third place every time. If the polls had been rigged, the riggers would surely have placed Ouattara in second position, not third. In any case, it shows the truth of the matter and the forces that were at work to bring me down. It also shows the extent to which supposedly respectable politicians or representatives of a great power are, in reality, nothing more than small-time crooks who, today, boast about their fraud! If Jean-Marc

Simon and the others are telling the truth, that means they're admitting to having organized everything to cheat, even though they claimed the opposite... I'd rather believe they drew the dice because they knew I was on the verge of winning. Just look at a map of the results: in almost every region, from East to West, and in the South, I'm ahead, while Ouattara is only ahead in the North. That's where it all happened, under threat from armed rebel militias.

This will undoubtedly lead Gbagbo, too used to storms and dangers - but he won't say so - to overconfidence. He insists:

I would have controlled the chain of events, had the rules and institutions been respected. My strategy succeeded, I won the election. But I was betrayed, right from the first round. Then again in the second round, they did what had to be done. Alassane Ouattara never came second, and was therefore not qualified for the second round. It was Bédié who came second. Bédié is Esau: he sold his birthright for a plate of lentils.

The information gathered at the time, and that which has come to light since, will help us understand why Ouattara and his followers had no desire to see the votes recounted, and to proceed with a definitive audit of the ballot.

On October 3, 2013, opening with great fanfare the 12th Congress of the party he chairs, the PDCI, Côte d'Ivoire's oldest, founded by Houphouët-Boigny, Henri Konan Bédié launched a diatribe against most Ivorian political leaders. Among them, of course, *"the dictator"* Laurent Gbagbo. The speech is full of bitterness and attacks, including those of his militants who *"like to dry their laundry where the sun shines", and* the *"(threats), (the) bloodletting, (the) buying of consciences"*, terms used to describe the maneuvers of Ouattara's RDR. A full-blown indictment of the PDCI's efforts to drain it of its lifeblood. The most interesting part of the speech comes just after these jabs at the audience, which he has just shampooed vigorously without provoking any reaction. The bomb explodes when he asserts: *"Following the first round of the 2010 presidential election, it's worth remembering that the rank I occupied was not mine! Despite the poor organization of my campaign management, I was able to note, with supporting evidence, that I had been robbed of at least 600,000 votes, and I informed various chancelleries of this, including ONUCI, the Constitutional Council and the Independent Electoral Commission, which I referred the matter to."*

An explanation of the text, in the form of primary arithmetic, will help to understand the significance of this revelation: the *"600,000 votes"* stolen from Henri Konan Bédié, added to the 1,165,532 votes (25.24%) he received in the first round, put him ahead of Alassane Ouattara, with 1,181,091 votes (32.07%), and within reach of - or ahead of - Laurent Gbagbo with 1,756,504 votes (38.04%).

In this configuration, Ouattara is not even in the second round, as Bédié publicly reminds him, without being denied in any way - he is eliminated. Between the two rounds, Bédié threatens to lodge a protest, but then, for some reason, fails to do so. Negotiations took place. Numerous rumors, some from people close to the candidates, suggest a meeting between Bédié and Gbagbo. There is also talk of Ouattara calling Bédié to order. There is also talk of Sarkozy pressuring Bédié to step aside. Enigmatically, Gbagbo confirmed this confidential information in one sentence: **Sarkozy and Ouattara had put pressure on Bédié to change sides.** Then, on Bédié's determination to remain at the head of his party, the PDCI, at the age of eighty: **He wants us to keep buying him**. At these words, I can hear Ambassador Jean-Marc Simon's words to me over coffee at the Berkeley: *"Bédié, he's counting the envelopes."*

When the news of the theft of 600,000 votes from him broke out of Konan Bédié's own mouth in October 2013, to the embarrassed silence of his political partners, it drew no protest from him in Côte d'Ivoire, not a line in the mainstream press in France. Perhaps because Abidjan's electoral tribulations had long since been cast in the concrete of certainty.

"Gbagbo didn't expect Ouattara and Bédié to get along so well. They summoned magic, secret practices, and it worked," Jean-Marc Simon tells me, who doesn't believe a word of it, and boasted to Jean-Christophe Notin of having manipulated Gbagbo, avoiding to dissuade him from his forthcoming victory, in complicity with Guillaume Soro. "[...] *His*

long-standing advisors, like Bernard Houdin," writes Notin, sang the same tune to him.

From the first day I saw him in prison, and well before Bédié's thunderous exit, Laurent Gbagbo had assured me that the fraud had begun with the Sagem manipulations, and then from the first round of voting. Between the two rounds, he also told me how someone had tried to set another trap for him.

The people at the IEC wanted me to change the date of the second round. They wanted me to delay it by a week. In fact, it was to get the Burkinabe, who were also voting in their own country, to come and vote in Côte d'Ivoire.

With Esau-Bédié out of the picture, the second round on Sunday November 28 was barely over when, the following day, Monday November 29, Young-jin Choi, for the UN, and Canadian La Tortue, for the Commission d'observation de la Francophonie, declared that *"despite a few incidents, the elections went well"*. They hope *"that the turnout, which was lower than in the first round, will still reach 70%"*.

On December 3, 2010, an article published on Abidjan.net had already reported Youssouf Bakayoko's remarks that 500,000 votes had been fraudulently cast in the second round of voting in the North. A region where the elections were under the control of the armed rebellion. Or 9.35% of votes cast. This gives, after a quick calculation, once this bonus has been deducted from Ouattara's score, out of 5,784,490 registered voters, 70% of whom - 4,049,143 - would have voted: 2,107,055 votes for Gbagbo, or 52.04%, and 1,942,088 votes, or 47.96%, for Ouattara.

In a particularly important region of the north, the Bandama valley, for example, the records show that the RDR candidate received 149,598 votes, whereas the regional IEC communicated to the central IEC the figure of 244,471 votes: 94,873 fictitious votes.

"Where have the voters gone?" asked Ivorian newspapers close to Ouattara, commenting on the second round, and worried about the abstention rate.

In the late afternoon, the Independent Electoral Commission announced a lower turnout of 70.84%, compared to the record 83%

of voters in the first round. *"We're approaching 70%,"* said Amadou Soumahouro, one of the IEC's vice-presidents, on RTI, the Ivorian public television channel. *"We are surprised that the turnout is so high, contrary to what we thought yesterday, Sunday. We feared we wouldn't even reach the 60% turnout mark,"* he added.

Already, Pascal Affi N'Guessan has announced that Laurent Gbagbo will lodge challenges to fraud in the northern provinces controlled by armed rebels.

In the evening, the results from the diaspora were publicly announced, after deducting votes from France, and showed Ouattara as the winner among Ivorians living abroad.

On Tuesday November 30, observers from the African Union, led by Joseph Koffigoh, former Prime Minister of Togo, thanked ONUCI for releasing three of their observers who had been blocked and threatened by rebels, and who had been unable to carry out their mission. They state that the competent courts will have to assess the impact of the incidents on the ballot: *"The mission noted with regret serious acts of violence, in particular loss of human life, attacks on physical integrity, kidnapping, intimidation and attempted abduction. [...] In addition, the mission deplored the late opening of some polling stations, the lack of stickers in some polling stations, and the relatively heavy atmosphere in the vicinity of polling stations. Lastly, the mission deplores the kidnapping of two of its observers, and thanks the UNOCI agents for the timely resolution of the situation."* I was able to speak to Mr. Koffigoh by telephone, as he was waiting to leave Côte d'Ivoire for his flight to Lomé at Abidjan airport. He expressed his disgust at the contempt in which his mission was held by representatives of the international community, *"because it was made up entirely of Africans"*. There have been rapes, voters prevented from voting, polling stations where Alassane Ouattara received 100% of the vote - Gbagbo's own scrutineer would not have voted for his candidate! - 2,200 reports out of 20,000 polling stations where there were more voters than registered voters.

On Thursday December 2, at the Hôtel du Golf, Youssouf Bakayoko, in a solo performance that went against the grain of all legality, not only announced Ouattara's victory, but also a formidable 82% turnout! Choi even went as high as 83%. Forget the 70% announced by the Independent

Electoral Commission on Monday. The official figure is 81.10%. Of which 54.10% for Ado, and 45.90% for Gbagbo. A real sleight of hand.

This 12% magical increase in voter turnout, which represents roughly 400,000 votes, is one of the keys - if not the only one - to the inversion of the second-round result, following the rigging of the first-round result: we wanted to get Ouattara through, not Bédié, not me, and we did: for Ouattara to win, we knew we had to get 50% of Bédié's first-round voters to turn out, but many Baoulés abstained, because they have old grudges against the RDR and Ouattara. They were the ones who abstained. So we had to correct the turnout to make Ouattara's victory mathematically credible.

As for the argument that explains Bakayoko's solitary announcement, supervised by the American and French ambassadors, at my opponent's campaign headquarters, by the "pressure" prevailing at the Commission's headquarters, it doesn't hold water: the UN was there to guarantee the smooth running of the ballot, and it was up to them to see what measures needed to be taken to achieve this. What they have done, on the contrary, is nothing legal, nothing sensible: it's a simple scam.

Ahoua Don Mello, Ponts et Chaussées engineer, former minister and spokesman for the Gbagbo government, and also head of Sils-Technology, which was involved in processing the election for the FPI, had the merit of publishing his analysis of the election in a widely circulated text[20], back in August 2011. It is based, according to him, on the minutes provided by ONUCI, Sils and the CEI. In all, 19,041 reports, out of 20,073 polling stations, i.e. 1,032 missing reports, were never transmitted to the IEC. Don Mello asked that his study, carried out PV by PV, be compared in public with the PV held by ONUCI, and the Sagem polling station directory. To no avail. No one wanted to put their cards on the table. Disturbed by the disappearance of 1,032 PVs, representing 306,889 voters, and after calculating the number of falsified or invalid PVs, he attributed responsibility to the

---

20. *Ma Part de vérité*, document distributed to the media on August 7, 2011.

CEI commissioners, *"responsible for the zones under rebel control [...]
and the presidents of the local commissions, who were able to make some
1,032 procès-verbaux disappear without any official explanation. When we
realize that almost all these commissioners and local commission chairmen
are [...] pro-Ouattara, and that they had the results of the first round, there
was nothing to stop them from creating situations that invalidated PVs
favorable to the opposing candidate, as in Paris."*

According to Don Mello, the second-round vote ended with the
following figures: 71% turnout, *"which roughly corresponds to the figure
announced by the IEC at the close of polling stations"*, *"figures based on voters'
lists, which are far from the 81% obtained on the basis of PVs"*. According
to Don Mello, the results put Laurent Gbagbo, with 52.45% of the vote,
ahead of Alassane Ouattara, with 47.55%.

For the record, on Friday December 3, 2010, Côte d'Ivoire's outgoing
president was declared winner of the November 28 presidential election by
the Constitutional Council, with 51.45% of the vote, against 48.55% for
his opponent. While the provisional results of the Electoral Commission
had given victory to Alassane Dramane Ouattara with 54.1% against
45.9% to the outgoing president.

Following challenges lodged by Laurent Gbagbo, the Constitutional
Council annulled the votes in seven departments of the rebel-controlled
north, for reasons explained by Paul Yao N'Dré, who was immediately
accused of having been appointed by Gbagbo. The reasons for this
massive cancellation include the absence of opposition representatives
in certain polling stations, obvious ballot box stuffing, the absence of
polling booths, the increase in the number of votes - sometimes excee-
ding the number of registered voters or voters - and the transportation
of ballots by unauthorized persons. No one took up the challenge, which
was worth proposing.

**In any case, how can you take seriously an election in which, as in
the northern town of Bouaké, Ouattara's stronghold, there are more
than 250,000 votes cast for some 150,000 registered voters? Was this
the election called for by the international community?**

Over and above all the accounting, despite the recount that should have taken place but never will, Henri Konan Bédié's admission settles the issue once and for all, officially, publicly and uncontested. Ouattara did not win the 2010 presidential election in Côte d'Ivoire. His best enemy, and political ally, cannot lie. He has no interest in doing so. According to him, a usurper is now running the country, and has sent Laurent Gbagbo to the ICC.

In the service of Laurent Gbagbo in the United States during the post-election crisis, Lanny Davis, Bill Clinton's former communicant, declared on CNN that the UN *"hadn't even bothered to read the text of the Ivorian Constitutional Council's decision"*, and that Laurent Gbagbo wanted to *"stop the violence and negotiate a peaceful solution"*. Similarly, Thabo Mbeki, in a report never published, advocated a recount. One senator, James Inhofe, went so far as to write to Hillary Clinton to request the same operation. Nothing came of it. Not even the Ivorian clergy took a stand in favor of Gbagbo: Cardinal Agré defended the Constitution. The bishops followed suit, calling on CDEAO and the UN to respect Ivorian sovereignty. As Jean-Christophe Notin recounts in his own way, going so far as to impute to Laurent Gbagbo the statements of an American politician he doesn't even know: *"Religious anathema is a Gbagbo classic that finds echoes as far away as the United States, where the Reverend Pat Robertson, a former candidate in the 1988 presidential primaries [...] declared on CNN in April: 'The problem is that this country, which was run by a Christian, is going to be in the hands of Muslims. So it's a new Muslim nation that's going to help build this arc of Sharia law around the Middle East.'"*

Everyone sees the problem through their own glasses. But we are entitled to ask why all the attempts at direct dialogue and controlled recounts proposed by Gbagbo have been rejected by Ouattara and his allies. The record cost of these elections. 261 billion CFA francs (398 million euros) - of which 242 billion CFA francs (369 million euros) will be borne by Côte d'Ivoire - leave us hoping for a better end than war, and thousands of dead.

On March 30, 2011, the general offensive began, including the shelling of Laurent Gbagbo's residence. European economic operators, blocked for weeks by the embargo imposed to stifle Gbagbo, warn that the end of March will be the last acceptable deadline. After that, it's back to business as usual, whatever the political and military situation. For Sarkozy and his allies, the key was to move quickly and knock out Gbagbo, who would have been relieved by the resumption of economic activity. With French forces engaged, the final military act was a foregone conclusion. As Gbagbo's supporters would say: *"We won the elections, but we lost the war."*

"THE OUATTARAS AREN'T A COUPLE, THEY'RE A BUSINESS"

We think we know the facts, we skim over appearances. The media don't write history; they don't have the means, the time or the vocation. In France, few audiovisual media will have deserted the highway of one-track thinking, secreted in high places by Nicolas Sarkozy's Élysée Palace. The French president's involvement was more striking than that of Jacques Chirac in his dealings with Gbagbo, between 2000 and 2007. A question of style. His involvement was also more personal: the friendship between Alassane Ouattara and Nicolas Sarkozy goes back more than twenty years. According to the online newspaper *Le Post* of April 12, 2011, which pretends to wonder how much their complicity might have weighed in Gbagbo's downfall, Ouattara has often spoken of this special relationship:

"*He and I are friends first. And we were friends long before this crisis. When I'm in Paris, I go and see him. To tell the truth, if I have five or six real friends in the world, he's one of them,' the Ivorian president told L'Express* [...]." According to the same article: *"Alassane Ouattara confirmed this 'long-standing' friendship the same month on Canal+, claiming at the same time to have friendly ties with Dominique Strauss-Kahn and Laurent Fabius, forged when he was No.2 at the IMF from 1994 to 1999.*

"*In 1990, as Prime Minister of Félix Houphouët-Boigny, President Ouattara entrusted the private concession for water and electricity in*

Côte d'Ivoire to Martin Bouygues, a close friend of Sarkozy. So it was only natural that the two politicians got to know each other, appreciate each other and forge ties."

"Ouattara then became very close to Bouygues," explains Antoine Glaser, former editor-in-chief of *La Lettre du Continent,* to the *Post.*

On August 24, 1991, Alassane Ouattara married Dominique, widow of Folloroux, at the town hall in the 16th arrondissement of Paris. *"Martin Bouygues was in the front row,"* recalls Glaser, who attended the ceremony.

But it wasn't Nicolas Sarkozy who united the Ouattara couple.

"This rumor is complete nonsense!" says Antoine Glaser. *Contrary to the persistent rumors circulating on the Web and elsewhere, it was a deputy mayor of the arrondissement who married them."*

"From this marriage onwards," says *Le Post, "Nicolas Sarkozy and Alassane Ouattara cultivated their relationship against a backdrop of business and politics. Via Martin Bouygues, Nicolas and Cécilia Sarkozy became close to the Ouattara couple."*

Ouattara's wife, a Frenchwoman born in Algeria, continues *Le Post,* became a mutual friend of Martin Bouygues and the Sarkozy couple. She proved to be a highly influential businesswoman. She built her fortune by managing Félix Houphouët-Boigny's substantial real estate holdings. It's true that Côte d'Ivoire's first president, whose fortune at the end of his life was worth between 7 and 11 billion dollars, was very fond of her. It was common knowledge that they were intimate. A former close associate of Houphouët's remembers the pinball games that occupied some of his afternoons at the local café when he was waiting for the old president, who was visiting Dominique in the apartment she owned on avenue Victor-Hugo. With Ouattara now Prime Minister, thanks to her, the young couple based their financial success on the former President's fortune. He on the kitchen side, she on the garden side. Until the death of the "Old Man" in December 1993. Houphouët disappeared without a written will. After arriving in Côte d'Ivoire in 1975, Dominique Folloroux took on modest jobs, first at the Ascott bar, then as a secretary at the Canadian Embassy. Her fierce determination to get ahead, her charm and her dazzling blond hair soon attracted the attention of men of power. She set up and developed her real estate company AICI (Agence immobilière de la Côte d'Ivoire) in 1979, with the support of Abdoulaye Fadiga, Governor of the BCEAO, who also became a close friend. She recovered the real estate assets that Houphouët-Boigny had entrusted to her, at a time when there was no difference between the state coffers and the pockets of the Head of State. She went on to manage Omar Bongo's portfolio. The late Gabonese president entrusted her with the management of his "ill-gotten gains". The name of Dominique Ouattara and that of her agency should therefore logically appear in the files of Sherpa, the association involved in tracking down these misappropriations of public funds, generally invested in real estate, which has focused its attacks on Denis Sassou-Nguesso. This has not prevented the handsome Denis from receiving Christine Ockrent in Brazzaville for the launch of *Forbes Afrique* magazine, or Bernadette Chirac in Paris, at the Hôtel Meurice[21], in April 2013. Teodoro Obiang, of Equatorial Guinea, and Omar, then his son Ali Bongo, of Gabon, are also targeted by the anti-BMA (Biens mal acquis) crusade. The Guinean and Gabonese presidents have entrusted Richard Attias, a former Publicis executive, with the task of "smoothing" their image in the West through international economic forums organized in their respective capitals. A total hypocrisy emerges from Sherpa's actions, which are strangely silent on the complicit system that covered up the embezzlement denounced, facilitated and sometimes organized it, and on those who benefited from it.

When William Bourdon was asked - as I was when I visited him at his rue de Rivoli office on July 15, 2013 - why he, the specialist in ill-gotten gains, had never taken an interest in AICI, Dominique Ouattara's agency in the case of the Bongo's "ill-gotten" real estate, which could legally be likened to complicity, he replied that his association *"does not take matters into its own hands"*, and that it needed a *"precise file"*.

Alassane Ouattara's assets, and the enigma of the origin of Dominique's immense fortune, remain a taboo subject that doesn't excite the masses. The mainstream press is not concerned. Quoting a *"former Africa advisor to the Élysée Palace"* in the book *Reines d'Afrique: le roman vrai des*

---

21. According to La lettre du Continent no657.

Premières dames[22]: "[…] *it may be that Dominique got his hands on some of Houphouët's grisbi. At least, that's what some heirs who claim to have been robbed are saying.*" In 1993, when Houphouët died, there was still no talk of ill-gotten gains. Only a complete biography of Dominique and Alassane Ouattara could untangle the golden threads weaving their shared history, and tell the origin of their fortune and success-story. The elements that do exist, however, allow us to sketch a few outlines.

Everything has been said about Dominique Nouvion-Folloroux's alleged affairs after her husband's death. She denied it. The fact that the young blond widow found herself at the head of a real estate business endowed with the assets of the head of state came as no surprise to those close to the Ivorian president. According to Michel de Bonnecorse, Africa advisor to the Élysée Palace, Houphouët was deeply affected when Dominique set her sights on Alassane Ouattara, and then married him: "*Jacques Chirac saw her cry. […] That's probably why he always mistrusted Ouattara, who was thought to have stolen Houphouët's wife.*" Dominique Ouattara swears that this gossip "*killed her*", and that she "*loved Houphouët very much*", who considered her "*his daughter*".

The Ouattaras skilfully make useful friends: from Michel Camdessus, Managing Director of the IMF for fifteen years, to Martin Bouygues, or George Soros, the famous billionaire and speculator: **Dominique Ouattara herself told me that he was one of their close friends.** Alassane Ouattara's status as a senior official at the International Monetary Fund gives him a powerful circle of friends, optimized by Madame's intense public relations work. This alchemy gives the couple every advantage. Dominique Ouattara communicates extensively through her Children Of Africa foundation, whose godmother, Princess Ira von Fürstenberg, and guests, all volunteers, claims the foundation, such as Alain Delon, Adriana Karembeu or MC Solaar, traveled all the way to Abidjan for a charity dinner on February 24, 2012 at the Hôtel Ivoire. On March 14, 2014, it's fun again in Abidjan. "*Maman Dominique*", as an article in *Le Figaro* dated Friday, March 21, 2014, calls her, has brought in a new charter of celebrities, for a charity gala. This time, the aim is to

---

22. Vincent Hugeux, *Reines d'Afrique: le roman vrai des Premières dames*, Perrin, 2014.

fund the construction of a one hundred and fifteen-bed children's hospital in Bingerville, eighteen kilometers from Abidjan. The guest list, gathered at the Sofitel convention center to attend the show inspired by Patrick Sébastien and his "Grand Cabaret", is just as impressive as in 2012. Richard Berry, Adriana Karembeu, MC Solaar, the inescapable Ira von Fürstenberg, as well as Jean Todt, President of the Fédération Internationale d'Automobile, Édouard Nahum, the jeweller, the film-maker Alexandre Arcady, Professors Alain Deloche, founder of Chaîne de l'Espoir, Professor Marc Gentilini, Miss France 2014 alongside Miss Côte d'Ivoire 2014, Ivorian singer Alpha Blondy, American actor Gary Dourdan from the series *Les Experts*. And let's not forget the guest of honor, Her Royal Highness Lalla Salma, wife of Moroccan King Mohamed VI. In an interview with the fortnightly *Afrique Éducation*[23], Mamadou Koulibaly, as president of his party, Lider, and as a professor of economics, gives a different view from that offered by the journalist inter-viewing him. The latter presents the new First Lady as *"solely concerned with social issues"*, and not with politics, as was Simone Gbagbo: *"She's not into politics, you say? The Children Of Africa Foundation, owned by the First Lady, was established as an organization of public utility by a decree[24] issued by her husband. This means that the foundation will benefit from Ivorian money for its operations. Clearly, state money is being used for charity. Good governance is suffering. Why doesn't the Ministry of Social Affairs do this work with public money? [...] What's more, on December 6, 2011, Mrs Ouattara was elevated by her husband, via the Grand Chancellery, to the dignity of Commander of the National Order of the Republic of Côte d'Ivoire [...]."* Mamadou Koulibaly points out, not without irony, that neither Madame Houphouët-Boigny, nor Henriette Bédié, nor Simone Gbagbo, the three previous First Ladies, had the honor and advantage of receiving the country's highest distinction. Moreover, the fact that Children Of Africa has offices in a large number of capital cities, with bases in Paris and Abidjan, obviously represents a parallel circuit of private financial flows, while being linked to the state budget.

---

23. *Afrique Éducation*, no348, May 16 to 31, 2012.
24. Decree no. 2012-232 of March 7, 2012.

All those in the know agree that Dominique Ouattara played a central role in her husband's rise to power, securing his appointment to the head of BCEAO and then to the Prime Minister's office. She helped build his glamorous image, which she promoted in the French media. Her constant public relations work gave the beginning of her husband's reign in Côte d'Ivoire a very international, if somewhat glitzy, tone. Ranked among the twenty-five most influential *businesswomen* on the continent by *Jeune Afrique* magazine in 2013, the current First Lady has founded a powerful group of hairdressing salons and products in the United States, managed under license from the Dessange brand. Her sister, daughter and son are also involved in the family business. Loïc Folloroux was also Africa Director of the Anglo-Saxon group Armajaro, specializing in the cocoa trade, until the end of 2013. In this capacity, he had his say in the redistribution of cocoa profits following the fall of President Gbagbo. As for Ibrahima, a true look-alike of his brother Alassane (hence his nickname "Photocopy"), he's a kind of "President bis", assigned to budget management and distribution. **The Ouattaras aren't a couple, they're a business,"** comments Gbagbo with a smile.

Dominique Ouattara, like her husband, is quite adept at using polished, truthful language. A discourse that says almost the exact opposite of the realities it conveys. She claims, for example, to have made a great sacrifice by giving up her business as soon as she became First Lady. She's not one for gender confusion! Of course, her sacrifice needs to be put into perspective, by pointing out that through a few unconditional and historic collaborators, and above all the members of her family, she remains at the center of a sprawling apparatus, which she can monitor from her office as First Lady, where she has some forty collaborators at her disposal.

With Elisabeth Gandon, one of the most loyal of the faithful, now at the helm of Malesherbes Gestion - a real estate agency with 250 portfolios to date - and the real estate agency AICI (with Nathalie Folloroux-Bejani, the boss's eldest daughter), and a member of the board of directors of Children Of Africa, Dominique is never far away. The communicating vessels between the various components of the galaxy are assured. Her son Loïc, having left the cocoa business, is now in charge of the Radio

Nostalgie network in Africa, another of his mother's properties. His sister Nathalie, in addition to her real estate duties, assists him. As for Ouattara's son-in-law, Benedict Senger, husband of Fanta Catherine Ouattara-Senger (Ado's daughter), he was awarded a series of customs, port and airport control contracts by mutual agreement in 2013, with his company Webb Fontaine. A company registered in Dubai, with headquarters in Geneva. In March 2014, an IMF mission to Côte d'Ivoire pointed the finger at the company's management and the significant revenue losses it was allegedly generating for the state: 46.36 billion CFA francs (70 million euros) were missing from the Ivorian customs accounting forecasts.

"In the Nouvian family, the brothers […] *Patrick is a general practitioner in Hyères* [Var]. *Marc, fifty-three, founded Sonecei in 2012* [one year after his brother-in-law Ado was elected president!], *an international trading company specializing in cocoa beans (of which Côte d'Ivoire is the world's leading producer) with his sister Noëlle. As for Philippe, also in his fifties, he may have left the management of AICI's Gabonese subsidiary, but he presides over the destiny of Gecmo, a firm well-versed in the secrets of project management and property management. It was to him, in particular, that the invitation to tender for the Bingerville hospital, so dear to his eldest daughter, was entrusted, as was the supervision of the renovation work at the Presidency*[25].

From charity to family business, we've come full circle. Honni soit qui mal y pense…

And we're having a blast in Abidjan! 10 million to see singer Rihanna on December 29, 2012, for Ado's birthday, which coincides with the Koras (African music celebrations). The pretty singer accompanied her then-fiancé, Chris Brown, who came to sing at the Houphouët-Boigny stadium, which remained half-empty, the overpriced seats having discouraged Ivorians. Even the announcement of the distribution of free tickets late in the evening failed to attract the crowds. And while the two American stars were performing at the private party in Ado's honor, a stampede left 60 spectators dead and 200 injured. Fireworks shot over the Cocody plateau. It is said that organization and security measures were

---

25. Vincent Hugeux, *op.cit.*

inadequate, and that Hamed Bakayoko, the Minister of the Interior, was responsible for the fiasco. Chris Brown did not go to the Hôtel Ivoire as planned to present the Koras trophies, but instead slipped away with his sweetheart, both a little richer than when he arrived. The operation was intended to "reposition" Abidjan in the concert of world capitals…

François Loncle, former Socialist minister and member of parliament for the Eure region, has spoken out about the *"maneuvers"* that helped sow trouble within the Socialist Party over the Côte d'Ivoire issue, and turned it against Laurent Gbagbo. Another aspect of the Ouattara family's actions before coming to power. In a series of interviews recorded and broadcast on the Internet by documentary filmmaker Nicoletta Fagiolo, he says that the intense lobbying of Dominique Ouattara, who *"achieved her goals thanks to her colossal fortune"*, *made* all the difference.

François Loncle mentions the names of well-known pro-Ouattara Socialists. For example, current Foreign Minister Laurent Fabius, or Dominique Strauss-Kahn. These friendly networks forged by the Ouattara family may explain the repeated refusals to set up a commission of inquiry into France's actions in Côte d'Ivoire, as proposed by Communist Alain Bocquet. Or Jean-Marc Ayrault. At the time, the aim was to shed light on the role of France and its army in the coup d'état launched against Gbagbo in September 2002. Let's not dream: transparency in relations between France and Africa is still a figment of the imagination.

"Sarkozy got to know Ouattara in 1993, when he devalued the CFA franc," says Antoine Glaser. The head of the Ivorian government helped the French Prime Minister with this operation. Ouattara then had to deal with Nicolas Sarkozy, the French Budget Minister at the time.

"In 1997, Nicolas Sarkozy made his first trip to Côte d'Ivoire. He accompanied Martin Bouygues as a business lawyer to Abidjan to meet Henri Konan Bédié [president of Côte d'Ivoire from 1993 to 1999] *and defend the contracts his friend had signed in the country,"* explains Gilles Labarthe. *Ouattara was then a personal friend of Sarkozy. He was part of Sarkozy's family circles, and it's possible that they met during this visit, which was more economic than political.*

After that, the ties between Ouattara and Sarkozy grew ever closer. *"When Sarkozy was Interior Minister, he and Cécilia received the Ouattara couple on several occasions,"* explains Antoine Glaser. *And since he became president in 2007, Ouattara has dropped by the Élysée for an aperitif at least four or five times,"* adds the journalist.

In August 2011, President Sarkozy rested in the villa belonging to the family of his new wife, Carla Bruni, at Cap Nègre on the Côte d'Azur. He made an exception to their summer seclusion for the Ouattara couple, who were invited to dinner.

On January 25, 2012, President Ouattara was invited on a state visit to France. All the pomp and circumstance of the republic was reserved for him: the Republican Guard on horseback accompanied the couple from their arrival at Les Invalides, after helicopter transport from the airport, to their hotel. For New Year's Eve 2013, it was Nicolas and Carla Sarkozy's turn to be received privately by the Ouattara family at their splendid seaside property in Assinie, a little paradise a few dozen kilometers east of Abidjan.

This intimacy has never wavered, even in bad times. Shocked by his electoral defeat on May 6, 2012, Sarkozy saw only one head of state rush to the Élysée Palace to comfort him: Alassane Ouattara. According to Alpha Condé, President of Guinea-Conakry, Ado didn't make the trip for nothing… Condé is indignant that he still hasn't received the 5 million euros France promised him. Whereas, as he asserts in the magazine *Challenge*[26], Alassane Ouattara *"who paid a private visit to Sarkozy the day after his defeat, is said to have left with 150 million".* The Guinean president would not be denied by anyone. In the same way, the two men gave free rein to El Hadj Abou Cissé's inflammatory statements, regularly reproduced by the Ivorian press. In his homeland, this unbearable man has a reputation for knowing everything about Ouattara's private life. As he has often recounted, like the griot of the Ado saga, he is his uncle, not by blood, but "in the African way". His sister, Nabintou Cissé, married to a Burkinabe - Ouattara's biological uncle - lived in Dimbroko, Côte d'Ivoire, and was entrusted with little Alassane Dramane when he was orphaned. He was born in the village of Sindou, Burkina Faso, in December 1941 - and not in Dimbroko or Konk, Côte d'Ivoire, as

---

26. *Challenge*, no301 from May 17 to 23, 2012.

stated on a second birth certificate, falsified for the purposes of the 1995 election - where he was raised until his father came to collect him at the age of six. This would explain why there is no trace of Ouattara's youth in Côte d'Ivoire, since he attended school and university in Ouagadougou, Burkina Faso, then, thanks to a scholarship, in the United States, as well as starting his professional career under Burkina Faso nationality, far from Côte d'Ivoire. *"Every Ivorian constantly refers to his village, returns there often, and builds his house there,"* say Ouattara's opponents. *"He doesn't, because he can't."*

El Hadj Abou Cissé has been involved in Ouattara's story from the outset, and claims to know all the details. No one in Côte d'Ivoire openly doubts this. Especially as he is also one of the founding members of Ado's RDR party, and has often been portrayed in the past as a "wise old man": *"I sold two houses to help him,"* he once declared, *"when he had problems with Bédié in the 90s."* This loudmouth publicly criticizes Alassane Ouattara for having sent Gbagbo *"to whom he owes everything"* to The Hague, as well as *for "having hidden 14 billion in the Cayman Islands",* and *"three boats"* acquired during his governance, in the 90s. He also recently referred to him as his friend Sarkozy's *"banker",* adding fuel to the river of unverifiable rumors that constantly flood Africa. It's true that you only lend to the rich: *"[…] the loot in the possession of the former French head of state is under Ouattara's guard. Sarkozy chose Ouattara to finance his campaign for the French presidential election […] Ouattara is the one who will coordinate everything*[27]*."*

Unleashed since Gbagbo's transfer to The Hague, which he finds shameful, he has never ceased to publicly attack the man he calls *"the beggar of Abidjan".* Laurent Gbagbo has known Abou Cissé for a long time, without ever having met him.

We met in the late 90s. He was in the RDR, which had been created in 1994 by Djeni Kobina, who was a friend. At the time, we had good relations with the party, until Ouattara took control in 1998, after Kobina's death, and colonized it with his people. Abou Cissé saw me, du-

---

27. Lecridabidjan.net

ring the troubled period when we were all going to prison, personally looking after the RDR people, giving them assistance and showing them friendship. After that, I kept in regular contact with him and some of them, often by telephone. What makes him react against Ouattara is not politics, it's a feeling of injustice on a human level. He's seen me in action, and knows that I've never harmed Alassane Ouattara - quite the contrary, since I've helped him become eligible, and always taken care of his security. So he doesn't understand why so much malice has been developed against me. He's a free man, and no one dares contradict him. Maybe because there's some truth in what he says?

"Some people have suggested that he change his address for his own safety. But he refuses. Because he believes he is in the right. And that his life is in the hands of the Lord", says Yacouba Gbané in *Le Temps*, as Abou Cissé has refused to obey the directives of delegations sent by Ado to ask him to tone down his intemperate declarations. Since then, he has reportedly received anonymous death threats. But he hasn't changed his address or his rhetoric. And no one has ever taken him to court, or officially denied his claims. This passivity lends weight to his accusations in African opinion. In *Le Quotidien d'Abidjan* of May 16, 2014, he struck again very hard, accusing the Ouattara clan of being responsible for the disappearance of journalist Guy André Kieffer in 2004.

Let's try to answer the *Post*'s question as to whether this long-standing friendship between Sarkozy and Ouattara *"favored the fall of Gbagbo"*, far from African rumors, fantasies and realities mixed, on a continent where tales run faster than the wind. The impact of such a strong personal relationship is questionable. Especially as none of the contracts between the major French groups and Côte d'Ivoire have been broken, or even threatened by Gbagbo, the reason for France's bias against Gbagbo was not fed by the bosses of these major groups, even if Martin Bouygues is a friend of Ouattara. It's even said that Vincent Bolloré, who got on well with Gbagbo, wouldn't have taken such a dim view of his re-election.

I have never opposed the work and interests of French companies. To say that I was, that I am, that we are anti-French is an abuse of semantics. Besides, you'd think it would be! I was simply defending my country's interests. If foreign companies win, Côte d'Ivoire has to win too. Our policy was to encourage entrepreneurs to invest, provided they respected the law and free competition was established. For example, Ouattara's son, Loïc Folloroux, entered the cocoa business in the early 2000s without encountering the slightest problem.

I let the institutions do their job. I've never interfered in business life. There have been obscure episodes: in January 1993, during an extraordinary session of the National Assembly, Bédié's PDCI deputies criticized the conditions under which Prime Minister Alassane Ouattara had sold Ivorian electricity and water to the Bouygues group, and asked questions about the unclear - to say the least - financial terms of the sale. A document exists, which can easily be consulted in the archives of the National Assembly.

I remember, in 2005, it was the end of this contract with Bouygues, which had been signed in 1990. We told them I didn't want to renew the contract. Martin called me and sent his son Olivier. I told him I had nothing against Bouygues, that the normal procedure would apply, but I made it clear that the Ivorian state now wanted to be present on the board of directors of the national electricity company to verify the reality of the figures declared to the Ivorian administration. Until then, no one had ever obtained credible, verifiable figures from Bouygues. I'd seen enough with oil: when I came to power, Côte d'Ivoire only received 12% of the price of each barrel. Things worked out well with Bouygues, even though their director in Côte d'Ivoire, Zadi Kessi, openly took a stand against me. I haven't ruled out the idea that Bouygues wanted to place people in government: Zadi Kessi made no secret of the fact that he wanted to be Prime Minister.

So who was so angry with Gbagbo, apart from the Élysée Palace? The involuntary answer came to me over lunch with Jean-Marc Simon on March 19, 2013. *"If it hadn't been for Nicolas Sarkozy, obviously, things would have gone differently: power-sharing, a gas factory,"* he told me. For once, Laurent Gbagbo agrees with him.

I don't think anyone else would have acted so brutally. Sarkozy is someone who has no perspective on events. I remember an interview I gave to the newspaper Le Figaro on January 27, 2011, at the height of the post-election crisis. He phoned me the next day, very upset, as if I'd spoken directly to him, to reply…

If I'd wanted to talk to him, I would have. That wasn't my intention, but he makes everything about himself. I had the feeling that he treated everything to do with Côte d'Ivoire as a personal, private matter…

He was Ouattara's friend, and he didn't like me, I always knew. I insulted him by not accepting his invitation to the June 2010 France-Africa summit in Nice, and to the July 14th festivities "to celebrate the fiftieth anniversary of African independence" (what independence?), with a parade of African troops on the Champs-Élysées. I was the only African president not present. He took offense. He just doesn't take the time to think. I had my reasons: how is it that Ivorian troops and a president who are accused by the French authorities of having caused the death of nine French soldiers in a bombardment in Bouaké in November 2004 are invited? Please explain! The French army massacred dozens of civilian demonstrators in the streets of Abidjan in the hours that followed. So we had to have a few discussions, and make a few clarifications, before parading off to Paris. I was astonished by Sarkozy's inconsistency. It was yet another reason to have my hide.

"I BELIEVE IN BUILDING INSTITUTIONS IN AFRICA"

I've always believed in building institutions in Africa, and I've never wavered from this conviction. Even if their incumbents make mistakes. Am I going to criticize the Constitutional Council that crowned Sarkozy? The person who proclaimed François Hollande the winner was Jean-Louis Debré, appointed by Chirac, and I was proclaimed the winner in 2000 by a relative of Robert Guéï. Institutions are designed to place political life above the contingencies of the moment, and the higher interests of the State at the heart of political life. This is the indispensable basis for our progress. Tribalism - that is, life and votes based on ethnic affiliations, or clans, as you might say - is an African reflex that is still very common, and very dangerous, in that it provokes conflict. Some people exploit it, watering it down like a weed. Only democratic institutions and a strong State can transcend political life, through multi-ethnic parties and institutions of universal value. "Above parties," said De Gaulle, "above clans: it's the law of the general interest against that of the mafias, and against outside interference".

Daniel Mayer, French humanist and politician, President of the Ligue des droits de l'homme, President of the Conseil constitutionnel between 1983 and 1986, said: *"The law expresses the general will only in compliance with the Constitution."* More recently, François Hollande indirectly reminded Nicolas Sarkozy of this intangible rule, who had been critical of the Constitutional Council after fraud on his 2012 presidential election campaign accounts came to light on July 4, 2013. From Tunis, where he was, Hollande the very next day, July 5, declared, *"The Constitutional Council must be respected, fully respected, fully respected, and no one can suspect, call into question, this institution without calling into question all the institutions."* He concludes: *"Its decisions are binding on all."*

One might well ask why no one in France made the connection between François Hollande's statement and what had happened in Côte d'Ivoire two years earlier. When the decision of the Constitutional Council designating the winner of the presidential election was held to be null and void, on the pretext that the President of the Constitutional Council had been appointed, as is the rule, by the President of the Republic, Laurent Gbagbo... In vain, only the supporters of the *"Hague deportee"*, as they call him, have noticed the double standard. African institutions are simply not held to the same standard as those in the West. This episode in African history was written elsewhere. In Paris, Washington and Brussels, but not in Abidjan.

Today, Francis Wodié sits unashamedly at the helm of Côte d'Ivoire's Constitutional Council, legally appointed by his long-time friend Alassane Ouattara. The other six members of the institution (former presidents Laurent Gbagbo and Konan Bédié are ex officio members) were also appointed by the current president. No one, least of all Ouattara's French friends, would dream of casting doubt on the institution's competence, arguing, for example, that Wodié has long been close to the current head of state. Gbagbo was given a trial in the second round, when the President of the Constitutional Council declared Gbagbo the winner. Yesterday as today, the President of the Republic is, in any case, the only one empowered to designate who should occupy this post to guarantee the stability of the institutions. This was the case for Paul Yao N'Dré, appointed by Gbagbo, or previously under President Konan Bédié: the lawyer Noël Nemin, a close friend of many, who was none other than his chief of staff...

In France, from Pierre Mazeaud to Jean-Louis Debré appointed by Jacques Chirac, from Daniel Mayer, Robert Badinter or Roland Dumas appointed by François Mitterrand, the same tradition of affinity between the President and the person he appoints to head the Council of Elders has been respected since the advent of the 1958 Constitution. Even so, Gbagbo chose only some of the members of this Council, the others being appointed by Mamadou Koulibaly, President of the National Assembly and No.2 in the regime. Whereas Ouattara himself chose, without exception, all the people who sit on it today. This Council will be called upon to validate the forthcoming 2015 elections and proclaim the winner. Francis Wodié will be stepping down eight months after his appointment....

The Ivorian Constitution clearly stipulates that the Constitutional Council alone is empowered to proclaim the final results of a presidential election, in Côte d'Ivoire as in France. But in a casino, whoever throws the ball, deals the chips and counts the points wins every time. And it's always the player who loses. Especially if the croupier isn't his cousin. Gbagbo understood this too late. He was the only one who believed that democracies would not dare trample on the highest institution, the symbol of Côte d'Ivoire's sovereignty. An African friend from Togo, one of the countries where France, so concerned about democracy in Côte d'Ivoire or Libya, has allowed the son to succeed his dictator father as president, because he is one of the most docile to Paris, told me of Gbagbo: *"He hasn't understood a thing! Doesn't he know that his country was sold to France by Houphouët-Boigny fifty years ago? He thinks he's the owner, when in fact he's just a tenant or, at best, a manager!"* To survive and last, many African politicians have integrated this dependence, this submission. This cynicism forms the *"mental pre-structures"* described by Jean-François Kahn in *L'Horreur médiatique*[28].

At The Hague, on February 28, 2013, Gbagbo reiterated his fundamental point: *"Our countries, our states - and this will be my last point - are fragile. And every time a European or Western head of state said to me, 'Do democracy in Africa', I said, 'We need democracy not because you say so, but because we ourselves actually need it to build our states."*

"Madam, look at Côte d'Ivoire, if we don't use democracy, how are we going to choose the head of state?

---

28. Jean-François Kahn, *L'Horreur médiatique*, Plon, 2014

"In the east, leaning against the Ghanaian border, the Akan have their own way of choosing their village or canton chiefs or their kings. In the West, we have a scattered power base. In the north, we have the Islamized Malinké, who gather around mosques, and alongside them, the Senoufo, who meet in the sacred woods.

"Which electoral method are we going to use?

"So democracy helps us. Because it wipes the slate clean and gives every individual, considered as a citizen, a voice. That's why I joined the fight for democracy. […]

"But democracy isn't just about voting, it's about who […] says what the result of the vote is. That's democracy too.

"When you go and take the president of the electoral group (the Independent Electoral Commission) one night, take him to a candidate's electoral headquarters, invite a foreign TV station to tell him to speak, film him and broadcast it the next morning. That's not very democratic, that's not democracy.

"Democracy means respecting the law, starting with the most important legal norm, the Constitution. Anyone who does not respect the Constitution is not a democrat.

"Madam, I was told to come here because I respected the Constitution. So I'm here, but I'm counting on you. I'm counting on you because I hope that all the Africans who support me and who are here all the time in front of the Court, in front of the prison, who are in their countries demonstrating, marching, all these Africans, that they understand that the salvation for African states is respect for the Constitutions we give ourselves and the laws that flow from them."

Who heard Laurent Gbagbo? Apart from *Jeune Afrique*, whose core business is obviously this, few Parisian newsrooms saw fit to send a journalist to attend the February 28, 2013 hearing.

Ouattara hasn't understood that tribalism is outdated. Who built the Republic and who broke it? We had an army and a police force, but he set them aside and replaced them with tribal militias. For example, Cherif Ousmane, known as "Le Guépard", one of the rebel leaders who organized the very first putsch against me, the so-called "black

Mercedes plot" in January 2001. He is now head of security at the Presidential Palace.

There are many rebels promoted by Alassane Ouattara. In 2002, Koné Zakaria, a Dozo initiate, led a unit of 1,500 Dozos, the "warriors of light". According to International Crisis Group, in May 2003 he had thirty traditional dancers and civil servants murdered in Manokono. When he was in charge of the Adjamé camp, he is said to have tortured and killed many civilians: Ouattara appointed him commander of the military police. As for Wattao, he is suspected by the same NGO of having repeatedly destabilized the peace process through targeted attacks, and of being responsible for a massacre in Bouaké in 2007. In 2008, Wattao ousted Koné Zakaria from his zone of influence in order to take control of diamond mines: Ouattara appointed him second-in-command of the Republican Guard. Raised to the rank of commander, and now one of the bosses of the Special Forces, Losseni Fofana took control of Duékoué on March 29, 2011, and his men massacred hundreds of people in the Carrefour district. Ousmane Coulibaly, known as "Bin Laden", and his men were responsible for numerous massacres, acts of torture and rape against civilians in Man during the 2002 crisis. Crimes denounced by major international human rights organizations. In May 2011, Bin Laden was appointed by Ouattara as commander of the former BAE camp in Yopougon. He carried out widespread torture and arbitrary arrests. On August 15, 2012, he was placed by Ouattara at the head of troops conducting operations in Dabou, where numerous civilians were arbitrarily arrested, tortured and murdered. On September 26, 2012, Alassane Ouattara appointed him Prefect of the San Pedro region. Soumalia Bakayoko was Chief of Staff of the Forces armées des forces nouvelles, the FAFN. His headquarters were based in Bouaké. He was in charge of the parallel army and administration set up by the rebels in the north of the country. Under his command, the Forces Nouvelles looted, racketted, stole, burned and killed. On July 7, 2011, Alassane Ouattara appointed him Chief of Staff of the Forces républicaines de Côte d'Ivoire (FRCI), the highest position in the armed forces of the Republic of Côte d'Ivoire, a post he has held ever since.

"FRANÇOIS HOLLANDE CAME TO SEE ME AT MY HOTEL EVERY TIME I WAS IN PARIS"

France's approach to African affairs is dictated "from above", from the Élysée Palace, in the name of France's economic, strategic and political interests. This was also the case under Mitterrand, who did not hesitate to appoint his son Jean-Christophe to head the Élysée's African cell, whose existence he had criticized under De Gaulle. With François Hollande, there is no longer any African cell. But the President retains control over Africa, *the most visible theater of the partnership between France and the United States*, explained the joint communiqué from the Élysée Palace and the White House with unusual frankness on this subject, prior to Hollande's trip to the United States in February 2013. At least the notion of strategic interests is clear. In economic terms, it's more likely to be the bosses of the CAC 40 who are spearheading France's efforts on the continent. Is "Atlantiquafrique" more pragmatic and uncomplicated than "Françafrique" in the face of the advent of Chinafrique?

François Hollande came to see me at my hotel every time I was in Paris. I never expected anything from him. Ouattara's lawyers here in The Hague are his close friends Jean-Paul Benoit and Jean-Pierre Mignard. Ouattara certainly didn't choose them at random. He knows what lobbying means...

French socialists have a complex… They want people to believe that they govern like the right. In the early 2000s, Villepin manipulated them all, telling them what a monster I was… They were afraid of being splashed, so they let me go. "Gbagbo is infrequentable", said Hollande at the time… Because I wasn't organizing an election… in a country occupied by armed men, in a permanent state of war, with an undefined electorate due to the absence of a census because of the war. To carry out a real census, I needed the rebels' cooperation, and they didn't commit to it until 2010. But then it was a trap, because the company organizing the census "covered up" the registration of tens of thousands of false voters. It was a French company obeying the French authorities.

In 1990, when I dared to run against Houphouët, after my years of exile in Paris, in the first multi-party elections, the kindest of "my socialist friends" gave me 1%… I got 18.3%… Afterwards, they all invited me.

There are some, however, of whom I'll say nothing bad, even if they weren't favorable to me, like Dominique Strauss-Kahn. He knew Ouattara better than I did, because of the IMF. I met him twice to solve problems when he was president of the IMF. Once in Ouagadougou with the West African leaders of the CFA zone. Another time, I phoned him to ask him to come and talk about the debt crisis and Côte d'Ivoire. He came. We had an excellent working session with the ministers of my government. He's brilliant, a hard worker. He had a good grasp of the issues, and things went well with him. He was neither arrogant nor interventionist in our African affairs. I spoke to him before the 2012 French presidential elections. I asked him "if he was going". He replied that he had to talk it over with Martine Aubry, that he wanted her opinion. He was listening, even if he wasn't for me. Just like Jean-Louis Borloo, whom I met in Yaoundé where I had gone to celebrate the fiftieth anniversary of the reunification of Cameroon, at Paul Biya's invitation, on May 20, 2010. He suggested we get together. I gave him the number of my suite at the Hilton Yaoundé, and he came, in all simplicity. We chatted for three quarters of an hour. Those two would never have had me bombed…

I also had a good relationship with Dominique Paillé, a UMP deputy. He's an open-minded man, like the first two, with an ability to listen. Their approach is different from that of Mitterrand, Chirac and, before them, De Gaulle, who still had old ways of thinking in mind. The three I mentioned knew the issues, and their culture meant they weren't always cocardiers. Even if they don't favor you, they listen to you, hear you and respect you.

Sarkozy is something else. I met him for the first time in New York, at the UN, in 2007. It was Robert Bourgi who suggested I make the trip, to see the new president, after all the problems I'd had with Chirac. So I had no negative preconceptions, quite the contrary. He left the area reserved for the five members of the Security Council as soon as he saw me, and came over to shake my hand. "President, when are these elections going to be held?" he asked me, just like that… I simply replied that we had to be patient, and that I wasn't the only one involved. We got to talking, standing up, and that was that. With him, instead of ideas, there's arrogance. George W. Bush was the epitome of this type of man. These are men without deep thought. It's in this category that I place Sarkozy. Or Villepin. Arrogant men, who use their arrogance in place of thought. That's how they think they're showing that France is big, when all they're proving is that it's become small. We're small and weak, so those with big muscles think they're smarter. What the hell! This is our country we're talking about!

But since the fall of the Berlin Wall, political thought in the West has collapsed. In Asia, South America and Africa, however, there are still those who aspire to give meaning and vision… The spectacle of French political life saddens me. Your public debates and your societal questioning show the decline in the level of general culture and pedagogy: marriage for all? But didn't the emperor Caesar say he was "the man of all women and the woman of all men"? The West is afraid of the Muslim jihad, but there was a Christian jihad, in the days of orders of warrior monks like the Knights Templar, and the Americas were conquered and colonized in the name of Catholic kings and in the name of Christ…

The last real politician in France, among those I knew in power, was Jospin. He had political thought and ethics. Chirac was content to win elections, he didn't govern.

I knew Lionel Jospin when he was Prime Minister. He refused French military intervention when Bédié was overthrown, and he did the right thing. He left us alone to manage our affairs, set up our Constitution and move forward. Neither indifference nor interference, I think he used to say. He put his ideas and principles into practice, and he had integrity. At least we can't imagine him phoning Africa to ask for money...

In Adieu, Abidjan-sur-Seine![29], Guy Labertit reports on François Hollande's total distrust of African affairs: *"In Africa,"* he used to say, *"there's nothing but trouble."*

When De Gaulle defied the great powers to say that France would have the atomic bomb, and thus its independence, when Mitterrand spoke of medium-range rockets to the German Bundestag, it was a different dimension of politics. I've reread the works of De Gaulle, and Roland Dumas's book on Mitterrand - times have changed! I never even resented Mitterrand for having always supported Houphouët-Boigny. They had belonged to the same governments, they were friends. Houphouët rendered every possible service to France in Africa. What's more, there was the East-West Cold War, and the whole Western world supported Houphouët, and forgave him everything: it really was a different era...

In 1970, there was no French protest when Robert Guéï, on the orders of Félix Houphouët-Boigny, crushed Bété dissent - opposed to the Baoulés, Houphouët's ethnic group - in the Guébié region, killing between 4,000 and 6,000 people. A genocide for which the survivors are still demanding reparation, to no avail. Who would have dared disturb the Wise Old Man of Africa, our friend, for so little?

---

29. Guy Labertit, *Adieu, Abidjan-sur-Seine! Les coulisses du conflit ivoirien, op.cit.*

"SARKOZY WENT ALL OUT—BUT THEY FOUND NOTHING: NO HIDDEN ASSETS, NO 'ILL-GOTTEN' GAINS"

Back to Scheveningen, a suburb of The Hague, Saturday, June 3, 2012, 1:30 pm. My first visit to the place's most famous inmate. I had to pass through a glass door, a first control desk: passport, verification of registration on the list of *bezoekers* - visitors… Badged, and now spied on all along the way by cameras whose big fish eyeballs follow you everywhere, you pass through another door, operated remotely, you enter a space filled with lockers, to empty your pockets… You take off your shoes, before the metal detector… Yet more doors, a waiting room, a guard in navy blue uniform who comes to fetch you, opens yet more doors. We cross a large courtyard… and finally arrive at the political detainees' block, surrounded by other walls, lined with other doors… a new counter, a new check, the badge, the identity document, yet another metal detector, removing shoes, belt, watch. Accompanied by a huge, blue-uniformed man from Batavia, who opens the last door on the left, with two big letters on it: BO. A corridor runs alongside the common room where families come, watched over by two clean-cut guards, sometimes including women, one of them a bodybuilder with ear piercings and tattoos on her arms. The private visiting rooms, *bezoekamers,* are small rooms equipped with a washbasin, an electric kettle and a white wooden table with two chairs. This is where he comes to sit opposite me. Each of my visits lasts about three hours, minus the time spent on control procedures, under the dark eye of the camera.

I'll always go through the same rituals. After escorting me, the guard leaves me there, before going to fetch Laurent Gbagbo from his cell.

This time, dressed in an Adidas tracksuit jacket, canvas pants and trainers, he sits down opposite me with difficulty on the small wooden chair, taking care not to rest his forearms too heavily on the table. **My wrists, kidneys and shoulders hurt**, he explains immediately, as if to avoid my questions. **But I'm doing better than when I arrived at the end of 2011.**

The first time I had occasion to smile, I think, was when three ICC officials came to ask me how I was going to pay my legal fees. I told them that the bank accounts from which I received my only income, i.e. my salary since becoming president in 2000, had been blocked, and that I had nothing else. They certainly didn't believe me, and decided to launch international investigations. I joked: I told them that if they found anything, they should keep it to themselves. They searched everywhere: France, Switzerland, the United States, tax havens... No matter what they did, they found nothing: no hidden assets, no "ill-gotten" real estate abroad. Sarkozy, too, went out of his way to have them search everywhere... Of course, they didn't find anything, because I don't have much: when I was a teacher, I was able, like all other university professors, to obtain a low-interest loan that enabled me to buy a small house in Abidjan. In the village, I inherited the family land on which I built a modest house for my mother.

If there's one person who knows I'm not venal, it's Ouattara. Every time he came to see me in Abidjan, which was very often, he'd phone me, and I'd protect him, because he was always afraid. He'd say to me: "You know what amazes businessmen? That you never ask them to do anything for you." He himself was astonished by my attitude.

At a loss to prove any enrichment, my opponents try to portray me as a man who sometimes resorts to violence. This has been said about the Kieffer affair, the journalist who disappeared in Abidjan in April 2004, or the Frenchmen abducted from the Novotel in Abidjan

in April 2011, and then murdered. I hardly knew Guy-André Kieffer. I met him once, and saw him another time in the midst of journalists at a press conference. At the time of his disappearance, the judicial authorities ordered a search that was carried out within a hundred-kilometer radius of Abidjan. I don't know what more we could have done. I know that a number of journalists have investigated Kieffer's death and that they have followed different leads. According to them, at the time of his death Kieffer was investigating scandals in the coffee and cocoa industry.

It is interesting to note that the French judge in charge of the case, Patrick Ramaël, of the Paris Tribunal de Grande Instance, seems to have obsessively followed the Gbagbo trail and neglected all other leads. In 2013, this judge became an advisor to Alassane Ouattara. Isn't this extraordinary?

As for the Novotel victims, it was in the midst of the battle of Abidjan, and we should perhaps look at those who were on the ground there that day: the rebels. But it's easier to blame everything on us. We'd known the people at the Novotel for ten years; they were my neighbors.

Yves Lambelin, president of Sifca, the country's largest private enterprise (27,000 employees), his colleagues, the Malaysian Chelliah Pandian and the Beninese Raoul Adéossi, and Frantz di Rippel, the Novotel manager, were abducted on April 4, 2011, then allegedly tortured and executed, their bodies thrown into the lagoon. Yves Lambelin's body was found two months later, and formally identified. The new government's justice system immediately attributed responsibility for these four murders to Gbagbo's men, even though other versions are circulating. The repentant rebel "colonel" Séméfia Sékou, otherwise known as "Colonel Sékouba", a key member of the Invisible Commando in Abidjan, accuses the rebel forces in his book[30] of having carried out the murders, in great detail.

---

30. In his confession to journalist Germain Séhoué, *Le Commandant invisible raconte la bataille d'Abidjan*, L'Harmattan 2012.

His own men, and those of Koné Zakaria, are said to have carried out this punitive operation. The testimony is signed and assumed. But is it credible? Sékouba has never been summoned by the Ivorian justice system, nor by the ICC, which could have verified this. We are entitled to ask why they have not done so.

Attempts have been made to consign to oblivion the death of Philippe Rémond, a French professor at Yamoussoukro's Institut polytechnique Houphouët-Boigny, who was murdered in his hotel room on March 31, 2011, after rebel forces had entered the city, even though no fighting had taken place. Philippe Rémond was the representative of Europeans living in Côte d'Ivoire, and a staunch supporter of Laurent Gbagbo. A sin for which he paid with his life. On several occasions, he had spoken out harshly on television about the French army's abuses in Abidjan in 2004, which had caused the death of over sixty civilians, and more generally, about France's policy of scandalous alienation from Côte d'Ivoire. A legal action initiated by his widow is underway in Paris, amid a general - or embarrassed? - media silence. Do we choose, even among French victims, according to their opinions, those whose murder is worthy of interest? Philippe Rémond was not an adventurer, just a teacher who openly expressed opinions contrary to those spread by the rebels and the Élysée. That's what got him killed. Once in Yamoussoukro, by bullets, a second time by indifference and oblivion.

Selective indignation and selective investigations are the hallmarks of the Ouattara system, and of the French authorities. But they say not a word about the hundreds of deaths caused by the rebels during their coup d'état in 2002. The expression "death squads", imported from South America, was used for the first time on our soil by Alassane Ouattara, on the very day of the coup d'état he had instigated. Not a word about Dagrou Loula, a gendarmerie colonel shot in the back in his Bouaké home during their offensive, the assassination of Dali Obré, another gendarmerie colonel killed in his sleep in Korhogo, or the death of my Interior Minister Boga Doudou, shot dead as he tried to flee his home... Not a word either about the assassination of some sixty unarmed gendarmes and their wives and children in Boua-

ké, in October 2002, by Guillaume Soro and his followers. The list of the names of these poor people exists, and the facts are proven. The gendarmes paid a heavy price: the gendarmeries were small and vulnerable, and for months the rebels were determined to liquidate all those who could not only intervene against them, but also investigate as judicial police officers and protect the population. They were systematically murdered, often in terrible conditions. And I'm not talking about the cold-blooded massacres committed against specific populations to spread terror and drive them from their lands in order to monopolize them. The genocide against the Wés is documented, and the file on their martyrdom has been deposited on the ICC prosecutor's desk...) as is the martyrdom of the Guéré people. The mass crimes committed over ten years by the rebels now in power in Abidjan are innumerable. I would remind you that the first populations to suffer were those of the North. From 2002 to 2010, the rebels cut off the northern part of the country, which they occupied. Their crimes are documented. In 2010, just after the elections, rebel groups infiltrating Abidjan attacked civilians. In March 2011, with the help of the French, rebel mercenary units swept from the north to the south, committing numerous massacres.Has a single investigation been opened since the rebels took power?

To complete the delegitimization process, the French press portrayed President Gbagbo as a devout Christian. Nothing could be further from the truth. Laurent Gbagbo is a highly Cartesian intellectual, a rationalist believer who has been nurtured by French secularism. A left-wing Christian, as we would say in France.

When people remember that I'm a Christian, they say I'm an enlightened man, a "God nut". That's more dangerous than a savage! No effort has been spared to caricature me. For example, when I said at the end of a public speech: "May God bless the Ivory Coast"... I was mocked, as if I thought I was God's chosen one... The truth is much more prosaic: I heard God bless America at the Republican Convention to choose their candidate for the presidential race, in 1980, in the

United States. I loved it, I embraced it! As for my religious practice, it was Sunday service, and in the afternoon, after mass, the pastor's visit to the house for prayer. Those who tried to demonize me in France, a country with a Christian tradition, never dared criticize the Muslim heads of state who discreetly go out during conferences to say their five prayers. The President of Benin, Yayi Boni, when I visited him, would always say at some point: "Come brother, we're going to pray" - he prayed in his study. Wade and Gaddafi organized their meetings around prayer times. We always recognized their right to do so. I don't steal, I don't kill, I'm not rich, but nobody can believe it, I'm an African head of state.

In January 2011, during the post-electoral crisis, the US Treasury announced that it was "freezing the assets of the Ivorian president and those of his wife and three of his relatives in the United States". This mock seizure was never heard of again. On the 5th of that month, Michèle Alliot-Marie, who had not yet been concerned by the courts over her family's real estate investments in Ben Ali's Tunisia, gave an interview to 20 Minutes. When asked whether Gbagbo could be granted asylum in France at this stage of events - he and Ouattara both claim to be elected representatives and look at each other with bated breath - she replies, in the tone of someone who knows: "If he left normally, why not? I think he owns property in France…". Media hype guaranteed. Sow the seeds of lies, and something always remains. Gbagbo laughs. **Nothing, I don't have a studio, I don't have a parking space!**

On December 28, 2011, the charges concerning alleged assets belonging to President Gbagbo having been proven empty, the latter was granted his recognized indigence, and legal aid.

For months, the Prosecutor of the ICC, backed by the intelligence services of the major powers, investigated to find traces of hidden assets, without success. Further investigations since then have not changed the situation, despite the efforts of pseudo-experts acting under the cover of the UN, who claimed to have found traces of several hidden Ivorian accounts. It is interesting to note that Laurent Gbagbo's defense team explained on this occasion that *"a careful reading of the experts' final report is enlightening: while they claim that President Gbagbo has several bank accounts on which capital movements appeared until recently, even a cursory analysis shows that these assertions are false and at best stem from errors of analysis revealing serious incompetence, at worst from a deliberate desire to fabricate incriminating evidence against President Gbagbo. [...] The experts claim that President Gbagbo has at least eight accounts. [...] If one examines the numbers of the two accounts of President Gbagbo appearing on the account statements reproduced in appendix 47, one realizes that they overlap with the numbers of two of the accounts listed in appendix 68. [...] These are therefore in reality the same accounts, which, according to the experts, are frozen; the numbers appearing in appendix 47 are simply more complete than those indicated in appendix 68. It is therefore clear that of the eight alleged accounts, two do not exist, those mentioned in appendix 68 whose numbers are exactly the same as those in appendix 47. For two other accounts [...] the experts provide no information whatsoever. Finally, for the two accounts in appendix 68 whose numbers are not exactly the same as those in appendix 47, these are not accounts in the strict sense of the term, but mere accounting locations for the circulation of amounts during a transaction [...]. The only proven accounts are: the account used to collect the President's monthly salaries and the account to which these salaries were then transferred, earning interest, accounts which, according to the experts themselves, have been frozen."*

Laurent Gbagbo's honesty and lack of personal enrichment are to be compared with the greed of all those who contributed to his downfall. Let's not talk about those who surround Alassane Ouattara and who take a dime from every transaction or operation taking place in Côte d'Ivoire. And let's not talk about the rebel chiefs, now endowed with the attributes of state authority, who are cutting the country to shreds and destroying piece by piece what was, until the fall of Laurent Gbagbo, one of the rare examples of a functioning state in sub-Saharan Africa. Let's talk about the French: Claude Guéant, the former Minister of the Interior and Secretary General of the Élysée Palace, has set up a branch of his law firm in Abidjan, where he frequently travels back and forth to develop his own business and that of his son-in-law, Jean-Charles Charki, who has become an advisor to Alassane Ouattara. The French justice system has put a stop to Guéant's affairist impetus, by calling him to account for his particular practices with cash and works of art… The former French ambassador has become a consultant and spends his life in close proximity to Alassane Ouattara; the military chiefs have also become "consultants" and have been entrusted with the modernization of the Ivorian army; Judge Ramaël is based in Abidjan. Not to mention the host of their military assistants, lawyers, publicists, communicators, etc., who are now more likely to be found in Abidjan than in Paris. A journalist and former director of the France 24 channel has been put in charge of restructuring Ivorian television, and organizing a defense and security fair through the Phil Média company[31].

---

31. *La Lettre du Continent,* no681, April 30, 2014.

19.
"I WANTED TO MAKE HISTORY"

Why am I so cursed by France? You can't understand it if you don't know the history of my country, Côte d'Ivoire, and its special relationship with France since independence in 1960...

Just before this, in 1956, Gaston Defferre's framework law created a Territorial Assembly in the colonies, with a native government under the supervision of a French governor. This was autonomy, the first step towards independence. The leader of the majority party became vice-president of the Council presided over by the governor: in Côte d'Ivoire, this was Auguste Denise, West Indian by his father and Ivorian by his mother. He was the man delegated by Houphouët... He was the General Secretary of Houphouët-Boigny's party, who had joined Guy Mollet's government in Paris, at "Abidjan-sur-Seine", as my friend Guy Labertit puts it.

In 1958, in the brand-new Franco-African community, the matrix of Françafrique, the territorial assemblies continued to exist, but the government of each territory was headed by a Prime Minister. The President of the French Republic is also President of the territorial community. The government runs the country, with the exception of Foreign Affairs, Defense, the Mint and Higher Education, areas over which France retains the upper hand in accordance with Article 12, relating to the Franco-African community. It's a curiosity that few French people are aware of: this article 12 still exists in the texts of your Constitution...

In 1959, Félix Houphouët-Boigny became Prime Minister of our country, then Head of State in 1960, at the time of independence, without an election. De Gaulle had to force his hand to accept the independence of Côte d'Ivoire, which was being prepared at the same time as that of Upper Volta, Benin and Niger. Houphouët didn't want it for Côte d'Ivoire. It has to be said that France had no choice: American and Soviet pressure, the Indochina and Algerian disasters, had placed France in a position of extreme weakness. It was under these conditions that the French authorities decided to proclaim independence for the colonies. But this independence was purely formal. Houphouët became President within a system of total dependence on France, of which he was one of the pillars. He had helped draft Defferre's Plan Cadre, and the 1958 Constitution... From then on, there were no elections in Côte d'Ivoire for thirty-three years!

In October 1990, who broke it? Gbagbo! I ran against Houphouët, who was forced to authorize pluralism, for which I had been campaigning for a long time as a leader of the democratic opposition, and which, incidentally, had landed me in prison. International upheavals and the dismantling of the Iron Curtain helped us, and the domestic opposition, embodied in particular by my party, the FPI, finally succeeded in getting elections organized. But the authorities insisted on controlling these elections. They tell me to withdraw. All the other candidates do it, but not me. I maintain my candidacy. I'm told the election will be a sham - and it was - but I wanted to make history. It's my original sin, the reason I'm here in The Hague. By obtaining more than 18% of the vote against Houphouët, I became an unavoidable leader of the opposition. I was already upsetting the established plans for the continuity of Françafrique...

In December 1993, when Houphouët died, it was this continuity, organized by him and France to put Bédié in place, that was imposed. No election. Thanks to a reform of the Constitution, the President of the National Assembly, Konan Bédié, automatically became President.

He immediately came up against Ouattara, then Prime Minister, who tried to steal the succession from him. It should be noted that Houphouët had taken Ouattara on as Prime Minister under pressure

from the French authorities, but had never thought of him as his successor. It was Ouattara's wife, Dominique, who saw in him a national destiny... Ouattara quarrels with Bédié, rushes to announce the death of the Head of State before he does, Bédié reacts, and Ouattara is forced to step aside...

In his book of interviews, *Les Chemins de ma vie*[32], Henri Konan Bédié was the first to write an account of what he described as Ouattara's intrigues to outmaneuver him and seize power.

"Alassane Ouattara knew very well that the mission entrusted to him required him to stay out of political issues, especially as he was not an Ivorian citizen."

Ouattara had a passport from Upper Volta, and did not meet the criteria defined by Article 35 of the Constitution, implemented by Bédié in 1994, according to which one had to be Ivorian, born of an Ivorian father and mother, to be a candidate. The concept of ivoirité, as Ouattara put it, was created by Bédié to prevent Ouattara from running for the throne.

"The President had told him and entrusted it to me," continues Bédié, *"as well as to numerous Ivorian and foreign personalities [...] in very clear terms and with precise facts. Shortly after his appointment, the President asked Alassane Ouattara to travel to neighboring capitals to emphasize the purely economic objective of his mission. The proof that his action was temporary was the President's request to keep his post vacant at the head of the Central Bank* [this is the BCEAO]. *For two years the post was kept open, and its occupant, Charles Bany, acted only as an interim."*

"But he had taken Ivorian nationality? [...]

President Houphouët had granted him a diplomatic passport when he had difficulties with the authorities in Burkina Faso. At the time, it was used by the Central Bank, which was shared by the seven West African states. As you know, a diplomatic passport is not a civil status document.

Even so, he had been Prime Minister and, as such, head of government. [...] This was not the first time in his history that President Houphouët-Boigny

---

32. Henri Konan Bédié, *Les Chemins de ma vie*, Plon, 1999.

had called on outside technical expertise. [...] In any case, he was Burkinabé through his father and still held the nationality of Burkina Faso, so he had no business meddling in our succession affairs [...]."

Before the 1995 election, Bédié had had the Electoral Code amended, which made it impossible for Ouattara [because of his Burkinabe nationality] to run, but he resigned himself to the fact that he'd just landed an interesting job at the IMF anyway. I made fun of these questions of origin, saying during a visit to Paris that all those of our generation who were over forty - the minimum age required to run for president - were born before 1960, i.e. before independence, with French nationality.

In 2010, Bédié was only able to present his candidacy because President Gbagbo had agreed to sign an exceptional dispensation in his favor. Bédié had already exceeded the age limit by one year: he was seventy-six. A measure taken using article 48 of the Constitution - the equivalent of our article 16 - against the advice of his political friends to contribute to appeasement in Côte d'Ivoire. Always in the hope of including as many leaders as possible in a democratic debate, and allowing everyone to express themselves, including politically. President Gbagbo issued a special decree under this same article 48, to allow Alassane Ouattara - who did not meet the criteria laid down by the Constitution - to stand in the presidential elections. It was a courageous move - suicidal in the view of some of his friends - but one that was difficult for his voters and supporters to accept. Today, the Constitution remains unchanged: *"The President of the Republic [...] must be a native Ivorian, born of a father and mother who are themselves native Ivorians. He must never have renounced Ivorian nationality. He/she must never have claimed any other nationality. He/she must have resided in Côte d'Ivoire continuously for five years prior to the date of the elections, and have had a total effective presence of ten years. [...] Candidates for the Presidency of the Republic must be in a state of complete physical and mental well-being, duly certified by a panel of three doctors appointed by the Constitutional Council from a list proposed by the Conseil de l'Ordre des Médecins. These three doctors must take an oath before the Constitutional Council. They must be of good character and integrity.*

He must declare his assets and justify their origin." Moral: Konan Bédié, because of his age, and Alassane Ouattara, because of the question of nationality, do not meet the established criteria. If the Constitution were respected, they could not stand in the 2015 elections. We know that constitutions and principles, in Africa as elsewhere, evolve according to circumstances and needs. Alassane Ouattara, if his illness does not prevent him from doing so, should stand. But to do so, he will have to remedy the constitutional text he approved in July 2000. He who lives will see.

In 1995, to show our solidarity with Alassane Ouattara, who had been ousted by Bédié, and to demand that a genuine democratic process be set up that would allow a real opposition to express itself, we formed the Republican Front with all the opposition parties. I boycotted the presidential election that took place that year. Without Ouattara and without me, Bédié became virtually the sole candidate. He was elected with over 95% of the vote, with the support of Jacques Chirac and the RPR, whose general delegate Jean-Pierre Bazin came to Abidjan to hold a meeting and publicly endorse him. I've often wondered why a man as clever as Houphouët chose Bédié to succeed him. Was it a tribalist reflex? They were both Baoulés. That's not enough... There were other young Baoulés in the ranks, some very gifted and brilliant. I was very close to Madame Houphouët, and we were on very good terms. Whenever anyone asked her if Houphouët's preference was due to the fact that Bédié was Houphouët's natural son, she would laugh and reply: "Oh, you know, he's much too ugly to be my husband's son!"

It was at this time that the Ivorian Constitutional Council was created [in August 1994] and set up to arbitrate any electoral disputes. It was chaired by Noël Némin, Houphouët's former Minister of Justice and Bédié's former chief of staff. Six of the nine members of the Council were appointed by Bédié himself, and three others by his friend Charles Donwahi, President of the National Assembly. It's worth remembering this today. Since then, the Council has had the task, as supreme jurisdiction, of monitoring the elections: the

regularity of candidacies, of course, but also of proclaiming the results of the ballots, assessing appeals and making rulings. I've said
it before and I'll say it again: in Africa, we need our institutions to
be respected, even if we may have reservations about the people
who embody them and the way they operate. Otherwise, the state
will collapse, and anything that seeks to provoke this is harmful. I've
already criticized Jacques Chirac, who has always done his utmost
to bypass me and empty our Constitution, adopted in a referendum
by 86% of the Ivorian people in 2000, of its content, when in 2003-
2004 he tried to put pressure on us to make way for the rebels, thus
emptying the Ivorian institutions of their meaning. But the shame-
lessness of the French when it comes to Africa is obvious. In October
2006, France's ambassador to the UN, Rochereau de la Sablière, even
dared to write in a draft resolution that "the decisions of the Security Council take precedence over the Ivorian Constitution and the
country's legislation". Within the Security Council, China, Russia and
the United States opposed this bracketing of our Constitution. You
see, whether by force or diplomatic pressure, any attempt to call into
question the democratic expression of a people and any attempt to
deny the representativeness of the holders of institutions necessarily
leads to calling into question the very existence of institutions and to
dismantling the structure of States. Didn't the French understand that
a pro-Ouattara victory, following the violent coup attempt in September 2002 or after the diplomatic and political threats we suffered
at Marcoussis in 2003, would lead to the same result: the collapse
of the Ivorian state? You can't support those who don't respect institutions and don't play the game according to democratic rules, and
pretend that this would have no effect on these institutions, and that
democracy can be preserved.

Marcoussis, Villepin's "Grand Œuvre", is a model of perversity:
pseudo opposition political parties have been created ex nihilo, and
are merely the civilian screen behind which the armed rebel groups
hide. These are the ones who are invited to pretend to discuss a solution freely, whereas this "solution" has already been drafted by
Villepin's advisors, even before the representatives of the "opposition

parties" arrive at Marcoussis. And to make sure he gets his way, Ville-pin is careful not to invite the President of Côte d'Ivoire, government representatives and representatives of the legalist political parties to these so-called "discussions". In other words, it's a crude farce pulled off by amateurs. France has always done its utmost to rescue my opponents after their electoral failures and failed putsches. That's what I call the plot against Côte d'Ivoire and against me. It was necessary to circumvent the Constitution, and to circumvent me. Before eliminating me.

20

COUP D'ÉTAT

The time for coups d'état was clearly announced by Alassane Ouattara as early as Saturday September 11, 1999, in the north of the country, his stronghold. In front of members of his party, the RDR, he delivered a speech, some of whose famous phrases he would no doubt prefer to be forgotten today: *"I will strike this corrupt power at the right moment, and it will fall like ripe fruit[33]"*. His intentions, and the means he envisaged to achieve them, are implicit in his words. On the following December 24, General Guéï's troops overthrew Bédié, who fled…

At Christmas 1999, on December 24 to be exact, General Robert Guéï overthrew Bédié at the head of a military junta that included people close to Ouattara, such as Ibrahim Coulibaly (IB), Ouattara's bodyguard. Guéï was simply Ouattara's armed wing, doing the job for him. But instead of stepping aside, Robert Guéï developed a taste for power. He settled in. He called all parties to the table, and formed a transitional government that lasted ten months, until the 2000 elections. A constitution accepted by all was drawn up, laying down laws and electoral rules. It was voted in July 2000. Strangely enough, Ouattara accepted and voted for the texts, even though article 35 of the new Constitution excluded him, still in the terms defined in 1994 by Bédié, since he was not born Ivorian. The famous concept of "ivoi-

---

33. *Le Patriote*, September 13, 1999.

rité" invented by Bédié. Ouattara gave the impression that he had lost interest in power. He was already planning something else. As for Bédié, in exile in Paris following the coup d'état, he prefers not to return to Côte d'Ivoire. The Constitution stipulates that candidates must undergo a medical examination in Côte d'Ivoire. Bédié underwent his in France, so he was excluded. I was left facing Guéï, with three other candidates. Ouattara said: "Guéï will win." I won in the first round, with 59% of the vote, while Guéï took 32%. They were all surprised, they hadn't prepared any arguments against me because they were so sure of themselves. Robert Guéï tried to oppose the result with arms, but he was not followed. It's the only truly democratic election to have taken place so far in Côte d'Ivoire. There was unrest in the streets provoked by Ouattara's supporters, who wanted to re-run the elections, and then when Bédié in turn contested them. However, the result was a genuine consensus between the elected representatives and the people.

One explanation for Alassane Ouattara's deceptive fair play (at the time, he said he wanted to respect republican legality) was unwisely given by Francis Wodié. This brilliant jurist, founder of a political party, the PIT (Parti ivoirien des travailleurs), is an old hand in Ivorian politics, recruited from electoral debacles. He won 3.5% of the vote in the 1995 election, just over 5% against Laurent Gbagbo in 2000, and 0.29% in 2010. In a book of interviews recently published in Abidjan under the title *Mon Combat pour la Côte d'Ivoire,* Wodié recounts how he sought the support of Ouattara and his constituents for this election. Many of his closest friends had rallied behind Gbagbo, to whom he has since dedicated a tenacious hatred. Promising Francis Wodié, in hushed tones, the leadership of a future transitional government, Ouattara confided to him *that he was convinced that this regime, which had emerged from the ballot box, would not last long*. His words hinted at the likelihood of violent destabilization. It's true that since 1993, and his failed attempt to establish himself as Houphouët's heir, Ouattara had been on the lookout, pretending to fall into line… He was chewing on his resentment.

As soon as he was elected, Laurent Gbagbo became the one to be destroyed, for having snuck in between the two favorites of France and the United States, thanks to their disagreements. After that, they never stopped trying to get me. On January 7 and 8, 2001, a first military coup, known as the "Black Mercedes", led by IB against Gbagbo, elected two months earlier, failed. Then, on March 21, 2001, still in his preferred region, the north of the country, Ouattara publicly declared: *"I will make this country ungovernable."* The next coup d'état took the form of a military attack on September 19, 2002, which split the country in two. More than half the country's surface area (60%) is occupied by rebels, notably Guillaume Soro's MPCI, the military wing of Ouattara's party. According to the then RDR mayor of Bouaké, Fany Ibrahima, who unashamedly claims to be *a "rebel mayor", "The MPCI is a military force of which we are proud. MPCI means RDR, that's how it is…".* The proposed arithmetic is as follows: Ouattara (political leader of the rebellion) + Soro (military leader of the rebellion) = coups d'état by the rebellion. Everyone knows this equation, and the international community, led by France, reputed to be the UN Security Council's expert on the subject, has been quick to endorse this terrible addition.

Ouattara repeatedly failed in his attempts to seize power for ten years. The French finally decided to impose him, in 2011, through a maneuver on the occasion of the presidential elections, which they did their utmost to organize while at the same time rearming the rebels with a view to seizing power by force. In one fell swoop, Ouattara had France - which under Chirac voted for Bédié - on his side, thanks to Sarkozy, and the United States, where he made his nest in finance. In particular, he benefited from the active support of George Soros. As Sarkozy was more Atlanticist than his predecessors, there was no contradiction in supporting a candidate whom the Americans supported. Historical Gaullism would have prohibited the French authorities from supporting Ouattara. Sarkozy has abandoned the Gaullist line of independence from the Americans. But to be president, you have to play politics. A bazooka coup doesn't make you president. After my victory in October 2000, Ouattara cried "hold-up" because

the Constitution he himself had approved a few weeks earlier had forbidden him to run. He publicly called for a new election, and threw his supporters into the streets. I first allowed him to return to Côte d'Ivoire by lifting the arrest warrant issued against him by Bédié for forgery. Then I reintegrated him into political life by giving him the opportunity to run for the highest office in 2010, and he refuses a simple vote recount!

Ouattara is praised by the international community on the pretext that he has put an end to the crisis. But it was he who provoked the crisis twelve years ago. It was he who sustained it for ten years. It was he who plunged Côte d'Ivoire into chaos. Today, he is the one who is tribalizing political life, choosing people from the North to occupy all positions in the name of "ethnic catch-up", as he puts it. It is he who impoverishes the population, when, as he says, "money works, but doesn't circulate". It is he who wants to naturalize hundreds of thousands of Burkinabés and foreigners - we have over 30% foreigners on our soil - who live in Côte d'Ivoire, to turn them into voters for his cause. They are arriving by the truckload from neighboring countries.

"GBAGBO WILL BE CRUSHED, BECAUSE THEY'RE GOING TO BRING OUT THE STEAMROLLER[34]"

November 30, 2011. When his lawyers arrive at Scheveningen prison, they see an exhausted, cold man. To prevent their client's state of health from worsening, they run out to buy him warm clothes and a suit for his first appearance. President Gbagbo was spared nothing: outbreak of war, bombardment of his residence by French forces, attempted murder, capture amidst the cries of the wounded and the rales of the dying, intimidation by his jailers at the Hôtel du Golf, transfer to the north of the country, illegal detention in undignified conditions, physical exhaustion perhaps programmed, legal farce authorizing his extradition to The Hague, brutal transfer to Scheveningen while the appeals lodged by his lawyers have not yet been examined, arrival in a blouse in a country where the temperatures that day are below zero…

His health appears to be failing. Over time, he confided to me that nothing had been done to follow up the recommendations of the specialists dispatched at his request. Months later, he still seems to be feeling the shockwaves of the bombings that hit his home. His eight-month detention in Côte d'Ivoire under particularly difficult conditions has not helped matters. He seems to be suffering physically. Eight months

---

34. A former *Jeune Afrique* journalist.

without seeing the light of day, without knowing what was going on outside the small house where he was held by the men of Commandant Fofié, a warlord close to Soro, accused by the United Nations of letting opponents roast exposed in containers for hours until they died. In a way, if President Gbagbo is in front of me, he owes it to his courage, his inner strength. Another man would have stayed there. Gbagbo, as he does every time he defends his ideas, stands up and resists.

No one will be able to say I'm the one who ran away.

Not a word in the French press about President Gbagbo's scandalous conditions of detention in Côte d'Ivoire, despite his lawyer's press releases of August 10, 2011 "President Gbagbo, a mistreated hostage", and September 16, 2011 "President Gbagbo's lawyers prevented once again from seeing their client". Not a gesture from the French authorities to ease his ordeal. And yet the French ambassador and French civilian and military officials are aware of the appalling conditions of his detention.

Not a word either about the fact that his son was detained for months in appalling conditions; Michel is a French citizen, after all. Not a word, finally, about the hundreds of political prisoners of the Ouattara regime, victims of the victors' vindictiveness. Yet the French state knows everything. What's more, it is consulted. The fate of the "big fish" is discussed between Alassane Ouattara, those close to him, his French advisors and representatives of the French authorities.

Little by little, he'll look better to me. Does President Gbagbo's state of health justify his release? Every time his lawyers have asked for his release, something has happened, as if by chance, a few days before the hearing. An event which the prosecutor is quick to echo to dissuade the judges from releasing the President. Each time, the prosecutor tries to frighten the judges: If you release him, he suggests, you will be responsible for the clashes that will inevitably take place in Côte d'Ivoire. Because, he says, the pro-Gbagbo want to put the country to fire and blood to regain power and put their leader in charge. To lend credibility to such accusations, the prosecutor pulls out of his hat incidents that always occur a few days before the judges examine the case. Incidents and armed clashes, acts of banditry on the border between Ghana and Côte d'Ivoire are invoked in the first debate. This avoids having to respond to the lawyers' legal arguments. Gbagbo is presented as a public danger, manipulating his sprawling African networks from his cell. The same scenario applies to the appeal of this decision, handed down on October 26: Gbagbo supporters detained at the Maca - Abidjan's prison - are transferred to the north of the country 48 hours earlier, on October 24, suggesting public unrest or an imminent coup d'état. They were brought back on the 30th, but nothing had happened, apart from a further refusal to release Gbagbo. The process is so consistent that it seems to be taken from a book entitled Fatou Bensouda's Good Recipes.

The next request, again in the same year, was answered by the sudden denunciation of an alleged Gbagbo plot by friends in exile, including Marcel Gossio, the former boss of the port of Abidjan. Fatou Bensouda took at face value a UN report and several newspaper articles whose authors clearly preferred not to investigate. The President's lawyers at the ICC will be delighted to dismantle the accusations, show their inconsistencies and reveal who really ordered them. Those quickest to jump on this wonderful suspicion of subversive activities will eventually agree that no such project ever existed, and that Marcel Gossio never left Morocco, where he resides, nor mounted any operation. On other occasions, the prosecutor would claim to have uncovered a network of activists fed by inexhaustible funds. Here again, President Gbagbo's lawyers revealed the deception and dismantled the accusations. There is no money. President Gbagbo's so-called hidden accounts, allegedly discovered by pseudo-experts to the delight of the prosecutor, turned out never to have existed. In the chapter on the use of risky expedients, which betray the feverishness of the prosecutor, and the undermining work he is carrying out against Gbagbo's defense, the statement of the discovery of eight *"hidden bank accounts"* at the Société Générale de Côte d'Ivoire, by an investigation by UN experts. *"Hidden accounts"*... in his name, and in his usual bank! Did you say bizarre? James Stewart, one of Bensouda's deputies, develops this thesis in court, which collapses like a house of cards after a simple counter-investigation by the defense. First of all, it was revealed that the experts had mistakenly noted down two of the accounts, leaving only six to examine. Of these, two were completely empty: not a single movement, not a single franc. Of the remaining four, one is the account into which his salary (8 million CFA francs, or 12,215 euros) was paid each month, and which stopped being paid in February 2011. Do the investigators speak of *"movements"* that continued after Gbagbo's arrest? These are agios. Another account, fed by the first, was used for savings, and earns interest. These interests are the other "movements" detected by the experts. A sub-account dedicated to the circulation of money between the two accounts, and a last account, used by the bank for a one-off operation, and on which we find… 3 euros complete the list. So much for Laurent Gbagbo's *"eight secret accounts"*. All we had to do was check. Which the Court was quick not to do. Unless, having changed its strategy, it is now trying to gain time and wear down the defense, after having tried in vain to speed things up and wrap up the case quickly. The time given to the prosecutor to glean *"new evidence"* argues in this direction.

Funds available for opposition refugees in Ghana? The exiles don't have a penny to their name and are surviving as best they can in a foreign country. Just because a particular exile tries to put himself forward in order to obtain either refugee status or a few subsidies does not mean that a "network" exists.

As for the pseudo destabilizing network made up of pro-Gbagbo, which, according to the prosecutor, contributes to insecurity in Côte d'Ivoire, it doesn't exist either. There is no more pro-Gbagbo network than there is a chocolate factory in Côte d'Ivoire, the world's leading cocoa producer. In its October 28 issue, *Jeune Afrique* devoted an investigation and a special report to the UN report, concluding that *"there is no proof of the existence of a skilfully prepared politico-military plot"*… The prosecutor, either through ignorance or bad faith, is helping to mislead the judges by stirring up the scarecrow of the famous pro-Gbagbo. Above all, it allows them to talk about something other than reality: it's better if international public opinion continues to ignore the fact that the country is being cut to shreds by the warlords who conquered the South in 2011 after conquering the North in 2002. They are destroying state structures, engaging in constant extortion, imprisoning and killing with impunity. The widespread insecurity they have created is exacerbated by the presence in the country of tens of thousands of pro-Ouattara fighters who have been idle since the end of the war, but still have weapons. Mercenaries from Burkina Faso and Niger who have remained in Côte d'Ivoire rub shoulders with gang members, former rebel soldiers and thousands of traditional Dozos hunters who are trying to make the most of their 2010/2011 investment in Alassane Ouattara. These Dozos are the infamous Kamajors who operated in Sierra Leone, the ones who cut off hands: *"In the judgment concerning Charles Taylor by the Special Court for Sierra Leone, it is stated [...] that the Kamajors ate people who were accused of being RFU sympathizers[35]."* All these ex-combatants are bitter, frustrated, abandoned and armed. They are multiplying coups de mains, racketeering operations on populations, looting and land seizures, as was the case with ex-Burkinabé rebel leader Amédé Ouérémi, in the west of the country. His arrest in May 2013 led to a marked reduction in terrorist activity and improved security. The issue of land appropriation by newcomers is crucial. This is the real source of tension in Côte d'Ivoire, and the very thing that could lead to the country's downfall. Every day, hundreds, perhaps thousands, of immigrants from Burkina and neighboring countries, members of the same ethnic groups as the rebel warlords and Alassane Ouattara, are being ferried to the south and west of the country to reinforce those who have confiscated the rich agricultural land, particularly in the west, from its rightful owners. They settle in, bring in their families and push the natives further and further away. An excellent article by Fanny Pigeaud in *Le Monde diplomatique* of September 2012, "Un territoire hors de contrôle, Guerre pour le cacao dans l'Ouest ivoirien", describes the incessant noria of vehicles filled with immigrants from Burkina and the consequences of this substitution of one population for another.

Back to the possible release of President Gbagbo. On the following November 24, there was a new incident. Two days before, on the 22nd, the secret of the arrest warrant for Simone Gbagbo was lifted. Up until then, Fatou Bensouda had denied that the warrant even existed, even

---

35. Confirmation of charges hearing at the ICC, February 25, 2013.

21. "GBAGBO WILL BE CRUSHED, BECAUSE THEY'RE GOING TO BRING OUT THE STEAMROLLER"

though it had been in place since February 29, 2012. The press, which has seized on the information, is therefore once again talking about the so-called "death squads". When they attack Simone Gbagbo for refusing Laurent Gbagbo parole, it's a reminder that the monster has two heads. Apart from the media hype this may create, the prosecutor undoubtedly also sees it as a way of weakening the defense before the eventual trial. Not a word is said about the decisions of the French courts in 2006, which ruled that accusing the Ivorian presidency of having set up death squads was defamatory. The prosecutor also pays little heed to what the President's lawyers had demonstrated before the judges in February 2013, namely the implementation since 2002 by Franco-Ivorian pressure groups of a defamation campaign against Laurent Gbagbo, which was designed to legitimize the violent seizure of power by the rebels. Exactly what will happen again in 2010: the same men at the helm on the French side, the same people on the ground on the Ivorian side.

Any pretext justifies measures of defiance. Or the appearance of land-mines deliberately planted in Gbagbo's path to destroy him. This type of procedure has plagued the Ivorian crisis from the outset, and continues to weigh heavily on the current proceedings.

At the end of 2013, a Cameroonian journalist, Saïd Penda, a BBC alumnus, made a two times fifty-two minute film: *Laurent Gbagbo ou l'anti-néocolonialiste, le verbe et le sang.* What is the writer-director's motivation? Public opinion and the media in Cameroon were mostly in favor of Gbagbo during the post-electoral crisis, and mostly opposed to his transfer to the ICC. But Saïd Penda, for his part, declared in an interview with the daily *Le Patriote,* which is close to Alassane Ouattara: *"I too don't understand why the ICC would have difficulty finding concrete evidence of Laurent Gbagbo's responsibility for what happened, when an investigative journalist like mine has been able to find, with supporting evidence, that Laurent Gbagbo gave chilling orders to men to crush any attempt at opposition to his power."*

Is its aim to provide arguments, if not evidence, for the ICC, or to discredit it in anticipation of its collapse, in order to mitigate its effect?

It will be recalled that on June 3, 2013, the ICC judges considered that the prosecutor had not presented sufficient evidence in support of his case for them to order a trial.

The author presented his film to an audience of journalists at the Maison de la Presse in Abidjan, in December 2013. Some skeptics were astonished by the powerful financial means at his disposal. It was very generously endowed with a budget of 108 million CFA francs (around 165,000 euros, a large production in Africa), unusual. It was produced by Sentinelles Productions, an unknown Abidjan-based company with unsuspected resources. Such an expensive and crude firebrand reminds me of the remark made by a journalist friend, familiar with the Ouattara team, who warned me, when we were talking about the forthcoming trial in The Hague: *"Gbagbo will be crushed, because they're going to roll out the steamroller: they have all the financial means, and all the connections for that."*

Michel Galy, a political scientist and professor at the Institut des relations internationales (Ileri), is highly critical of France's treatment of Côte d'Ivoire and Laurent Gbagbo. Since then, Ouattara's regime has been the focus of his attention. He denounces it as a *"Gulag"* where 800 political prisoners are imprisoned in arbitrary conditions and denied their full rights, under a mendacious cloak woven at great expense by communications agencies.

Michel Galy notes that, in the semantics of the Ouattara system, *"words are the opposite of things"*: they can say the opposite of what they actually mean: *"war"* is *"peace"*, and *"irreversible democracy"* actually means *"continued repression"*.

For those who remember, it also resembles the 2001 appearance of Belgian sociologist Benoît Scheuer's documentary-ovi *"Côte d'Ivoire, la poudrière identitaire" (Ivory Coast, the powder keg of identity)*. It, too, was mysteriously financed, and hostile to a newly-elected Gbagbo, whom no-one was charging with any criminal responsibility at the time. Through this film, an association called "Prévention Génocide" laid the foundations for the communication still used today by Soro: the evocation of an alleged genocide project conceived by people close to Gbagbo against the Muslim populations of Côte d'Ivoire. The living proof of this discrimination, according to Scheuer, was of course Alassane Ouattara, prevented from standing for election because he was Muslim. Like a devil out of a box, this film foreshadowed - and justified in advance - the armed coup d'état launched in 2002. This in turn followed the failed coup d'état in Abidjan in January 2001, led by the late IB (Ibrahim Coulibaly), one of Alassane Ouattara's bodyguards, against a Gbagbo who had been elected for barely seventy days. In 2010, this same IB became the leader of the notorious "Invisible Commando" based in the Abobo district of Abidjan, which launched numerous deadly attacks against regular forces and the population from December 2010 onwards. He had already distinguished himself alongside General Guéï, "Papa Noël en treillis", in the military coup that overthrew Henri Konan Bédié on December 24, 1999, bringing Guéï to power on behalf of Ouattara, before Robert Guéï discovered his own national destiny. As for IB, who had been involved in all the coups for twenty years, he knew too much, and was expecting too big a slice of the cake in payment for his services, when his boss Alassane Ouattara came to power in 2010. He was immediately liquidated.

22

THE INTERNATIONAL COMMUNITY'S WILFUL BLINDNESS

A stop at the foot of the "sacred tree" of the rebellion - decorated with garlands by the international community - to see if it is necessary that it is not a Christmas tree, and that it deserves to be replanted in The Hague, Netherlands, in the courtyard of the ICC. The violent history of the current regime, and its brutal methods, have long been obscured by the international community and the press. Guillaume Soro, in his book *Pourquoi je suis devenu un rebelle (Why I became a rebel)*[36], presents the movement he led, along with others, as the camp of the Right having defeated the forces of Evil. A *"civilized rebellion"*, he writes to an RFI colleague, which *"astonishes journalists, representatives of NGOs and institutions with our attachment to respect for human rights"*, with brigades of *"street sweepers in pink coats"* intervening three or four times a week. In May 2005, as the romantic hero of a fight against tyranny, he appeared on Parisian television to promote his book, announcing everywhere: *"There is a serious risk, I'm sounding the alarm for genocide in Côte d'Ivoire"*. Genocide is the key word. Aimed exclusively at white, Western ears traumatized by Rwanda. A pyromaniac in Africa, disguised as a fireman on the banks of the Seine, he shows only one of his many faces. Like so many others, Thierry Ardisson doesn't have the information to counter the intoxication. He could have found it in the book by Georges Neyrac (the

---

36. Guillaume Soro, *Pourquoi je suis devenu un rebelle*, Hachette, 2005.

pen name of Georges Peillon, former press officer for the French army in Côte d'Ivoire) *Nue*[37], published in March 2005, while Soro's book was published in April. On the same subject, the rebel's book received the media spotlight, while the French soldier's book, a beautifully written account of his first-hand experience, full of unpublished information but at odds with French policy, remained in the shadows. What's in it for us?

In *France-Soir on* May 13, Guillaume Soro justified his refusal to disarm his men, even though the Marcoussis Agreement of 2003, the Pretoria Agreement of 2005 and the peace agreement he signed with Gbagbo in Ouagadougou in 2007 obliged him to do so. He maintained this position until 2010, without respecting any of these agreements or any of the UN resolutions requiring rebel disarmament to balance the concessions made by President Gbagbo. The latter imposed this counterpart to the concessions made by President Gbagbo (majority granted to the opposition in the composition of the future electoral commission, admission to eligibility, against the Constitution and the advice of his own supporters, Bédié and Ouattara, participation in the rebel government, with Soro as Prime Minister)… Disarmament *"is an extremely sensitive and delicate subject, for which we need to give time"*, Soro replies to the *France-Soir* journalist. Sensitive and delicate indeed, since the rebels will never disarm.

I made two mistakes: going to the elections without the disarmament promised by the rebels having been carried out, and ceding the majority to the opposition in the composition of the IEC. My supporters blamed me. I wanted to move quickly so that the elections could be held quickly, as early as 2005, and so that reconciliation could take place as soon as possible. I did this in good faith, in April and May 2004, at meetings in Pretoria to seek a way out of the crisis. In South Africa, the mood was one of reconciliation, or so I thought.

Back in Pretoria, I was the only "pure" Francophile. Bédié and Ouattara spoke English with South African President Thabo Mbeki. I always refused, so Ouattara translated for me. But as far as the French were concerned, I was the black sheep… You'll have to explain!

---

*37. Georges Neyrac, *Ivoire Nue: chronicles of a lost Ivory Coast*, Éditions Jacob-Duvernet, 2005*

After Pretoria, Soro said to me: "And what do we have?" I had just given Ouattara and Bédié the opportunity to stand for election. I realized that "we" meant him and Compaoré. So we held the Peace Conference in Ouagadougou, Burkina, to satisfy them both. I was the one who always pleased everyone. I did my part, without reciprocating: they never kept their promises.

Let's talk about disarmament! All our agreements include the obligation to disarm rebels. All UN resolutions - and God knows there have been many - include the disarmament of rebels. And yet, we were pushed into the elections without this disarmament being carried out... the pressure was terrible: "Go to the elections", the international community told us, led by Sarkozy. Today, I understand that they wanted a brutal and definitive outcome.

I was wrong to agree to go to the 2010 elections without disarmament. But in any case, you can be sure that they would have found something else: the attack would have taken place on the pretext that I was refusing them. It was a stalemate, and I was determined to get my country out of it.

A civilized rebellion? From 2002 to 2010, pro-Ouattara warlords carved out strongholds for themselves in the north of Côte d'Ivoire, destroying state infrastructure and putting pressure on the population. Intimidation, extortion, theft, arbitrary confinement, torture and murder. Documented evidence of the crimes committed by the rebel leaders now in power in Abidjan is abundant and accessible. Curiously, the French press does not mention them. There are none so blind as those who do not want to see. It has to be said that if readers were to see the truth, it would *ipso facto* call into question all the conventional discourse aimed at demonizing President Gbagbo.

When the same *France-Soir* journalist pointed out that his name appeared on a list of 80 people published by the UN *"suspected of serious human rights violations"*, Guillaume Soro did not flinch, apparently certain that he risked no prosecution. Is he not the hero of the international community, the valiant knight whom Luis Moreno Ocampo - prosecutor at the ICC - will later congratulate on his accession to the presidency of the National Assembly? Who will be received in Paris, on July 2, 2012, at the Palais Bourbon, by his counterpart Claude Bartolone? *"When you're at the head of a rebellion that controls 60% of the territory, and you have to administer it… it's understandable that things can go wrong,"* Soro calmly professes.

Indeed. On May 31, 2005, Soro returned from his promotional tour of Parisian "pince-fesses" and signing sessions. Far from the TV sets, in the villages of Petit Duékoué and Guitrozon, over one hundred and twenty peaceful inhabitants, men, women and children of the Guéré ethnic group, sympathetic to Gbagbo, were massacred with machetes, or burned alive, in the middle of the night. Soro's MPCI men and, according to numerous accounts, the Dozos, were involved. A number of them were sentenced by the Ivorian courts to up to twenty years' imprisonment in 2007. Do we also know in France that during the attack of September 19, 2002, followed by the occupation of more than half of Ivorian national territory by the rebels, hundreds and thousands of crimes were committed?

All the evidence of the involvement of Soro's men can be found in an investigation report by the Abidjan prosecutor's office, which I have been able to consult, following complaints from the families. Another sinister exploit to be credited to Soro is the massacre in Bouaké, already mentioned by Laurent Gbagbo, of sixty gendarmes, their children and their wives, after they had been taken hostage by members of the MPCI. The information site Afrique2050.com provides a good summary, from which this extract is taken: *"Following an in-depth investigation, Amnesty International has been able to retrace the circumstances of this massacre on the basis of direct testimony. The gendarmes arrested on October 6, 2002 at the headquarters of the 3rd Gendarmerie Legion in Bouaké were not killed in combat. They were shot down in cold blood by armed elements of the MPCI while being held with some fifty of their children and a few civilians in the prison of the 3rd infantry battalion military camp in Bouaké. Moreover, some of them, including the wounded, were most likely shot dead at the mass grave where they had been forced to bury some of their comrades. The survivors of this massacre were only saved by an order given at the very last moment by an MPCI leader. Finally, the ten or so gendarmes still held in December 2002 were released after paying very high ransoms."*

In reality, this nebulous group of armed groups known as rebels was built up in a free-for-all, a series of armed clashes between factions, infighting, rivalries between men, and physical eliminations. Corporal Kassoum Bamba, known as "Kass", one of IB's close *com'zones* (zone commanders), was killed and found mutilated on June 21, 2004, a victim of the rivalry between his friend and Soro, the rebel's enemy brothers, as was Adam's, another rebel militia leader, executed a year later in an internal settling of scores. In this context, an episode already mentioned, nearly eighty of their men - young men recruited at random to fight for a few bucks - perished of asphyxiation in a container where they had been locked up. Martin Fofié Kouakou, militia leader (Gbagbo's chief guard after his fall), had ordered them to be left in the sun in Korhogo. Fofié has been prosecuted by the UN since 2004, for various crimes, including the enlistment of child soldiers, as *Le Monde* reported on December 25, 2013, stressing with the latest Amnesty International report, that the *"justice of the victors"*, and the impunity enjoyed by former rebels, responsible for mass crimes, but promoted to positions of responsibility by Alassane Ouattara *"undermine reconciliation"*.

Ibrahim Coulibaly, not yet the self-proclaimed general IB, but already a professional putschist, arrested and detained at Fresnes in 2003 for attempted subversion in Côte d'Ivoire, was strangely released by French justice after twenty days in prison, and disappeared into thin air. Already involved in the military coup d'état against President Konan Bédié in 1999, in 2007 he teamed up with a Frenchman, Jean-Paul Ney, in a new, completely botched attempt to overthrow power in Abidjan. An international arrest warrant was issued against him in 2009, but he continues to move around Africa unhindered, weaving the web he believes will enable him to gain political ascendancy over his partners, and who knows, ultimately, power?

On April 27, 2011, just a few days after the military victory over Gbagbo, it was his turn to be killed, on orders, by the men of his fellow travelers, Soro and Ouattara. His body was not returned to his family until several weeks after his death. Ouattara refused to allow an autopsy, insisting that Ibrahim Coulibaly had been killed in combat, and not murdered, as his friends claimed, despite the fact that, according to reports in Abidjan, his corpse was in a particularly gruesome state.

This was the final act in a struggle between rebel rivals for power that has yet to reveal all its secrets. On June 29, 2007, rockets and Kalashnikovs were fired at the plane belonging to Soro, then Gbagbo's Prime Minister in a "cohabitation" government. Four members of Soro's retinue were killed. Issiaka Ouattara, better known as Wattao, one of the rebel leaders, always claimed to know the name of the instigator of the attack. He never gave it. Nor has Soro, who has declared that he *has his own ideas on the matter*. In Abidjan, one name is on everyone's lips: Ibrahim Coulibaly, the notorious IB… Soro's promotion in the government of his sworn enemy Gbagbo doesn't please IB any more than it does many other rebels, who feel cheated. IB's death in 2011 was undoubtedly the culmination of this long-standing mutual hatred.

Soro's underground career has disoriented many of his partners, and fooled many of his adversaries. Which is hardly surprising. From armed rebellion against Gbagbo, whom he denounced as a dictator, to Prime Minister of the same horrible Gbagbo, after the signing of the Ouagadougou peace accords in 2007. Then, with arms and baggage, in the service of Alassane Ouattara following the stormy 2010 elections. In reality, he has never stopped working for him. Guillaume Kigbafori Soro, a former student of English, has no university degree. Initially trained as a trade unionist - he presided over the student federation, the FSCI - he then threw himself into politics. A close friend of General Robert Guéï, Soro was Ouattara's infiltrator throughout the years, assuming the role of political leader of the rebellion. Today, Gbagbo remembers.

It was my son Michel who brought his student friend Guillaume Soro home for lunch one day. That's how I got to know him.

He marked Gbagbo "by the scruff of the neck" from the moment he joined the national unity government after the Ouagadougou peace accords, playing a brilliant and permanent double game.

Some of Ouattara's vibrant public tributes to Soro, after his accession to power, on the occasion of public meetings in the North, attest to the fusional complicity between "the Father", "the Son", in the "Holy Spirit":

the Rebellion. The fact that such praise for the rebels contradicts Ouattara's own words a few months earlier, in an interview with Africa 24 during the 2010 election campaign, in which he *"condemned"* the rebellion from day one, and said that *"violence never brings definitive solutions"*, seems to have shocked no one. Not even himself.

Guillaume Soro himself revealed, in Kong on July 1st, 2013, the *"old ties that bind him to Ibrahim Ouattara"*, Ado's lookalike brother. Soro's old friend is now his brother's Minister of Presidential Affairs, i.e. President bis. In the 90s, Ibrahim and Guillaume, both students, fraternized. Soro says he became close to Ouattara and made a pact with him. He had met Ouattara in 1998 and was also a close friend of General Robert Guéï. In the roulette wheel of the race for power, the young Soro began by straddling several numbers. In his book, he explains: *"Because of my young age, I'm a bit like the son of Ivorian politicians…"* In the end, he recognized only one "father", Alassane Dramane Ouattara, to whom his brother Ibrahim Ouattara had led him.

"One day […] I said to him: 'Well, Ibrahim […] I give you my commitment: from now on, I'll support your big brother [Alassane Ouattara] *and I'll fight with you for him.' Since that day, I remember that it was Ibrahim Ouattara, returning from one of our stays here in 1998, who determined and enabled me to decide to lead the fight for Alassane Ouattara. That's the historical truth."* In any case, it couldn't be more convincing and definitive to say that Alassane Ouattara is indeed the godfather of the rebellion that has plunged Côte d'Ivoire into civil war for ten years. And that Guillaume Soro has never ceased to be his loyal lieutenant, even when, as Gbagbo's Prime Minister between 2007 and 2010, he simulated loyalty to the incumbent president to perfection. As soon as the results of the disputed December 2010 election came in, with two presidents instead of one, Soro came out of the woodwork. He declared his support for Ouattara, *"swearing on his Christian faith"* that Ouattara had indeed won the election. The rebel forces, this time officially but unsurprisingly, joined their long-time hidden leader. On March 17, 2011, by decree, they became the country's army under the name of Forces républicaines de Côte d'Ivoire, replacing the regular army.

Guillaume Soro owes his position to his weapons. He'll have to worry if one day he doesn't have them with him.

A change of president has never meant a change of army in Côte d'Ivoire: governments come and go, the army remains. The old army was, whatever one might say, rooted in republican legitimacy, with high-caliber cadres and officers. The new one is a motley conglomeration of uncontrollable ex-rebels, putschists and militiamen. The French army is therefore likely to be in Côte d'Ivoire for a long time to come, if only to protect Ivorians from their own army, which is incapable of not indulging in looting. This view is shared by Ivorian journalist Théophile Kouamouo, who comments ironically in a contribution to the online journal *Gri-Gri International: "It's the French taxpayer who's going to pay for police and gendarmerie duties in a country that's been independent for fifty years!"* Sure of himself, and of the impunity he enjoys thanks to the constant support of the international community that chose him, Ouattara admitted this complicity with his "loyal son" Soro in Korhogo, in front of an audience of militants, at the end of July 2013, barely three years after having declared the contrary in an interview with Africa 24 :

"Of course, Soro felt at one point that we, the elders, were on a path that would perhaps take too long to bring our fight to a successful conclusion.

"[…] Soro has shown courage, sacrifice and has fought so that the people of the North can recover their dignity through Ivorian nationality […]."

Speaking to convinced militants, he couldn't help but regale his audience with one last such daring touch, for someone who had launched three coups d'état and two wars:

"[…] in the midst of my parents, I would like, once again, to launch an appeal and invite our brothers of the FPI [Gbagbo's party] *to enter the Peace process…*

"[…] the FPI must have the strength to ask forgiveness of the victims and the victims' relatives…"

Koné Djakaridja, alias Zakaria, one of the rebel commanders, now appointed head of the military police by Alassane Ouattara, spilled the beans about the rebellion's secret affiliation in a speech in Malinké, filmed in a public square, back in 2002[38]. At a time when Ouattara was careful not to acknowledge, let alone claim, any link with Soro's men or other rebel leaders. In his speech, Zakaria clearly identified Ibrahim Coulibaly, IB, as the military leader, Ouattara as the political leader - the one *"who bought the arms"* - and France as his accomplice. As for his threats against certain other rebel leaders, they were carried out in blood.

"At the start of the war," recounts the Gbagbo-friendly daily *Notre Voie*, on October 16, 2010, *"members of the Ivorian rebellion toured the towns and villages of northern Côte d'Ivoire to explain the rationale behind their bloodthirsty actions and make themselves understood by their relatives. One of the leading figures of this armed violence, Koné Zakaria, in a meeting in Séguéla before the chiefs of the land gathered to say who is behind their movement, who financed it and why all, inhabitants of the North, must support it."*

Excerpts: *"Anyone who betrays Alassane Ouattara's policies will come to a tragic end, and IB knows this very well. We asked Kass to pull himself together.* [We saw how both were liquidated for forgetting these warnings]. *If you support the MPCI, don't do it for Zakaria or for IB* [Ibrahim Coulibaly] *or for anyone else, except for the man who bought our weapons, that is, Alassane Dramane Ouattara. [...] Sixty of us had to go into exile [...]. During our exile, IB was our leader. We agreed that he would not be a candidate in the presidential elections. Even if Laurent Gbagbo were killed, we need someone who can help our relatives in the North. We had planned to set up a security council chaired by IB, with the participation of France. I, Koné Zakaria, was in charge of recruiting gendarmes, policemen and soldiers for the rebellion [...]. We took the weapons, but it wasn't IB who bought them. Let this truth be known to all today. When we were in exile, I was the guardian of the whole group and I was ready to die for my brothers. I was the one who brought fighters and weapons into the country, from Korhogo to Abidjan. If you support the MPCI, don't do it for Zakaria, or for IB, or for anyone else, except for the man who bought our weapons, i.e. Alassane Dramane Ouattara. When we were in exile, it was Alassane Ouattara who looked after us. He regularly*

------

38. Who appears in Thierry Legré's film *Alassane Ouattara, le père de la rébellion.*

brought us rice and the sum of 25 million francs a month. Soro, IB, Adam's and I were all housed in the same place. God is our strength. We were angry with the RDR because IB had hidden from us for a long time that all the money he had came from Alassane Ouattara. IB and I went to Paris where we were received by the wealthy Zanga Ouattara and Zoro Bi Ballo. We each received a million francs. Zanga promised to send us money regularly. But we don't know where the money went. Only IB knows. Zanga can testify because he's not dead. We swore on the Koran, so no one had the right to betray us, whether civilians, soldiers or even Dozos. I'm the one who recruited them. So I know what I'm talking about. I'm asking you to support us, because it was for Alassane that we took up arms. It's not for IB or Soro."

When will the ICC's sleuths finally investigate those responsible for the new Duékoué massacres in 2011? On March 28, 29 and 30, 2011, while the two presidents continued to stare each other down in Abidjan in an increasingly dramatic face-off, Alassane Ouattara's forces launched their major offensive against the south towards Abidjan, in perfect synchronization with the French Licorne force, which began bombing family-run gendarmerie barracks, the RTI building[39] and Laurent Gbagbo's residence in the capital.

The rebels enter Duékoué, the pivotal city between North and South. After the battle, the massacre of civilians began. Traditional Dozo hunters, militiamen of all nationalities, took over the town and surrounding villages. They sorted the population and slaughtered those belonging to the Guéré ethnic group. A thousand or two thousand men, women and children were raped, shot, slaughtered and burned alive.

Has the slogan-making machine broken down? As Laurent Gbagbo rightly pointed out to me, we won't be hearing about "death squads" in the French and international press this time.

Less than a year and a half later, when Ouattara's new government had been legally in power for over a year, 2,500 survivors who had taken refuge in the Nahibly camp, supposedly protected by UNOCI troops stationed 500 meters away, were once again attacked and massacred by the hundreds.

---

39. Radio Télévision Ivoirienne.

To date, these are the only "genocidal" acts recorded in Côte d'Ivoire in the last ten years. They were committed under the leadership of Guillaume Soro and Alassane Ouattara. They have deceived Western opinion by denouncing the danger of an imaginary genocide, the better to conceal the genocide being committed by their troops. Not content with "covering up" the murderers, they then claimed that, thanks to them, the worst had been avoided! As political scientist Michel Galy explains, this is a technique of systematic perversion of information, which they have mastered to perfection since the start of the crisis.

In April 2013, Salvatore Saguès, Amnesty International's West Africa researcher, observed, "[…] *despite its promises of justice, the Ivorian government has made little progress in investigating the crimes committed during this attack.*" But who will bring them to a successful conclusion? Incidents broke out between the prosecutor and Gbagbo's lawyers, who were accused of politicizing the case when they described the nature and ramifications of the rebellion, demonstrating that they led to Alassane Ouattara. Yet the primary responsibility for human rights abuses lies with those who triggered the conflict, even if this does not mean absolving anyone when crimes have been committed. At the end of the day, however, the supposed neutrality of NGOs objectively benefits the victor, by equating his crimes with those of the vanquished. Even if the latter is the aggressor, only he will be prosecuted and eventually punished. The victor only incurs rhetorical blames, quickly forgotten, from organizations with no coercive power, but with strong influence over the media, international institutions and public opinion.

These NGOs are not all neutral, and can influence the outside world's perception of events to the benefit of powerful interests. Behind their action on the ground and the public communication they practice, naming the good guys and the bad guys, there are sometimes hidden agendas, a secret strategy. Such is the case with Human Rights Watch, whose main backer is George Soros.

"Ado, who has been preparing for this deadline for fifteen years, has been able to count on his personal fortune accumulated over more than two decades. In addition, American billionaire George Soros is said to have provided him with a 'Grumman 4', renamed 'RHDP Solutions'", reports *La Lettre du Continent* of November 25, 2010.

"George Soros gave much more than a private jet to Ouattara", comments *Nerrati Press,* which delivers its analysis of Soros' objectives in Côte d'Ivoire, and gives an article by Léandra Bernstein "Misanthropist George Soros' Secret War Across the World", the first few paragraphs of which are edifying. Here they are, as quoted, *in extenso.*

"For George Soros in The Deficiencies of Global Capitalism, in On Globalization, 2002: *'Democracy and the open society can only be imposed from outside, because the principle of sovereignty stands in the way of outside interference. […] Of course, it is difficult to interfere in the internal affairs of sovereign countries, but it is important to recognize the problem.'*

For a very long time, George Soros' actions and money have been used to dismantle the national sovereignty of states, filling the coffers of 'philanthropic' or 'droitdelhommist' organizations. We take a brief look at one aspect of this operation.

At the time of the first criminal investigation against him for stock market manipulation in 1979, George Soros launched the 'Open Society Fund', designed to 'open up closed societies'. Today, he is active in 29 countries. Asserting that 'states have interests, but not principles', Soros explains that 'an ideal open society would do away with specific national interests, while an international political and financial structure would take responsibility for defending the good of the people'. This explains his boundless admiration for, and collaboration with, the 'United Nations (especially the Security Council)', the 'WTO' and the 'World Bank'. […] To this end, Soros endows his philanthropic organizations with financial liquidity, which then 'buy' large sectors of the population, who in turn rage to bring down any government that tries to maintain a 'closed society'. 'If a nation wishes to control its own natural resources, it is a closed society. If a nation wishes to develop its economy and workforce through tariffs and regulations, it's a closed society. Any nation that rejects globalization (i.e., free-trade imperialism) is condemned in the same way' and will be attacked by Soros and his secret organization.

British-style organizations under Soros' supervision include the Open Society Institute (OSI), Human Rights Watch, the Soros Foundation and the Extractive Industries Transparency Initiative.

In 2002, Soros admitted to having disbursed over $2.1 billion in five years to these philanthropic enterprises. He writes of them: 'They work with *government when they can, and independently of government when they can't; sometimes they're outright in opposition. When foundations can coope-rate with government, they can be more effective; when they can't, their work is all the more necessary and appreciated, as they offer an alternative source of funding for civil society. As a general rule, the worse the government is, the better the foundation, because it enjoys the commitment and support of civil society'.*

George Soros has paid $100 million to 'Human Rights Watch' over the past ten years to secure the services of this 'NGO', whose investigations into Côte d'Ivoire have had a crucial media impact in the demonization of President Gbagbo.

George Soros' latest maneuver is the sordid attack on Ivorian cocoa farmers by the 'lobbying' group Avaaz, closely linked to George Soros according to Canadian Minister John Baird. George Soros has not only set his sights on Côte d'Ivoire, but on many other African countries, which he is destabilizing in order to leave them in the clutches of Anglo-Saxon speculators."

George Soros dreamt it, his champion in Côte d'Ivoire, and friend of the IMF, Alassane Ouattara, did it. The Ivorian market has now joined the global one, through arms and blood. *"As the facts given are verifiable, we are free to analyze them as we see fit. But everything indicates that the introduction of the 'externally imposed democracy' advocated by George Soros has succeeded in Côte d'Ivoire."*

In the immediate aftermath of the presidential elections, Human Rights Watch, largely funded by Soros, denounced alleged crimes committed by pro-Gbagbo supporters. Throughout the post-electoral crisis, Human Rights Watch does not appear to have clearly denounced the crimes committed by the pro-Ouattara side. So much so, in fact, that the ICC prosecutor based his indictment largely on Human Rights Watch's accusations. He was all the more able to do so because, at inter-national conferences dealing with international justice, the prosecutor's representatives rub shoulders with NGO representatives, notably those of Human Rights Watch. Indeed, the ICC has many employees who were formerly members of NGOs such as Human Rights Watch. And who "monitors" the ICC trials? Soros-funded institutions. And who organizes conferences on international criminal justice? Soros-funded institutions.

Today, all the inconsistency of the international community is contained in these contradictions. It is capable of providing political cover for war criminals, because it has supported them, and ultimately being their hostage, as Guillaume Soro has clearly understood. This is how history would be written, in the shadow of international justice.

"If a com'zone [former rebel leader who commanded a zone] *claimed by the ICTR were not handed over, that would pose a problem for the international community,"* says Phillip Carter III, the US ambassador to Abidjan, during a restricted press conference on February 6, 2012. Vincent Hugeux of *L'Express,* who has never been soft on the Gbagbo regime, told me himself that *"there should be representatives of the Ouattara camp in The Hague".*

And why not Ouattara himself, whose rebels, renamed FRCI (Forces républicaines de Côte d'Ivoire) by himself, committed crimes and atrocities under this label when they conquered Abidjan?

23

"WHEN I THINK THAT OUR 'GOVERNMENT OF PROFESSORS' WAS LAUGHED AT"

Jennifer Naouri, the youngest member of Emmanuel Altit's team, was tasked with highlighting, during the major hearing in February 2013, the links that have united the current Head of State and the main rebel leaders from the outset, all of whom have been appointed to positions of responsibility by Alassane Ouattara. How could the latter refuse anything to armed people who have opened the road for him?

On September 26, 2012, the Ivorian government appointed three former Forces nouvelles (FN) rebels as regional prefects. Ousmane Coulibaly aka "Bin Laden" has been assigned to San Pedro, Côte d'Ivoire's second-largest port and capital of the Bas-Sassandra region. He was previously in charge of security in the Yopougon district of Abidjan, after having reigned as zone commander in Odienné, the town where Simone Gbagbo has been held under heavy guard since the fall of Laurent Gbagbo in April 2011.

The second soldier concerned is Tuo Fozié, appointed to Bondoukou, capital of the Zanzan region. He was Minister of Youth and Civic Service in the post-Marcoussis government of national unity. The third new prefect is Major Koné Messamba, ex-director of the FN paramilitary forces. He has taken up his post in Guiglo, in the west, on the border with Liberia, in the Moyen Cavally region. These three appointments take place in security-sensitive regions.

Ouattara's "son", Guillaume Soro, was the head of the Mouvement patriotique de Côte d'Ivoire (MPCI), the main Ivorian rebel movement which later became the Forces nouvelles (FN). **He was imposed by Blaise Comparoé at the head of the rebellion.** He had *"under his command the Republican Forces of Côte d'Ivoire - the FRCI - which perpetrated numerous massacres, for example in Duékoué, [...] where on March 29 and 30, 2011, at least 800 people were killed. Today, he is President of the National Assembly, a position which gives him parliamentary immunity,"* said Jennifer Naouri. As Maître Altit pointed out, Ibrahim Coulibaly, known as "IB", was Alassane Ouattara's bodyguard and one of the main players in the ex-rebellion on the ground. The Defense adds that IB was the leader of the Invisible Commando, the main armed rebel group in Abobo - a district of Abidjan - active against civilians and law enforcement forces from February 2010 to March 2011. IB was liquidated by his own friends. As for Soumaïla Bakayoko, who became Chief of Staff of the Forces républicaines de Côte d'Ivoire (FRCI) created during the post-electoral crisis by Alassane Ouattara, he was - recalls the Defense team - the Chief of Staff of the ex-rebellion and consequently one of those who benefited from the population being cut off. Ousmane Coulibaly, nicknamed "Bin Laden", the commander of the Movement for Justice and Peace (MJP) based in Man in the west of the country, was during the Battle of Abidjan the most active rebel leader in Yopougon - another district of Abidjan - where massacres of civilians took place. His links with ex-president Taylor are well documented. In 2012, he was appointed Prefect of the San Pedro region, the world's leading cocoa port, west of Abidjan. Chérif Ousmane, nicknamed "Papa Guépard" or "the Cleaner", is accused of *serious blood crimes"* in the west of the country. As for "Wattao", he became famous for being accused of being one of the most important diamond traffickers. Today, through his father, he reigns supreme over the Doropo region, where he parades around in a Maserati, flaunting a $40,000 watch, racketeering and pillaging with impunity. He lives in a sumptuous villa, whose garage is filled with Ferraris *"paid for in the USA and which I resell here"*, he explains to Christophe Hondelatte and Jacques Langlade, authors of a report broadcast on channel 13e Rue. He is, however, the deputy head of the CCDO (Centre de coordination des décisions opérationnelles). A new police unit tasked with securing Abidjan.

I've never held a gun in my hands, apart from during my military service. Nor gold: I don't wear, and never have worn, any jewelry: not a chain, not a ring, not even a watch!

The famous gold pistol was in fact stolen from the home of Lida Kouassi, Gbagbo's former Defense Minister, who had received it as a gift from his counterpart from an Arab country visiting Abidjan.

Wattao as he is, promoted and successful. Violent, boastful and self-assured. A mafioso capo who presents himself as a *"close collaborator"* of President Ouattara, *"of whom I am one of the sons"*, he adds. *"For the time being, the warrior and the president remain loyal to each other,"* he confides to Hondelatte. The former French ambassador to Abidjan, Jean-Marc Simon, told me in Paris that *"Wattao is indeed at home in the presidential palace."* According to Théophile Kouamouo, who commented on this report on the Internet, Wattao's fortune probably began with the robbery of BCEAO's Bouaké branch on September 24, 2003. Over a period of three days, the highly organized rebels emptied the vaults, taking away who knows exactly how many billions of CFA francs. According to *Jeune Afrique* of November 21, 2003, witnesses saw Wattao at the scene. A month later, still in the stronghold occupied by Soro and Wattao's men, on October 28, branches of the same bank were targeted by hold-ups, in Man and Korhogo, within 24 hours of each other. According to the local press, one of the attacks succeeded, the other failed.

Georges Peillon, former press officer with the Licorne military force in Côte d'Ivoire in 2003 and 2004, and author of *Ivoire Nue*, under the pseudonym Georges Neyrac, remembers this episode and the heavy machine-gun firefights between rebels, with the population mingled in, to grab part of the booty: 23 dead and 30 wounded, before French troops intervened. In the field, he formed a very precise opinion of the situation and the role of the French authorities, an opinion that led him to leave the army. His experience of the Ivorian conflict is irreplaceable.

He remembers the ambiguity of French policy, and the unease of French military leaders. When his book came out, he was told, Dominique de Villepin was furious: *"Who is this idiot meddling in our politics?"*

Peillon testifies: *"Michèle Alliot-Marie, who was Minister of Defense, came to see us on December 31, 2003. And General Joana, who was commanding Operation Licorne at the time, was waiting for the green light to put into action the defense agreement with Côte d'Ivoire, signed in 1961. Because we knew that there were exactions in the North, and that we still had to succeed in reunifying the country, which was completely split in two. Everything was ready, with a rapid offensive on three axes, and the resources we could deploy, added to the professionalism of our units, would have made the reconquest of the North very simple. In thirty-six hours, and without much damage, it was all over. The political decision to support Gbagbo's legitimate government, to restore peace and stabilize the country, never came.*

"France endorsed this partition of the country, and our commanding general, General Joana, understood that we didn't have the same conception of our mission as the political powers in Paris.

"I came into contact with the Forces Nouvelles during negotiations on issues such as disarmament and the restoration of traffic access. Apart from one or two, the rest were uneducated men with gri-gri. They weren't military men, they were gang leaders. I once said gang leaders, and I stand by it. They were people without faith or law, who held their power through violence, through the terror they wreaked in the north of the country, where the population went through hell on a daily basis. When I heard that Abidjan had fallen into the hands of these people, I said to myself: the brigands are in the square... It will always be a question for me: what was the deal made between these gang leaders and President Ouattara?[40]"

When I think that our "government of professors" was sometimes laughed at, it included Pascal Affi N'Guessan, a telecom engineer, Mamadou Koulibaly, associate professor of economics, Émile Boga Doudou, assistant professor of law, Oulaï Hubert, associate professor of law, Bohoun Bouabré and Aké N'Gbo, respectively doctor and asso-

---

40. *Naked Ivory, op.cit*

ciate professor of economics, Ahoua Don Mello, a Ponts et Chaussées engineer, and so many other graduates...

In addition to rebel heavyweights with a track record of killing, such as Tuo Fozyié, appointed Prefect of Bouna, and Ousmane Coulibaly, there is the former corporal and kitchen assistant Koné Messamba, promoted to Prefect of the Bas-Cavally region. They represent the first choice of Alassane Ouattara's victorious new regime. It would be more accurate to say that they invite themselves to the banquet of the man they have made king, and who can refuse them nothing.

At The Hague, the names of the warlords and cadres of the current regime are only mentioned in the defense pleadings, never by the prosecutor. As if all these individuals, suspected of the killings, didn't exist; as if their names had been erased to allow Alassane Ouattara to appear as the champion of democracies: Losséni Fofana aka "L'intrépide Loss", in the West, Martin Fofié Kouakou, the commander of the Compagnie territoriale (CTK) in Korhogo, Koné Zakaria, among others, are cited, and their "exploits" are recalled by Gbagbo's lawyers.

The defense team lists the names of the warlords and the accusations made against them by human rights organizations. For whose benefit were these exactions, extortions and crimes? *"The rebels were doing it on behalf of one man, Alassane Ouattara"*, explains Maître Altit's collaborator. She recalls that in a video, Koné Zakaria explained that rebel leaders acted on behalf of Alassane Ouattara, who transferred funds to them. She underlines the contribution of warlords to Ouattara's success. Proof of the complicity between the henchmen and the former IMF director? As soon as he came to power, Ouattara gave them positions and privileges. Yet they are liable to be prosecuted for war crimes and crimes against humanity. Unless they risk nothing. To remove suspicion, Fatou Bensouda suggests that some of them could be prosecuted. Thus, in *L'Express* on July 17, 2013, in response to a question from Vincent Hugeux about prosecutions aimed exclusively at the Gbagbo clan, she wields her tongue: *"The Gbagbo case is the first in Côte d'Ivoire, it won't be the last."*

The lords of the north," explains Jennifer Naouri, "were protected by the French authorities. What's more, it was foreign military advisors in Burkina Faso who trained the mercenaries recruited in 2010, who were to form the bulk of the rebel army destined to seize the South. Who financed their weapons and heavy equipment in March 2011, in violation of the UN embargo? - Who paid their salaries? Who paid for their transfer from Burkina to northern Côte d'Ivoire throughout 2010? Who organized them logistically so that they could flood south in March 2011? Who paved the way for them? The traces of French intervention are manifold. Boxes of ammunition stamped in France were found in the rebel camp. And that's exactly what Maître Altit's team has started to prove, as they are clearly ready to get to the bottom of their argument, with the evidence, if given the opportunity, at a trial.

It's easy to see why such an operation, aimed at seizing power by force regardless of the outcome of the presidential elections, was planned and organized well in advance. It materializes the constantly reaffirmed desire to topple President Gbagbo. In such a complex context, where numerous representatives of the French authorities - politicians, diplomats, military personnel and senior civil servants - were involved, decisions could only be taken at the highest level of government. One of the main thrusts of the offensive was to cut off the Ivorian authorities' access to funds belonging to them in banks and at the BCEAO. This raises a troubling question. Can a President of the French Republic and a handful of advisors and military leaders destabilize a foreign country, build up a rebel army from scratch, launch military attacks against the country's regular forces and seize a legitimate President by force without anyone being moved? All these preparations were carried out in broad daylight, even if some - French officials at the time, the ICC prosecutor today - tried to cover them up more or less clumsily. Is it not shocking to note that the French Parliament was not consulted, and that the military hierarchy was bypassed? The Ivorian affair reveals the flaws and dysfunctions of our political system, and the way it has been diverted to serve particular interests.

What's more, this operation will have been carried out in spite of common sense. Its brutality risks alienating the African members of our French-speaking family once and for all. The violence of the military intervention and the contempt shown towards a foreign government and institutions will have inflicted irreparable damage on the African psyche, and hence on the Franco-African relationship. In 2013, in the report drawn up by former minister Hubert Védrine and Franco-Beninese financier Lionel Zinsou, at the request of Pierre Moscovici, then Minister of the Economy and Finance, Africa clearly emerged as France's future. In a globalized context of cut-throat competition and economic warfare, our country, burdened by debt and unemployment, needs to work with Africa. *"But,"* comments Ahoua Don Mello, the exiled former spokesman for the Gbabgo government, *"if Africa is France's future, many Africans today consider that France is Africa's past."*

24.

"I ACCEPTED EVERY COMPROMISE"

Strange usurpers, such as certain lawyers from outside the Gbagbo case, sometimes take or have taken the floor in the media, claiming to speak on behalf of the President. When they are not some of his own friends, too well-intentioned. These are often the same people who, during the post-election crisis, refused to contemplate an attack by the French army in April 2011. Jacques Vergès, for example, was convinced that *"Côte d'Ivoire would be the tomb of the French army"*. And some of the President's advisors were somewhat boastful in their optimism, concealing the possibility of any warlike initiative on the part of France… Educated by these different experiences, and unable to intervene himself to correct the abusive language of his visitors on leaving prison, Laurent Gbagbo left it to the members of his party and those close to him.

In The Hague, his visitors, including Nady Bamba, his third wife, can see that President Gbagbo is still lucid and combative despite the after-effects of his detention in Korhogo. *"The first time I saw him on January 19, 2012,"* recounts Guy Labertit, *"I found a man who was still scarred by the eight months he'd spent in Korhogo in fairly disastrous conditions. He told me himself that he hadn't been out except for visits from Desmond Tutu, Mary Robinson and Kofi Annan - who, incidentally, had taken the liberty of saying that he was well treated, which is quite scandalous considering what he'd been through. President Gbagbo had also been more than jostled at the time of his arrest and at the Hôtel du Golf, contrary to what has been said. He still had after-effects; he still couldn't close his right hand."*

From the presidential palace - where I met him for the first time in 2005 during lengthy interviews, part of which were published in *France-Soir* - to the besieged residence in the Cocody district, via the house in Korhogo where he was detained, and finally to Scheveningen prison, the successive shocks were brutal. Memories come back, one by one, precise in spite of everything. The President recalls every stage of the fatal spiral, right up to his arrival here. Laurent Gbagbo speaks calmly, without bitterness, as an old hand at adversity and hard knocks. He was already in prison from March 1971 to January 1973, when he was in opposition to Houphouët-Boigny. Then, in 1992, when Alassane Ouattara, already Prime Minister, had him arrested, after he had run against Houphouët in the first multi-party presidential elections in 1990, and become leader of the opposition, then a member of parliament, under the FPI label. Sentenced to two years' imprisonment, the inveterate opponent spent only six months in prison, before being released in August.

I was sworn in on Saturday December 4, 2010, at the Palais, after the Constitutional Council had ruled on the appeals we had lodged following the massive fraud in the north of the country, and after it had taken note of the Independent Electoral Commission's inability to reach a decision within the allotted timeframe. The day before, on Friday 3rd, I realized that everything could end very badly. The Constitutional Council had just announced the results, declaring me the winner of the election. The same day, I received a phone call from Sarko. He was furious: "The Constitutional Council shouldn't have done that, no, no, they shouldn't have!" That's the approach of a madman, not that of a head of state. How can anyone in the 21st century afford to call another head of state and say such a thing? It was at that precise moment, when I hung up, that I had the feeling that everything could get out of hand. I know that they don't give a damn about the institutions of African countries! After all, it's just a matter of putting their man on the throne... but to sit on the Constitutional Council of a sovereign country, whose constitution is modelled on France's, with so much nerve, just like that, over the phone, is a bad joke. It's not a head of state I've spoken to on the phone...

When I asked Jean-Christophe Notin, who was close to official French circles at the time, if not a great connoisseur of Africa, why the decision of the Constitutional Council had not been respected, he replied: *"For Paris, it was a puppet Constitutional Council."* Pointing out that it functioned exactly like the French Constitutional Council, I slipped in, *"By puppet, do you mean Negro?"* Embarrassed silence. Jean-Christophe Notin, the Republic's unofficial historiographer, doesn't insist. I think he may have suddenly discovered another vision that, as a faithful Unicorn ghost-writer, he had never even considered.

On Saturday, just before I was due to leave for the Palais, where I was to be sworn in before the Constitutional Council, my chief of protocol came to tell me that a message had reached us saying that Nicolas Sarkozy had asked us to physically oppose the investiture. I decided to go anyway. He's acting like a thug, I told myself, I don't have to take that into account. It was a bluff, or a warning...

On Monday December 6, we formed the government, a government of technocrats, and started work. France had cut off our access to the BCEAO, hoping that we wouldn't be able to pay civil servants' salaries and government bills, which would have turned the population against us. Sarkozy ordered me to leave in a speech he gave in Brussels, in a tone closer to casse-toi de là, pauvre c., than to the masterful language of a head of state.

But at the end of the month, from December 22, we paid all the salaries, and the same in January. They realized they couldn't have us like that...

And I'm being blamed for it today...! because I continued to do my job, and to pay my civil servants. Same reason, same punishment for the measures I took to maintain order. I used a decree that has been in existence since 1961, and which opens up the possibility - it's not a foregone conclusion - of putting the forces of law and order on alert if the situation is such that incidents are to be feared. In short, I was doing my job to ensure the security of the State and the population, I was governing. The rebels had introduced armed commandos into the heart of Abidjan, a whole army. They were to join up with the hundreds

of rebel soldiers, most of them Burkinabe mercenaries, who had been stationed at the Hôtel du Golf, a vast complex on the banks of the lagoon, where the Ouattara family and rebel leaders had been staying since September.

From early December 2010, attacks against the population and the forces of law and order began in Abidjan, until the strategy of violent seizure of power by Alassane Ouattara and his supporters was revealed in the concerted general attack launched throughout Abidjan on December 16, 2010.

Politicians from my party, my government, even my son, and many others, are being prosecuted, and have been imprisoned, for "undermining national defense, attacking or plotting against state authority, forming armed gangs, leading or participating in an armed gang, participating in an insurrectional movement, undermining public order, a coalition of civil servants, rebellion, usurpation of office, tribalism and xenophobia". It would only be grotesque if it didn't entail so much suffering, so many deprivations of freedom, so much injustice. We're hunted down, made to look like criminals. It's the world upside down.

The death of Basile Mahan Gahé, a peaceful man and trade unionist, who died recently of ill-treatment in the prisons of the Ouattara regime, at the age of sixty, affected Laurent Gbagbo, like so many other brutal disappearances due to ten years of crisis.

There have been deaths, many deaths, so many deaths. Isn't it unworthy to try to attribute them to me, when I've always advocated reconciliation? I was so concerned that the situation could lead to deep and definitive tensions between Ivorians, that I did everything I could to reach a peaceful solution. I accepted all compromises. As I've often said, I've never owned a gun, I don't like guns, I don't like war, I've never staged a coup d'état... I've written books, Pour une alternative démocratique, Agir pour les libertés, and a few others. I suggested to the judges in The Hague that they bring them, because it's in these books that people can get to know me, who I am,

what my life's purpose is… I've always heard contradictory comments about me: some of my friends have criticized me for not being
tough enough, and for coming to terms, even with opponents. But
talking to everyone is what politics is all about! On the other hand,
my opponents claim that I'm a dictator. All my life I've fought for
democracy. I've spent months in prison and years in exile because
of my fight for democracy. I rejected the one-party system because
I believed that the future of Africa could only be organized within
a democratic framework. When I was in exile in France, I refused
Houphouët-Boigny's proposals to get me back. I've always played the
election game, I've always believed in the will of the people. And in
the end, that's what I'm being criticized for: being the spokesman for
the people. Giving voice to the people of Côte d'Ivoire. How many
African leaders represent the people? They can be counted on the fin-
gers of one hand. Who has allowed each sensitivity to express itself?
Who allowed rebel parties to exist on the Ivorian political scene?
Who integrated the rebels into the government and the army? Who
organized the elections? Who allowed Ouattara and Bédié to stand,
even though they did not meet the constitutional criteria? Who ensured that all candidates had the same speaking time and the same
resources? It seems to me that I have always acted like a true politician, concerned with the well-being of his fellow citizens, anxious
to allow democratic debate to take place, listening to others. Far, far
removed from the soulless technocrats with no moral structure who
now make up the political staff of your Fifth Republic. Coming back
to the great maneuvers of economic suffocation, in 2011 I decided to
cut all ties with the BCEAO headquarters in Dakar. The boa constrictor technique for suffocating us was implemented by the head of
the Treasury in Paris. [Rémy Rioux, Deputy Director for International
Affairs and France's representative at BCEAO].

Paradoxically, the same Rémy Rioux who, on official business, became
one of Gbagbo's executioners, gave him the French Treasury's seal of
approval for his economic management of Côte d'Ivoire. Despite the war
fuelled by the rebels, Mr. Rioux considered that the country… *"was in a*

favorable cycle after Gbabgo brought it into the HIPC[41] program, and was preparing in a few weeks to reach the completion point for debt cancellation."

Philippe-Henri Dakoury-Tabley, head of the BCEAO, was put in prison because he didn't give in, unlike other economic leaders turned around by Christine Lagarde. The European Community was enlisted by France, and there was an embargo on everything, including medicines, which penalized the population. Enormous pressure was brought to bear on economic operators, including cocoa exporters, to block the port. Around the 19th or 20th of February, all the branches of private French banks closed in the country: BCC [BNP Paribas], SGCI [Société Générale]... Their customers were unable to receive their salaries, which were domiciled there. We reacted very quickly, requisitioning all the small Ivorian banks to transfer our civil servants' salaries to them. The boa constrictor had bitten its own tail...

From then on, they became very nasty. I learned that between late February and mid-March 2011, planes were delivering weapons to Bouaké to attack us, despite the UN embargo. The mercenaries who were to form the bulk of the rebel troops had been recruited months earlier in neighboring countries. CDEAO said its army was going to attack us.

Then, with the help of the French on all fronts, the rebels advanced south towards Abidjan, aided by mercenaries from Burkina Faso, Mali and Niger... UNOCI and French troops opened the way and took part in the fighting.

The bombing of the residence - which many people confuse with the presidential palace - began on March 31. I no longer went out, but lived in the armored tunnel built by Houphouët to enable the President to get to the French ambassador's residence in a hurry in the event of a coup. Quite a symbol... The tunnel had been walled up. When the French forces intervened, I had it checked. I didn't want to risk an attack there, and so it didn't happen, contrary to what has been written. What is true is that there were French soldiers positioned in the French ambassador's

---

41. Highly indebted poor countries.

residence, a few meters from us. They were shooting at the occupants of the presidential residence, whoever they were. Easy targets. Many civilians were killed or wounded by these snipers. And there were snipers on the roof of the residence of the President of the National Assembly, Mamadou Koulibaly, who was fortunately no longer there.

We had provisions, enough to last a long time.

Désiré Tagro, Secretary General at the Presidency, came to tell me on the evening of Saturday April 9 that Gérard Longuet, Sarkozy's Minister of Defense, had called me. In fact, it was a phone call from Charles Millon, who had asked for my contact on Longuet's behalf. I went up to my room, where I showered, washed and changed clothes. I told Tagro to call Millon back in the meantime.

My aide-de-camp informed me that my Prime Minister and the head of Petroci [Côte d'Ivoire's national oil company] wanted to speak to me. I got my minister on the line, and then I spoke to the President of Ghana, John Atta-Mills. He was a good friend and reassured me. I was talking to the director of Petroci when a bomb hit the building and exploded exactly above my head. It must have been a tracking device, thanks to my phone call. In any case, I never got through to Longuet. The strikes were intended to kill. I would have been presented as collateral damage, not as a direct target, no doubt.

Government forces were fighting. They were retaking rebel positions. Yes, the Ivorian army had the upper hand, but every time they achieved a result, an advance, the French air force came to bomb them. At that point, my former Minister of Foreign Affairs took refuge in the French embassy: they thought I'd sent him to negotiate…

There were no heavy weapons at the Cocody residence. Yet that was the reason given for bombing the residence, where around a hundred civilians had taken refuge: all those of my ministers or friends who thought they were safer in my house than in theirs, poor things! In addition to my family, there were old people, children, babies and teenagers. Among them was the sister of footballer Basile Boli, who ran a charity for police officers' children. There were also some outside, around the residence, and many were killed.

French jumbo jets arrived in Abidjan with tanks on the night of April 2 to 3, 2011, and disembarked soldiers from the Foreign Legion, and combat equipment, including armor. The soldiers were stationed in the French camp near the airport. People phoned us from their cell phones to give us information on the movements of the armored vehicles. The number of French combat helicopters also increased.

It was with all this information in mind, and not in order to politicize the debate or make people feel sorry for me, that I was able to assert in my last interview - I gave it by telephone to the French channel LCI on Tuesday April 5 - that France had just gone to war "directly" against us in Abidjan. Before that, it had already been, but indirectly, by transporting rebel troops from one part of the city to another, arming them and giving them ammunition. I told the journalist Vincent Hervouët that my aim was not to die, and that all I wanted was the truth from the ballot box. I talked about negotiating, I didn't call for war. "Are you going to fight with your back to the wall?" the journalist asked me, still using the same logic that presented me as "the one clinging on to power": I replied that I wasn't fighting, that I was defending myself, that I had never in my life been a war-monger, a civil war-monger, or a coup d'état. For that, I said, you have to look the other way. I told him how incomprehensible I found the actions of the French authorities. Why had the French army intervene so violently against government forces when the issue was to settle an electoral dispute, which could have been done by a simple recount of the votes? Why bomb the residence of a head of state? Why destroy the national radio and television station? What I called for in the end was, once again, the truth of the ballot box. Because therein lies the question: who won these elections? A military ceasefire was still possible, but I wanted a political dialogue. I was the only one. On the other side, they wanted war. I've never held a gun in my hands - except during my military service! -I've never used weapons. Since the first rebel attacks in 2000, we've never been the cause of any violence.

In the meantime, I received a message - on the 8th or 9th - telling us that French soldiers had gone up to the airport control tower. To a woman who was there on duty, they asked: "Are you pro-Gbagbo or

pro-Ouattara?" She was a sensible, well-informed woman, and answered intelligently.

Around Sunday April 10, the officers said to me: "President, we
can't hold out any longer. Our equipment is destroyed, our men are
dead." I told them, "Everyone, get yourselves to safety." The military
boss of the Plateau, as well as the one commanding the residence,
went to see ONUCI, to hand over their mission: the protection of civilians and buildings. I knew it was over.

On the morning of April 11th, we received a phone call from Port-
Bouët, where there's a French airport and military camp, to tell us that
fifty French armored vehicles had come out and were heading our way.
They arrived shortly afterwards and took up position around the residence. The French helicopters set fire to the interior of the residence
with incendiary ammunition, walls fell down and the library was completely destroyed. My collection of classic books went up in ashes. It
immediately became unbearable for the families and civilians gathered
there. There were no soldiers left. We all went underground to safer
shelters, even though the smoke everywhere made the air unbreathable.

In a press conference held at the Maison de l'Afrique in Paris, Jacqueline
Chamois, the French teacher who was Laurent Gbagbo's first wife, and
who was then fighting for the release of their son Michel, reported the
testimony of her daughter-in-law, who lived through the siege of the
residence. Viviane Gbagbo told her that holes had been drilled in the
wall blocking the tunnel leading to the French ambassador's residence,
to pass gas and smoke through, and that she and her husband had been
beaten and abused, before being separated from him in the presence of
French soldiers on April 11.

French soldiers came up to the gate, and one of their tanks blasted
it with cannon fire. Then there were gunshots, bursts of gunfire, and
through the smoke I heard: "We want Gbagbo! We want Gbagbo!"
With us, in a small room plunged into darkness, was the mother of my
minister Sangaré, a ninety-year-old woman, children aged four, seven
and a baby. The rebels came down shooting. "We want Gbagbo!"

I stood up and said, "It's me, Gbagbo." They grabbed me. I recognized Wattao. He said, "You mustn't touch him." There was also Ouattara Morou, Cherif Ousmane, many rebel leaders. My shirt was torn, so I asked for another one, and Wattao brought it to me. While I was changing my shirt, I was filmed. As I said, always by French army cameras. From the beginning, everything was filmed by French soldiers, right up to the end…

It was Ouattara Morou who put the bullet-proof vest and helmet on me. From that moment on, I knew that anything could happen to me, to all my family… Ouattara Morou pushed me into a vehicle that ran at breakneck speed, and we went as far as the Hôtel du Golf. There, I was made to wait in a room, where I saw other prisoners lying on the floor, then I was taken to the fourth floor, to a room, I think 468.

The barons of the new regime came to see me: Soro, with a little cap, Hamed Bakayoko. What for? To savor their victory. They stayed about fifteen minutes, no more.

I saw Simone and my son Michel arrive, bleeding. I'd seen my relatives beaten up, just as I'd seen Tagro murdered. I saw the Minister of Health, my friend Sangaré… They were taken to another room.

Alphonse Djédjé Mady, Secretary General of the PDCI [Konan Bédié's party] comforted me. I saw my former Minister of Economic Infrastructures, Patrick Achi, who had gone over to the other camp…

I slept. No medical examination, no interrogation. On the 12th, Guillaume Soro came back to see me. He told me I was to be transferred to Korhogo the same day. I refused.

"- If you don't accept, they'll do it brutally.

- Korhogo for what?" I said.

- It's in a house that belongs to me," he replied. You'll be fine there.

 - I have a house in Gagnoa," I replied, "and there's also San Pedro."

He wouldn't listen. Cherif Ousmane came and brutally took me away. In the process, they took my doctor, Christophe Blé, away with me. On the way to the Golf course, a rebel almost slit his throat. And there he was, off with me for eight months' detention. He's a good man, Christophe Blé, a competent doctor and a good person.

It was because he was my regular doctor that he was almost killed and then detained without a warrant. We were put on a helicopter to Korhogo.

On the way, I thought of all those who had died and suffered, and I prayed for them. I wondered what would become of Côte d'Ivoire.

25

"THEY WOULD HAVE KILLED ME SLOWLY"

In Korhogo, a major town in the north of Côte d'Ivoire, my doctor and I lived in a tiny house, a three-room shack, in complete isolation. I wasn't allowed to set foot outside. There was a small common room. We each had our own room. A woman I didn't know came to bring us meals, prepared elsewhere. Meals calculated to weaken us. Did I think I'd been poisoned? Yes, I did. Someone was watching us eat: a UNOCI soldier and a rebel. Lunch was around 1pm, dinner around 8:30pm. The door only opened at these times to let in our food and a little daylight: at each meal, we could sometimes catch a quick glimpse of the sky. Otherwise, the door was closed. We lived for eight months under electric light or in the dark, all the shutters closed, never allowed to put our noses outside, to walk, to exercise. I could only tell it was raining when I heard the sound of rain on the roof. I couldn't go for a walk. I was going in circles. I stayed in this situation for eight months. They would have killed me slowly.

The President's real jailers are Fofié's men, not the UN soldiers whose officials claim to be protecting and caring for the notorious prisoner. To add to the confusion, both the UN soldiers present in Korhogo and the rebels have very similar uniforms and come from the same Sahelian regions. According to the lawyers who approached Gbagbo during this initial detention, the former were acting as auxiliaries to the latter, and not vice versa. The international forces were officially in charge of the prisoner, but knowingly abandoned him to his executioners. They implicitly covered up the ill-treatment to which he was *subjected*. The fiction perpetuated by the media that Gbagbo was "protected" by the UN, which was fulfilling its role and mission, is false, but no one ever went to check.

Since his first trip to Abidjan in June 2011, Emmanuel Altit has been able to form his own opinion of the situation. From then on, he predicted that Gbagbo would be brought before the ICC before the end of the year. His Ivorian colleagues did not believe him. In June, in Abidjan, he and his team met Jeannot Ahoussou, Alassane Ouattara's Minister of Justice, and then the heads of the UNOCI Human Rights Office.

A compulsory step for anyone wishing to see Gbagbo, especially as ONUCI was providing the air link to Korhogo at the time. The United Nations won't help him, even though in principle they are the guarantors of a detainee's rights, first and foremost the right to see his lawyer. Laurent Gbagbo remarked on this during his first appearance at the ICC in December of the same year.

The former lawyer for the Bulgarian nurses held in Libya from 1999 to 2007, then spectacularly freed under media escort thanks - among others - to Cécilia Sarkozy, flew to Korhogo in a small private plane, like a tourist. The plane had engine problems, and nearly crashed, with Altit, the pilot, and his accompanying collaborator on board.

Altit will return in July and August. The Minister of Justice, the Minister of the Interior, and United Nations officials all assured him that they would do everything in their power to enable him to see his client as soon as possible. But when it came to organizing the practical details of the visit, the interlocutors either disappeared or passed the buck. In particular, the UNOCI does not seem to be concerned about the violations of the prisoner's rights, despite the fact that he is being held without a warrant, in defiance of Ivorian legislation, and in very difficult conditions of detention. Yet no one is unaware that President Gbagbo is in the hands of a bloodthirsty warlord, and that he is being held in appalling conditions. Not the new Ivorian authorities, not UN officials, not French officials. On July 14, 2011, Prime Minister François Fillon was in Abidjan. He had come to assure Alassane Ouattara of the support of the French authorities. He will make an evening appearance at the reception given to mark the national holiday. At the same time, Emmanuel Altit and his team are in Abidjan. Knowing that he could count on France, the UN and the United States, why would Ouattara be concerned about the fate of President Gbagbo? Weren't the rebels hoping, or at least some of them, that the President would disappear? Despite the written authorization he had obtained from the Ivorian authorities at the start of his mission to meet President Gbagbo, Emmanuel Altit did not manage to see the President until October. At that time, Ocampo was in Abidjan for discussions with the authorities. The ICC Prosecutor, Moreno Ocampo, whom Emmanuel Altit had officially informed of the violations of his client's rights, in particular the fundamental right to meet his lawyer, did not seem to be moved by the situation any more than the others. Nevertheless, the travels of the French lawyer and his team have been fruitful: they have enabled him to meet important witnesses and build up a file.

The meeting between President Gbagbo and Emmanuel Altit took place at the Palais de Justice in Korhogo, which had been emptied of all its occupants. A few hundred meters from the palace, Fofié's guards stepped aside to let ONUCI soldiers surround the President, giving the impression that they were in charge. In fact, it was Fofié and his men who had repeatedly physically prevented Emmanuel Altit from seeing his client. And this despite the duly stamped authorizations that the lawyer possessed. At the end of the meeting, Emmanuel Altit and his two Ivorian colleagues were particularly worried: the President was clearly exhausted by his detention, and left at the mercy of the rebels. Anything could happen.

26

IS THE ICC AN AFRICAN COURT?

"I was dismayed to learn that the deposed President of Côte d'Ivoire, Gbagbo, was transferred to the International Criminal Court on Tuesday, November 29... in total violation of the International Code of Procedure and in defiance of the requirements of peace in Côte d'Ivoire. This transfer follows such a rapid procedure, that it can legitimately be described as a kidnapping..." declares Jerry Rawlings, President of Ghana between 1992 and 2000. Like others, he was surprised and shocked by the expeditious judicial procedure employed in Korhogo. *"This haste to charge and transfer Gbagbo* [who did not run to escape during the bombing of his palace] *as a common criminal defies the logic of a quest for true reconciliation and lasting peace in Côte d'Ivoire."* The coup was staged in Paris on Thursday November 24, 2011. Alassane Ouattara was there, on purpose to meet Nicolas Sarkozy and Luis Moreno Ocampo for a secret meeting. Gbagbo has fallen, it's time to finish the job. The ICC prosecutor returns from Libya, where he was the day before, trying to indict Gaddafi's son. Saïf al-Islam is the target of international justice. The prosecutor rushed back to Europe when he learned that the ICC judges had validated President Gbagbo's arrest warrant. He hops on a plane to Paris to discuss the terms of President Gbagbo's transfer with the operation's deus ex-machina, the French president and Ouattara. No dead time.

On Friday November 25, 2010, my lawyers learned from the file in Abidjan that I was to be questioned the following Monday, the 28th,

by an examining magistrate in connection with the economic crimes proceedings opened illegally, in violation of neither the law nor the Ivorian Constitution. The examining magistrate was due to travel to Korhogo. My lawyers immediately jumped into a car. From Abidjan to Korhogo there are 600 kilometers of difficult, poorly-bodied road, infested with "coupeurs de route" [highwaymen]. My lawyers took all the risks.

In Korhogo, surprise, they come across clerks and judges from the Abidjan Court of Appeal. When I was questioned by the judge at the Palais de Justice, I could smell a trap. At first, I refused to answer any questions. I pointed out that the whole thing was illegal. The judge postponed the questioning until the following day, Tuesday.

That day, Tuesday 29th, as the interrogation resumed, a magistrate rushed into the room where we were sitting and announced that the ICC was requesting my transfer to The Hague. My lawyers object that only the Court of Appeal is empowered to deal with such a request, and that if there is to be a hearing, it must be held at the Court's headquarters in Abidjan. "All the magistrates of the Court of Appeal are there," they retort, "there's no need to go to Abidjan!"

The trap… By e-mail, in view of the urgency of the situation, Maître Altit sends his colleagues a statement of defence, which they will use while requesting a legitimate postponement based on the provisions of the Code of Criminal Procedure and international standards. The judges refused. I knew that the die was cast, and I watched the whole shabby comedy with resigned eyes. The hearing began.

My Ivorian lawyers, those who were present, wanted to speak. The judges hardly listened to them. But they were courageous, they insisted and finally made the voice of law and reason resound. But it wasn't enough.

The Korhogo judges were in constant contact with ICC officials in The Hague, keeping them abreast of developments at all times. Koffi Fofié and his men in the room, armed with Kalashnikovs, became noisily impatient when they sensed that the judges were losing their enthusiasm.

It just happened, and it had nothing to do with the law… or anything normal, for that matter. I wasn't even given anything to eat all

day... After the hearing, the guards took me away, telling me I was going back to the house where I was being held, and that I could see my lawyers again the next day. The lawyers believed it!

Thus, the transfer to the ICC is taking place almost clandestinely, in a hastily cobbled-together legal framework.

In the car of Kouakou Fofié, my jailer, who was transporting me, I saw that we were passing the house road. I asked where we were going: "Aren't we stopping?" He replied, "No, we're going to the airport. It's not lit and your plane has to leave before dark, at 6:30 p.m." "Where am I going?" He didn't have the courage to tell me. He said, "Abidjan." I laughed, I understood that. He didn't dare answer. I think he was ashamed. In fact, we went all the way to Korhogo airport. From there, I was put on one of the two official presidential planes and flown to The Hague.

In Paris, the President's lawyers have also understood. Emmanuel Altit and his team take their ticket to The Hague. On the night of Tuesday November 29 to Wednesday November 30, the plane carrying Laurent Gbagbo landed at Rotterdam-The-Hague-Airport, from where the President was transferred, freezing cold, to The Hague. No one saw fit to give him a sweater on this wintry night.

In the cell van, President Gbagbo, dazed and tired, dressed in a simple flowered Ivorian shirt made in Abidjan - a "Pathe'O" made world-famous by Mandela - light pants and sandals, heads for the ICC prison. It was in this unsuitable outfit, to say the least, that the man who was his country's chief magistrate for ten years arrived in Scheveningen in the early hours of the morning.

Ouattara has sometimes said in interviews that I was more than a friend to him, I was a brother! I don't think so... I arranged for him to be able to return to Côte d'Ivoire after Konan Bédié slapped an international arrest warrant on him, forcing him into exile for falsifying identity documents. I then arranged for him to stand in the 2010

elections, even though the Constitution, which he himself had voted for in 2000, prohibited him from doing so. I never blocked his pension. During the ten years I was in power, I continued to make him pay his 8 million CFA francs for his former position as Prime Minister, and in the same way, Bédié and his wife, who had been President and First Lady, received for ten years, he, 22 million, and she, 8 million monthly.

Besides, I don't think that any legitimately elected statesman, illegally put in a difficult position by people up in arms, would have been more amenable to negotiation than I am.

Like the end of a reel, the last sequence speeds up, then suddenly stops. Gbagbo is in the box. Quickly done, well done, the film is wrapped up, we think in Paris, Washington, The Hague and Abidjan.

I told them in The Hague when I was first introduced to them on December 5, 2011: there's no point in acting like this. We can do things normally.

From the outset, barely able to stand on his own two feet, Laurent Gbagbo apostrophized the magistrates: *"I'm here, and we're going to see this through to the end. Madam Judge, there's no need to hide in order to transfer us to The Hague. I ran Côte d'Ivoire for ten years. I didn't do this. Madam Judge, take precautions so that in other countries, in other cases, this does not happen again. There's no point. They want people to believe that they don't want to appear before the ICC. If I've been accused, it's because we have evidence. When I appear, you'll have mine and you'll judge."*

At the very end of this flat country where *"the sky is so low, a canal is lost, with a sky so gray, that a canal is hanged"*, sings Brel. The Thalys crosses Flanders into the Netherlands, to Amsterdam or Rotterdam, before an "Inter city" takes you to The Hague Sport Hall or Central. A cab then takes just twenty minutes to Scheveningen. The prison is a red-brick building like all the other houses, villas and opulent apartment blocks in this wealthy suburb of The Hague, a seaside resort on the North Sea.

Peaceful, middle-class neighborhood. In front of the neat entrance reserved for visitors and staff, four stone planters, planted with holly, and neatly mown lawns. On the wall, next to the glass doors, are prohibited logos: cameras, telephones, cigarettes, lighters or matches, and in case I've forgotten, firearms... The other entrance to the prison, which opens at right angles onto the main carriageway, and through which the inmates are introduced and extracted, reminds us with its large black gate, piercing a sinister, never-ending rampart, that this is the entrance to a penitentiary, not a rest home. A terminus dedicated to war criminals and those guilty of crimes against humanity.

For the most part, these are second-rate militiamen whom the ICC has put away, from African countries chosen from among the one hundred and twenty-two that recognize the institution worldwide. Ignoring many other perpetrators, or suspects, of mass crimes, in other countries and on other continents, the ICC has made a geographically highly "targeted" selection.

What is the ICC? Three of the five countries that make up the Security Council and have veto power at the UN are not members of the ICC. Only the French and British have ratified the treaty. As for the Russians, Americans and Chinese, there's no risk of them getting lost here in the fog.

The international judicial institution currently has eight investigations underway, in exclusively African countries - Uganda, Mali, Democratic Republic of Congo, Central African Republic, Sudan, Kenya, Libya, Côte d'Ivoire - but is attempting to diversify its areas of investigation, and ultimately the prison population of its establishment. In Central and South America (Honduras and Colombia), Afghanistan, Georgia, Korea... a dozen countries likely to provide some future defendants and detainees. Frédéric Taddeï, a journalist with France-Télévision and host of *Ce soir ou jamais* on France 2, offers this polemical analysis[42]:

---

42. Internet Newsring, February 2013

"The judges of the International Criminal Court in The Hague are currently examining the evidence gathered against Laurent Gbagbo to decide whether or not to prosecute the former Ivorian president for crimes against humanity. Shouldn't we take this opportunity to examine the evidence against the ICC for ourselves, and judge whether or not the Court deserves to continue its work? Since its creation on July 1, 2002, in application of the Rome Statute, the ICC has only targeted Africans. Racism? Impotence? Blindness? Everyone can deduce what they want. The fact remains that over the last ten years, according to the ICC, massacres and war crimes have, as if by chance, been exclusive to Côte d'Ivoire, Libya, Darfur, the Central African Republic, the Democratic Republic of Congo and Uganda… The rest of the world? Nothing to report. Iraq and Afghanistan? Cool! Tibet? Syria? No problem…? Not content with invoking a so-called international law which, in reality, does not apply equally to all states, since countries such as Russia, China and the United States have not signed or ratified the Rome Statute, and member states of the UN Security Council can veto referrals to the ICC, the latter never attacks the victors, only the vanquished. Taking its cue from the International Criminal Tribunal for the former Yugoslavia, set up in 1993, which convicts all Serbs it can get its hands on and systematically exonerates their opponents, be they Croats or Bosnians, the ICC incriminates poor Gbagbo, but refrains from investigating Alassane Ouattara's supporters, backed by the major powers. Similarly, it waited until Gaddafi was on the verge of losing the war against the French, British and Americans before accusing him of crimes against humanity… Can we still speak of justice when we are so weak with the strong and strong with the weak? In fact, over the last ten years, the ICC has constantly distorted the concept of crimes against humanity. Born in the aftermath of the Second World War to punish and render imprescriptible crimes of exceptional atrocity, it is now confused with any massacre. As if the Auschwitz extermination camp, the bombing of Dresden and the Sétif massacre were the same thing! As if an attempted genocide and the repression of a demonstration in front of Ivorian television were exactly the same thing! With so much and repeated evidence of wrongdoing, isn't it urgent to put an end to this parody of international justice, which acts as yet another instrument of domination in the service of the powers that be, and ends up disgracing the 121 countries that have ratified the Rome Statute?"

Since its creation by the Treaty of Rome in 1998, its inauguration on July 1st, 2002, and its effective start-up in 2003, the ICC has arguably specialized in cases on the dark continent. It's almost as if the continent alone were home to almost all the world's war criminals. Are mass murderers and bloodthirsty lunatics all Africans? In any case, all the proceedings concern African leaders. The indictment of Sudanese President Omar al-Bashir for violence in Darfur, then that of Kenyan President Uhuru Kenyatta for the repression of post-election unrest, and now the detention of President Gbagbo have united Africans against the ICC. The African Union, through the mouth of its President and Ethiopian Prime Minister, Haile Mariam Dessalegn, did not hesitate to denounce a "racial hunt" by the ICC against Africans, during a closing speech at the fiftieth AU summit on May 27, 2013.

In June 2012, in Malabo (Equatorial Guinea), Jean Ping, former Foreign Minister of Gabon, inveighed against the ICC at the 17th Summit of African Union Heads of State, saying: *We have the impression that the International Criminal Court only targets Africans. Does this mean that nothing is happening in Pakistan, Afghanistan, Gaza or Chechnya?"* Speaking even more directly to former Argentine diplomat Luis Moreno Ocampo, the Court's first prosecutor and "star" at the time, Ping expressed distrust and contempt, without translating his words into strong action at the head of African countries: *"Apply the law,"* he told him, *"don't play politics!"* Quoting one of the heads of state present, he added without laughing: "[…] *Ocampo is a joke."*

To say that the International Criminal Court was struggling to establish its credibility prior to the arrest and transfer to The Hague of Mama's Woody[43] - Gbagbo's nickname in his homeland - is an understatement. Undermined from the outset by the fact that, of the 121 states that have ratified its existence (out of the 193 member nations of the UN), none are the United States, Russia, China, India or Israel. This deprives it of jurisdiction over many cases involving the nationals - and leaders - of these countries. The Court appears to be a biased instrument

---

43. "Woody" (good boy) from Mama (Laurent Gbagbo's home village).

of the UN Security Council, even though three of its most eminent members - the United States, Russia and China - have not signed, or have refused to ratify, the Rome Treaty. As for the Americans, while they do not contribute to financing the Court's operations - a budget of 100 million euros, 10 of which is provided by France - they are present at the annual review meeting: the eye of Whashington... Danish Judge Harhoff of the International Tribunal for the former Yugoslavia belongs to this nebulous group of international criminal jurisdictions. In June 2013, he echoed the African heads of state criticizing the ICC, himself denouncing from the inside the fact that *"massive and assiduous pressure is exerted on international magistrates." "These courts,"* he declares, *"are not neutral* and *obey the orders of the great powers, the USA and Israel in particular."* The Americans have warned that they will never accept that one of their own be referred to them, reserving the right to choose which of the crimes committed by their troops in Iraq or Afghanistan they will judge themselves. This is the root of our malaise. Such a philosophy ruins the ambition of the ICC. It's hardly surprising that Africans, and long before them Asians, see it as nothing more than one of the arms of Western political power wielding the judicial whip against the weak. A birthmark that is no longer a hidden vice, and justifies all criticism and growing resistance. However, the project to create an autonomous African court, often evoked but difficult to build for reasons of political and financial independence, needs to take shape. The handling of the case of Chad's Hissène Habré, whose file has been entrusted to Senegalese justice by the African Union for crimes committed when he ruled his country between 1982 and 1990, will be decisive. Hissène Habré has been living in total impunity in Dakar for the past 23 years, and was finally arrested on June 30. He is due to stand trial in 2014. This trial will demonstrate that Africans are beginning to take control of their own destiny. They will prove that impunity is no longer the rule in Africa.

Criticized, too, for its highly selective and highly political choice of cases, with all the less care taken as they affect African countries, most of which are too small and too weak on the international scene. The face of a justice system manipulated by the victors of conflicts, who send their vanquished to it, and thus gain international cover for their own crimes. This was the case in the Democratic Republic of Congo, where Luis Moreno Ocampo succeeded in having a few obscure militia leaders brought before the Court, without any of those truly responsible for the wars and carnage in the east of the country, which have caused 5 million deaths to date, being called to appear.

This hallmark of Ocampo's management, aimed at consolidating the institution's status - and his own - through easy successes, is one of the Hague Court's organic weaknesses. Since the arrest warrants against Sudan's Omar el-Béchir, which were never acted upon, Africa has reacted, rising up as one against its bogeyman. The scheduled appearance in The Hague of Uhuru Kenyatta, Kenya's current president - elected in 2013 - and his vice-president William Ruto, accused of having provoked bloody unrest in 2007, during the previous presidential elections, resulting in a thousand deaths, was postponed under pressure from members of the African Union. Some member countries threatened to withdraw from the ICC. It is foreseeable that the trial will never take place, and with the accused in power, that the country's prosecution witnesses will be brought to their senses, if they have not already done so.

When you enter Scheveningen, you don't come across many white people. Apart from a few Serbs, stranded there before the creation of the ICC, who are often seen with their families, surrounded by tall girls with very long hair in the common parlour. Six tables separated by wheeled screens, a kitchenette, a lounge area with a coffee table, two sofas and red fabric armchairs, a soda and sweets dispenser, and on the opposite side, the trunk of a wooden elephant gives shape to a slide for the very young, a TV screen with a loop of cartoons, a big plastic car on which I saw a blond, curly angel ride one Saturday afternoon: a two- or three-year-old girl, towed by a tired-faced Serb who has taken off his belt, turned it into a harness and transformed himself into a workhorse... Is this Vojislav Seselj, Serbia's ultra-nationalist leader? I wouldn't know.

Many were imprisoned in the Netherlands as part of the Special International Tribunal for the former Yugoslavia. Sloboban Milosevic, former president of Serbia, died in detention in Scheveningen in March 2006, as did Radovan Karadzic and Radko Maldic. Former president Charles Taylor was tried by the Special Court for Sierra Leone, and was in The Hague for the duration of his trial. Sentenced to fifty years' imprisonment, he will serve the remainder of his sentence in England.

The other detainees all represent trophies from what some are calling Luis Moreno Ocampo's "African safari", since the permanent Court came into operation to replace the various temporary jurisdictions dedicated to this or that theater of war (TIPR, Special International Tribunal for Rwanda, TIPY, Special Tribunal for the former Yugoslavia, or TIPS for Sierra Leone).

Among them, the Congolese Thomas Lubanga - sentenced to fourteen years, notably for having mobilized child soldiers, the Congolese officer Germain Katanga, prosecuted for massacres in the Kivu region. Or the former vice-president of the Democratic Republic of Congo Jean-Pierre Bemba, also a senator, and unsuccessful candidate against Joseph Kabila in the 2006 presidential elections. This giant of more than one meter ninety, whom I see on each of my visits with his wife Liliane, his daughters and sons, who live in Brussels, is accused of criminal acts, in particular rape, committed by his Congolese Liberation Army in neighboring Central Africa, during the war he waged against the regime of Désiré Kabila. Kabila's main gain was the elimination of Jean-Pierre Bemba, his most serious challenger, who through the marriage of a sister is related to the family of the late President Mobutu, and the exoneration of his own misdeeds, much to the satisfaction of the United States, which sponsors him.

Child soldiers in the Congo, rape and murder in the Central African Republic - the accusations and the accused also seem to have been chosen to correspond exactly to the raison d'être and specializations of certain NGOs, to legitimize their existence, and their budgets. Jean-Pierre Bemba was no longer in command of the soldiers involved in the crimes mentioned, and was first sentenced to 18 years in prison… then acquitted and released from prison by the ICC. Grotesque, after eight years in detention. His conviction, in September 2018, by the ICC for witness tampering - one year's imprisonment, already served, and a €300,000 fine - does nothing to change the substance of the bogus Bemba case.

Laurent Gbagbo was the first president to be imprisoned there. His transfer was, in extremis, the marshal's baton for Luis Moreno Ocampo, the ICC's first prosecutor, then at the end of his mandate, in his quest for the "big case" that was missing from his record.

Fatou Bensouda succeeded him after assisting him. She was tasked with crowning this operation with a spectacular trial, intended to definitively establish the ICC in the noble mission assigned to it at its creation in 2000: to put an end to impunity for those responsible for mass crimes. This is the justification and raison d'être of this young judicial institution, which is in need of a reference point and is the target of mistrust and criticism. In France, *Le Monde* of July 4, 2013 headlines - and pulls the trigger - with a double-page spread entitled "La Cour internationale sous pression" ("The International Court under pressure"). The journalist highlights the "bad mark" given to Bensouda by the judges a month earlier, when they noted that, as President Gbagbo's Defense had demonstrated, the Prosecutor was not providing sufficient evidence to support her accusations against Gbagbo. A return to reason, after the prosecutor had been credited in principle with articles in which there was not a shadow of a doubt, until the June sanction.

Since June 3, 2013, Fatou Bensouda's failure has become public, with the judges' decision to ask her, after two years of investigation, to start her work from scratch. You don't have to be a staunch supporter of the deposed President to know that the media-political mountain has given birth to a judicial mouse.

"MY LAWYERS CORNERED THE JUDGES"

Only the budget is worthy of the announced super-production. In 2013, the prosecutor's budget amounted to 28,265,700 euros[44] to which must be added the 2.8 million enabling the prosecutor to hire new consultants, investigators and temporary staff specifically to work on the Ivorian case. In The Hague, dozens of legal experts have been hard at work building a case against President Gbagbo: prosecutors, deputy prosecutors, legal assistants, trial specialists, appeal specialists, translators and so on. To these must be added the dozens of investigators from the prosecutor's office working in the field in liaison with the Ivorian authorities, magistrates and police. The Ivorians have provided the Prosecutor with all kinds of information to help him nail President Gbagbo's coffin shut. And behind the Ivorians, the French. Lawyers Jean-Paul Benoit and Jean-Pierre Mignard, close to François Hollande, are at the helm. Faced with these gigantic resources, Emmanuel Altit's defense team has only a limited budget at its disposal. For the entire duration of the trial, it will only be granted 76,000 euros for investigation costs. The disproportion of forces is blatant. And yet, with their experience and maneuvering skills as their only weapons, Gbagbo's lawyers were to defeat the prosecutor and all his international supporters, and turn the situation completely around,

---

44. ASP, ICC Draft Programme Budget for 2014, 12ᵉ session, 29 July 2013 (ICCASP/12/10).

putting the prosecutor on the defensive and forcing him to justify himself to the states parties[45].

After several successive postponements, the long-awaited hearing finally takes place from February 19 to 28, 2013. Over 10,000 pages of investigative reports and annexes, numerous videos, all assembled in close collaboration with the Ivorian authorities, to produce a "DCC" or Document Containing the Charges, i.e. an indictment, which was intended to be implacable and insurmountable. The prosecutor claimed to be describing a Gbagbo who led units loyal to him in order to practice terror between November 2010, the date of the second round of presidential elections, and April 11, 2011, the date of his downfall, in order to maintain his grip on power. According to the prosecutor, this policy against the civilian population led to the deaths of 1,080 opponents, and more than thirty rapes. The reason? Acts of terror were the only way for President Gbagbo and those close to him to stay in power. These actions, which for the prosecutor amounted to crimes against humanity, were premeditated. Gilles Dutertre, Fatou Bensouda's first collaborator, opened fire, then Eric Mac Donalds and Maria Belikova detailed, with images and videos, 41 criminal events, including the most important, such as the march on the RTI, the killing of the women of Abobo, the bombing of the Abobo market, and the massacres in Yopougon. An impressive battery of charges. In short, the future trial *from which Gbagbo would like to escape*", reads *Jeune Afrique*, May 26, 2012, is already presented as the announced triumph of the prosecutor. According to the journalists, the conviction should not make a ripple. The defense and its illustrious client are trembling… Today, it's more the international judicial institution that's wavering.

On the defense side, everything had been prepared. From the very first minutes of the hearing, the prosecutor was called to account for a number of procedural errors he had made. The prosecutor found himself on the defensive. Never, it seems, had the prosecutor worked so hard on a hearing and presented his case so well. But as soon as President Gbagbo's defenders struck the first blow, he began to falter.

---

45. The States Parties to the Rome Statute vote on the Court's budget each year.

After hearing the prosecution's case, the defense took the floor and, for two weeks, never let up. Emmanuel Altit frames the debate. He began by expressing surprise that only President Gbagbo was being prosecuted, whereas the prosecutor had constantly proclaimed that he would prosecute all perpetrators of mass crimes, regardless of their camp. *"Is it because the perpetrators of these crimes are unknown?"* he asks. On the contrary, they are known to everyone, he reminds us, and their crimes are documented in detail by all human rights organizations. The lawyer points out that those in power today are :

"Those who, since September 19, 2002, have been plundering, extorting on a massive scale and engaging in all kinds of trafficking in violation of the law.

Those who make systematic rape a policy.

Those who use mercenaries and dozo militiamen.

And those who continue to commit crimes today, particularly in western Côte d'Ivoire.

They are cited in reports by the United Nations, Amnesty International, Human Rights Watch, the International Crisis Group, Global Witness, the US State Department and others."

He points out that since the fall of President Gbagbo, it is these warlords, suspected of the most serious crimes, who head the army, the police and various militias, occupying decision-making positions and increasing their power. The lawyer notes that at no time after the second round of the presidential elections did the prosecutor attempt to contact President Gbagbo's government, even though he was in constant contact with the rebels and Alassane Ouattara. He is astonished that the prosecutor never warned *"rebel leaders and Alassane Ouattara's warlords, reserving his arrows or threats for the government camp alone"*. He is also astonished by the good relations that the prosecutor seems to have maintained with the winners of the conflict after the crisis. *"In these conditions, how can we be surprised that the document containing the charges only reflects the accusations made by the rebel leaders and the pro-Ouattara press at the time of the crisis? This document is just a press review, the review of a committed press."*

Above all, Emmanuel Altit highlights the absence of a prosecution investigation, let *alone* an exonerating one: *"The prosecutor provides no evidence to support his accusations: it is striking to note the small number of attestations he presents, their vague and unclear nature, and the fact that they often contradict one another.*

It is also striking to note that nowhere is there any trace of any order from President Gbagbo, or from political or military officials, which would corroborate - if only in part - at least one of the allegations..."

"The prosecutor's account is fragmentary and incomplete, for one simple reason: reality doesn't fit his accusations, so he has to try and transform it, and to do that he has to conceal certain aspects of it. But the facts are stubborn, and we're going to reiterate them, without omitting any important element for understanding the events."

"The prosecutor's narrative is biased for two reasons: one, as we have said, is that it depends on the elements transmitted to him by the [current] *Ivorian authorities; the other, more fundamentally, is that in order to place responsibility for the conflict solely on President Gbagbo's shoulders, he needs to adhere to the narrative constructed at the time of the crisis to* [...] *'delegitimize'* [President Gbagbo] *and to convince the International Community to support* [Ouattara]. *"*

"This explains the choice of the four events that structure his Document containing the charges, however vague, contradictory and debatable they may be", explains Emmanuel Altit. [...] *"Because these events* [constituted] *as many turning points in the Ivorian crisis, as many stages in the 'delegitimization'* [of the government] *of President Gbagbo, and at the same time* [as many degrees] *in the involvement of certain powers in the conflict."*

"The alleged repression during the attack on the RTI in December 2010 led to international condemnation of President Gbagbo's regime;

"Allegations concerning the women's demonstration in early March 2011, led to the immediate suspension of ongoing peace negotiations. The powers that be did not want a negotiated peace [...]*"*

"The alleged bombing of the Abobo market on March 17, 2011 led, a few days later, to the adoption of Security Council Resolution 1975 and the launch of the ground offensive that had long been prepared under the radar by French forces and UNOCI.

"And what about the accusations of fighting in Yopougon after the fall of President Gbagbo? They make it possible to conceal the roundups and

systematic human rights violations committed by the [...] pro-Ouattara forces after their victory.

"*The choice of these four events [...] allows [...] to read a narrative, to believe a story*" that would legitimize those in power today, explains the lawyer. This "narrative" enables the victors to present a history of the Ivorian conflict that is "acceptable" in the eyes of the international community. As Emmanuel Altit puts it, it paints "*a broad picture of a good camp and an evil camp*".

"*From this point of view, they therefore have a political significance; they built a 'legitimizing' reality that served as the foundation for the Ouattara camp's seizure of power.*

"*Rather than checking the veracity of this story, rather than investigating its reality, the prosecutor has taken it for granted. And the problem is that he can no longer deviate from it without jeopardizing the whole edifice,*" he continues.

"*But it doesn't add up: the attack on the RTI? All the evidence at our disposal proves it: it was not pro-Gbagbo forces who attacked [...] unarmed crowds, but pro-Ouattara militiamen who launched a premeditated and prepared attack against the forces of law and order.*

"*The repression of the women's march? The Ivorian press itself echoed the inconsistencies of the accusations. The prosecutor, for his part, took it for granted that the version of one side was the only correct one, without questioning it, without investigating, without verifying different hypotheses.*

"*The bombing of the Abobo market? The least we can say is that the case presented by the Ivorian authorities is not convincing, and the prosecutor has done nothing to clarify matters.*

"*How, moreover, can we fail to be surprised that those whom the prosecutor presents as the* [principals] *[...]* [those whose role would have been crucial] *in implementing the alleged policy he [...] blames* [President Gbagbo] *for, have been promoted and rewarded by Alassane Ouattara?*"[...].

"*But he preferred to read Ivorian reality through a simplifying prism: it's easier to be Manichean, to picture unarmed crowds being machine-gunned when you want to distinguish between the good camp and the evil camp; it speaks immediately to the imagination; it's already inscribed in the collective unconscious.*"

"Because he didn't investigate himself, because he relied on what the Ivorian authorities entrusted to him, the prosecutor is not in a position to grasp what the political reality on the ground was, and consequently can't show it to the Chamber."

"We'll show in the course of the debates just how serious the consequences of this temptation to the easy simplification are, and how it has led the prosecutor to misinterpret the events he's talking about."

"In order to write a scenario likely to lead to the indictment of President Gbagbo before the ICC, the prosecutor had to force the truth and reinvent a reality. Yet the truth is known to all specialists and inhabitants of Côte d'Ivoire: President Gbagbo's downfall was planned and organized"[…].

"It's a risky game that the prosecutor is playing by adhering to a narrative elaborated by others. Indeed, if the narrative on which he relies were to be called into question, the whole intellectual construction aimed at accusing President Gbagbo and, at the same time, the whole edifice aimed at legitimizing Alassane Ouattara would collapse. It would then become clear what lies at the heart of the accusations: the search for a scapegoat who is, in reality, a man guilty of having wanted to emancipate his country, a man guilty of having preferred freedom to servitude."

"The prosecutor is playing a risky game by focusing on the four most high-profile incidents, those with political consequences, because in so doing he's overlooking the countless crimes suffered by the Ivorian people.

"The Ivorian people would have deserved […] to have their suffering taken into account, they would have deserved a trial other than a political one, they would have deserved a trial of those truly responsible for the decade-long destruction of the country. "And the Court would have deserved to be able to look into what really happened in Côte d'Ivoire during all those years; it could then have played a beneficial role in national reconciliation."

Emmanuel Altit also points out that the Ivorian crisis is also a French affair, and can only be understood in the context of Franco-African relations. "Over the past fifty years," he continues, "France has intervened some forty times in Africa."

From that point on, everything followed one another relentlessly. One by one, the members of Emmanuel Altit's team took the floor and demolished all the prosecutor's arguments. They take each of the elements presented by the prosecutor in support of his allegations and demonstrate their inanity, irrelevance, vagueness and contradictions. At the end of the demonstrations by Professor Jacobs, Agathe Bahi-Baroan, Jennifer Naouri and Natacha Fauveau, nothing remains of the prosecutor's allegations. The shock is made all the greater by the fact that the hearings are broadcast almost live on the Internet via the Court's website, and repeated in a number of countries. In Côte d'Ivoire, the hearings are followed passionately on the Internet.

Members of the defense team are eager to point out the inconsistencies in the prosecutor's position, to explain his silences, and to demonstrate that many elements seem to have been established for the needs of the case, when they are not completely unrelated to it. For example, a video that the prosecutor claimed to illustrate atrocities that took place in Abidjan in 2011, when in fact it was footage shot in Kenya in 2009! Members of the defense team had noticed the exclamations in Swahili.

In view of the seriousness with which the counter-investigation was conducted, the prosecutor's position now appears very fragile. The absence of a genuine investigation is obvious. Her reliance on what the Ivorian authorities were willing to tell her or provide as incriminating documents is obvious. Her lack of understanding of the situation is appalling. It is a great victory for the defense to have succeeded in changing the public's perception of the case.

My lawyers were able to turn the situation completely around. My opponents thought they had won and used the International Criminal Court to their advantage. It now appears that they have everything to lose in a trial. Because a trial will reveal the truth. They're stuck. This is one of the great merits of Emmanuel Altit and his team: they immediately understood the reality on the ground and managed to show it to the judges. They destroyed the prosecutor's evidence. Everyone now knows that the evidence presented by the prosecutor in support of his allegations does not stand up to analysis. Finally, they showed the prosecutor's bias, which goes with the wind blown by the great powers. Why doesn't he prosecute those who have been denounced by NGOs as mass criminals? Why does he even maintain what appears to be a

cordial relationship with them? Probably because it doesn't see them as criminals. Because he operates on the basis of presuppositions and prejudices. My lawyers showed that these prejudices, conveyed by the media, were the result of a fabrication. We were able to use the judicial process to show reality. All the political accusations, designed to prepare the ground for international opinion to overthrow me, turned out to be false after truly contradictory debates. The debates before the Criminal Court will have shown that the accusations made by the Ouattara camp, in response to a strategy devised by its French communicators, were nothing more than a smokescreen designed to conceal the attempts to seize power by violence that took place over ten years against a legitimate government. What about the elections? Why isn't the prosecutor interested? After all, it's simple: if I lost them, we can talk. But if I won them, then everything collapses: the international community will have supported the loser of the elections and brought him - Licorne force and UN contingent combined - to power by violence. Why didn't the prosecutor consider the hypothesis that I had won the elections, when everything shows that I did. Why did Ouattara and his French backers have only one fear during the crisis: that an agreement would be reached to recount the votes, and why did they do everything they could to scupper attempts at mediation?

Informed - intoxicated? - by ONUCI, Jean-Christophe Notin believes he has solved the problem by writing in his book *that "once the ballot papers had been counted, they were destroyed"* in December 2010. As this argument has never been put to Gbagbo, it is false. If it turns out that this destruction did indeed take place, it would be a clandestine and illegal maneuver, aimed at destroying all traces of fraud, and thus prohibiting a recount. A common practice in electoral disputes everywhere.

What was supposed to be the prosecutor's triumphal march turned into the path of the cross. While he was strutting his stuff in front of the TV cameras, Emmanuel Altit and his team were investigating in the field. While the Prosecutor wasted his time meeting Alassane Ouattara and his deputies, and receiving encouragement from international officials, notably French, the Defense Department was building its case. The result was that, while the prosecutor was spreading the word on the airwaves and in the newspapers, assuring anyone who would listen that he had an airtight case, Gbagbo's counsel had already torn it to shreds. Hence the prosecutor's surprise at the February 2013 hearing: a fortnight of suffering as he endured criticism and lessons in professionalism. The prosecutor emerged groggy. At the end of the February 2013 hearing, President Gbagbo's victory seemed close at hand. All the journalists and specialists who had been following the case and had complacently echoed the prosecutor's assertions prior to the hearing immediately flipped their jackets and emphasized the extent to which, after the defense's demonstration, the prosecutor found himself exposed, with a fragile and above all political case.

In every legal skirmish leading up to the confirmation of charges hearing, Emmanuel Altit presents an argument that is always based on an essential principle of law: respect for the rights of the defense, equality of arms, procedural fairness, etc., all of which are essential to the implementation of fair proceedings.

This strategy is all the more necessary as the ICC aims to be an exemplary court. Now in a position of legal strength, it was easier for him to denounce the prosecutor's political approach in his opening speech on February 20, 2013. He played the professionalism card against a prosecutor oblivious to his obligations. The aim was to get the judges to step back from the prosecutor's arguments. To put them in a position to hear what the defense had to say. At the end of the two-week hearing, Emmanuel Altit delivered a second message to the judges in his closing speech: since the defense had just demonstrated how flimsy, incoherent and contradictory the prosecutor's evidence was; how it was based on elements that had not been verified by the prosecutor; and how it had been constructed to "fit" a political narrative, he asked the judges whether they were prepared to follow the prosecutor's lead and run the risk of putting the Court at an impasse.

The way Emmanuel Altit and his deputies organized the confirmation of charges hearing meant that the prosecutor lost all credibility. My lawyers advanced their pawns in such a way as to corner the judges.

They asked them to rule on something they had already destroyed: the prosecutor's evidence. We had to unveil reality as we went along, so as not to clash head-on with prejudices, and gradually bring it to the judges' attention. It's a lengthy work that restores historical reality.

The defense's grip on the confirmation hearing had been so tight that all observers expected that the charges would not be confirmed and that there would be no trial. The question the judges had to answer was whether the prosecutor had presented sufficient credible evidence for them to authorize him to go to trial.

On June 3, 2013, the judges handed down their decision. They found, as the Defense had demonstrated, that the Prosecutor had not provided any credible evidence to support his account of all the incidents on which he was basing his allegations of crimes against humanity. The judges noted, as the defense had shown, that the prosecutor had not conducted a proper investigation. Finally, the judges noted that the Prosecutor had not followed any "line of reasoning" of his own. Consequently, the judges refused to confirm the charges. A major victory for Gbagbo and his lawyers. The Statute, i.e. the Constitution of the Court, stipulates that if the charges are not confirmed, they must be overturned, which *ipso facto* should allow President Gbagbo to be released from prison immediately. But the judges are divided: one of them, the senior judge, was the prosecutor's right-hand man for several years. This judge strongly opposes the reversal of the charges. Perhaps this is why the judges are going to re-read the statute, authorizing the prosecutor to start all his investigations from scratch, even though the statute makes no provision for this. A compromise? Having made this devastating assessment of the Prosecutor's shortcomings, and having endorsed the defense's case, the judges consider that the Prosecutor may have disregarded his duties, failed to understand his evidentiary obligations, and was unaware of the need, at this stage of the proceedings, to provide the judges with sufficiently probative documents. The judges even consider that the prosecutor could have been mistaken about the meaning of the applicable law! In layman's terms, does this mean that he doesn't know his job? In any case, it is on this fragile and curious basis that they are authorizing him to start all his investigations from scratch on the basis of charges already formulated. Unheard of! A strange way of saving him, to say the least. The prosecutor is not punished for his professional shortcomings, but President Gbagbo pays for the prosecutor's lack of seriousness, and has to spend several more months in prison. It's odd to give the prosecutor a second chance - a catch-up of sorts - when professional misconduct should result in a sanction, in this case the reversal of the charges. To everyone's surprise, the ICC tolerates and encourages incompetence at the expense of the imprisoned, and the international taxpayer. The new masters of Côte d'Ivoire and their French friends had a field day: Gbagbo already had one foot out the door, but was caught in extremis.

The significance of the non-confirmation of charges is weighty: it means that judges who cannot be suspected of a *priori* favoring the President have found that the prosecutor did not provide any evidence to support his allegations. This is not even evidence in the sense of a trial. Since we are at the stage of confirmation of charges, i.e. pre-trial proceedings, all the judges had to do was examine whether the elements presented by the prosecutor had any appearance of truth, whether they carried any weight. Before the actual trial phase, the standard of proof that the prosecutor has to achieve is very low, a long way from the standard of proof that the prosecutor would have to achieve in the trial phase to secure a conviction. He would then have to prove guilt beyond all reasonable doubt. Even this minimum standard of proof is unattainable by the prosecutor. In other words, the judges found that the prosecutor's account of events during the post-election crisis was unsupported. Which also means that this account is not based on any reality. Since the "narrative" used by the prosecutor was (if we follow the defense) nothing more than a legal rehash of the political "narrative" used at the time by the Ouattara camp and its French communicators to legitimize their violent seizure of power, this means that, for the judges, this political "narrative" is unfounded. The judges admit this after careful examination of all the elements at their disposal.

If President Gbagbo had also been released, this would have constituted an *urbi et orbi* proclamation by the judges that the French army's intervention was truly a colonial war at the service of particular interests, and that the intervention of UN contingents - for the first time in its history, the UN is taking part in a civil war by siding with one of the competitors - was illegitimate.

The prosecutor immediately appeals the decision. After some heated legal exchanges, the defense once again wins the day. The prosecutor's appeal is rejected.

On January 13, 2014, he filed a new DCC, the fruit of his new investigations. Surprise! The prosecutor had not complied with the judges' instructions, and while he had kept the appearance of the allegations, he had changed their content. As a result, he has largely dropped the charges he made in 2012 and 2013.

On April 4, 2014, the Defense files a 320-page document in response to the prosecutor's DCC entitled *Redacted Public Version of the Second Corrigendum Regarding the Defense's Written Observations on the Prosecutor's Evidence*. It takes up the prosecutor's new argument and, argument by argument, tears it to shreds. After reading the Defence's observations, nothing remains of the Prosecutor's accusations. President Gbagbo's lawyers have done a convincing job. The version available to the public has been redacted. The crunchiest part is hidden. This is the problem with this procedure, which claims to be exemplary, but is not totally transparent. According to all observers, the prosecutor can no longer hope for a frontal victory against President Gbagbo's defense. It is now clear that he has very little chance of winning a trial, should it ultimately take place after a hypothetical, surprising or even improbable confirmation of charges.

Just a few hours after the defense had submitted its observations, the prosecutor was hard at work negotiating with the Ivorian authorities, advised by their French lawyers, to bring Blé Goudé, the former youth leader with an arrest warrant, to The Hague. So far, Fatou Bensouda has not seemed at all interested in Blé Goudé, but perhaps she feels that he is her last card in the Gbagbo case. The request for Blé Goudé's transfer was announced on March 20, 2014, three days after President Gbagbo's Defense had filed its devastating submissions for Fatou Bensouda. Perhaps the prosecutor, reading the observations of President Gbagbo's lawyers, realizes the weakness of his position? He then attempted what looked like a final maneuver: to circumvent President Gbagbo's defense by attacking Blé Goudé. Blé Goudé was a young political activist. He was transferred to the ICC. After, it seems, strong pressure on the Ivorian authorities, who were apparently not enthusiastic. Blé Goudé had been locked up for over a year, without ever seeing his lawyers. The Ivorian authorities were not particularly happy to lift the veil on the abominable conditions in which political prisoners are held. But it was mainly a question of trying to please international criminal justice, to prevent the judges from taking too close an interest in the country's new masters, many of whom are suspected of serious crimes.

"The aim here is to use Blé Goudé as a prosecution witness against the man he defended by mobilizing thousands of young people and taking them to the streets", writes *Jeune Afrique*[46]. An emergency timetable, a lifeline for Bensouda, which suggests the pressure Blé Goudé will be under to perform the service expected of him: bringing down Gbagbo. In Abidjan, some people are talking about Blé Goudé's negotiations - with the Minister of the Interior - and his friendly ties with Wattao. Others have no doubt of his loyalty to Mama's Woody.

In the end, those who believed what they read or heard about Laurent Gbagbo will have to come to terms with it. After four months of deliberation by the three judges of the Pre-Trial Chamber, the grievances presented against him were deemed insufficient, almost non-existent, to risk the decision to open a trial, since the defense had demonstrated that they lacked substance, coherence and consistency, and were not supported by any evidence... The prosecutor appealed against this decision, but it was curtly dismissed. Then, on December 16, 2013, the institution disowned her a second time. The Appeals Chamber, which sanctions the prosecution, is headed by the current President of the ICC, the Korean Song Sang-hyun, leaving the impression of a split between the institution and Fatou Bensouda. The message seems to be: she is her, we are us. As if it were a question of not allowing ourselves to be dragged into her future shipwreck. The foretold "African

---

46N° 2776, March 23-29, 2014.

Nuremberg" turns out to be short-lived. From that moment on, we knew that one or other of the protagonists would be left out in the cold. Prosecutor Fatou Bensouda is well aware of this.

Paradoxically, in its current state of failure, the ICC could draw on the resources to finally raise itself to the level the Rome Treaty had placed it. If only to save itself from disaster, and finally to establish its credibility once and for all. With the transfer of Charles Blé Goudé, it is not moving in this direction.

28

"THEY'LL NEVER CHANGE"

No charges confirmed. Fatou Bensouda is asked to go back to the drawing board. I gauge the extent of the sensation among Gbagbo's opponents when I hear the news by telephone from Jean-Marc Simon. He came to the news and exclaimed: *"No charges, it's not possible!"* without concealing his disappointment. He had been worried about the disagreements between the judges at the end of April, and had told me so on the phone, hoping for a final consensus at the time of their decision. Always very active on the case, he agreed to meet me the first time, knowing that I saw Gbagbo regularly. Over the course of two meetings and several telephone conversations, interspersed with Jean-Marc Simon's frequent trips to Abidjan, he confided in me the wish of his friends, the new masters of Côte d'Ivoire: *"If Gbagbo would just admit that he lost the election! Well, I understand, it's difficult. I think I might be able to plead with Ouattara, who might implicitly agree to Gbagbo's release and exile to a host country, pending his trial. The problem is, I can suggest it to him, but he'll have to talk to Hamed Bakayoko* [the Minister of the Interior], *Guillaume Soro* [the President of the National Assembly], *in whom he has every confidence, Gnenema Coulibaly* [the Minister of Justice], *Blaise Compaoré in Paris…"* There's no need to transcribe Laurent Gbagbo's reaction when I told him about this extravagant idea. He looked up at the ceiling, clasping his hands together, with the apologetic air of one who is underestimated. He sighed:

"They'll never change!"

The ambassador can't believe the turn of events. Like *Jeune Afrique*, the mirror and unofficial cog in the incestuous relationship between France and its former colonies. The change in the balance of power brought about by the defense team in The Hague caught him unawares. Reputedly unfavorable to Laurent Gbagbo, the magazine ran the headline "Présumé coupable" (Presumed Guilty) before the famous February hearing. The prosecutor's office was supposed to crush Gbagbo under an avalanche of irrefutable facts and send him to trial without discussion. This was the dominant leitmotiv at the time, a direct result of the post-electoral crisis, when the media hype was predominantly hostile to Gbagbo. Any different assessment, even if only more nuanced, triggers hysterical or skeptical reactions. Gbagbo's guilt, at that time in Paris, was not debatable. No more so than at the worst moments of the post-electoral crisis, or during the Battle of Abidjan. Periods during which any reservations about the election result immediately put you at odds with the petty princes of the media world. Some, sincere and convinced, feed the general anti-Gbagbo consensus. Most remain closed to any critical examination of French military interference in the crisis. A few are already on the meter. I remember the insults of a colleague working on the management team of the France 24 channel, who went into a kind of hysteria, elegantly accusing me of wanting to *"smoke him out"*, when I was talking to him about information on the incidents that had marked the elections, which I wanted to compare with his sources and his judgement. I saw it as a simple exchange of information between journalists. Of course, I didn't know that in 2012 he would set up a company whose first contract would be to restructure RTI, Radio Télévision Ivoirienne, thanks to his personal links with prominent members of the Ouattara team. We've seen better since. A political journalist from a major weekly, a close friend of Dominique Ouattara, invited and received in Abidjan like a star, with a Mercedes 500 at the airport to take her to a five-star hotel. The Ouattaras know how to attach themselves to the people they need to create an entourage of journalists and celebrities. In fact, a number of French journalists act as advisors, even on the board of the Children Of

Africa Foundation, which includes a former founder and owner of one of France's most cutting-edge weeklies.

Jeune Afrique changes its tune after the June 3 verdict. "CPI l'épine Gbagbo". This time, the title appears in a discreet cartouche at the top of the front page, *minimally* sanctioning Bensouda's slap in the face, and the frustration and anxiety of anti-Gbagbo supporters. On the inside pages, "Le bénéfice du doute" ("The benefit of the doubt") caps a well-documented and well-crafted factual article. An assessment of the damage, which does not rule out the prosecutor's next move in a second round. As Alassane Dramane Ouattara's opponents say, there's no need to despair in "Dramanistan", the nickname given to his regime.

The successive titles of the magazine specializing in Africa, based on the rue d'Auteuil in the 16th arrondissement of Paris, perfectly reflect the changing balance of power in the battle at The Hague. Even when thwarted by events, it remains the best indicator of trends, provided you know how to decipher it by reading it, if possible, upside down in a mirror. For example, on October 27, 2013, the cover of the magazine featured an improbable headline: "Et s'il était libéré?"[47] The result of the shockwave of the previous June 3, as much as of the echoes that subsequently reached the editorial staff about the divisions between the three judges of the Court.

Another red flag for observers: Fatou Bensouda's trip to Abidjan in July 2013. She returned there urgently in search of new elements to prepare her catch-up session. The government in power, winner of the 2010 crisis and Gbagbo's political enemy, which ordered his referral to the ICC, tried to help her find evidence. For the Gambian, a magistrate shaped by her predecessor, this is called an investigation.

It is known that she will not be received by Alassane Ouattara, President of the Republic, nor by Guillaume Soro, President of the National Assembly and former Prime Minister, major players in the post-electoral crisis. She reviewed her copy with the Minister of Justice, Gnenema Coulibaly, and urgently set about enriching it with new testimonies. At the risk of exposing more than questionable evidence, which

---

47. And if he were released?

28. "THEY'LL NEVER CHANGE"

would appear to be as disguised as stolen cars. We still remember the video showing the violent repression of demonstrations… in Kenya… Fatou Bensouda is no longer popular. She has been reduced to hitchhiking. The Rolls-Royce of international justice has broken down.

In Abidjan as elsewhere, doubts have been raised. This allowed the Paris-based African weekly to publish this issue, destined to remain on newsstands for two weeks due to the All Saints' Day long weekend. It's a good commercial operation, because Gbagbo is a "seller", but also a figure imposed by the collapse of the case against Gbagbo at the ICC. It's all about not being caught unawares by events. You can imagine the headaches of the journalists, torn between two imperatives: they had to work together to write precise texts that would not anger Alassane Ouattara, one of the newspaper's shareholders, while at the same time preserving their credibility. A difficult exercise, in which the rue d'Auteuil magazine excels. Like its founder and boss, Béchir Ben Yahmed, who is as much a passionate journalist as a shrewd businessman. Stapled by *Le Canard Enchaîné* for his contracts with Ben Ali's Tunisia, he confirms in his response letter to the satirical weekly that Ouattara's Côte d'Ivoire is one of his generous backers.

Alassane Ouattara has never disguised his links with the press owner: on November 4, 2013, in Paris, in his entrance speech to the Académie des Sciences d'Outre-Mer, Ado saluted Béchir and Danielle Ben Yahmed among his guests, *"who have always been by my side"*, he explained. A perusal of the issues of *Jeune Afrique* covering the period of the electoral campaign, then the post-electoral crisis, attests to this well-deserved friendly tribute.

On that day, Ado also thanked Jean-Marc Simon, his ally and accomplice during the four months of crisis, *"for everything he has done, and continues to do, for Côte d'Ivoire"*, as well as *"[…] my friend and brother the President of Burkina Faso, Blaise Compaoré"*. The "handsome Blaise" is one of the most "sulphurous" heads of state on the black continent. He came to power in a bloody coup on October 15, 1987, during which he was implicated in the assassination of his predecessor and "friend" Thomas Sankara. The latter, fiercely committed to the fight for independence and dignity of his people, one of the poorest in the world, had earned the enmity of the West, and France in particular, through his criticism and uncontrollable Burkinabe revolution. People died for less in Africa in those days. Sankara was dubbed "the man of integrity" when he renamed Upper Volta after its colonial name: Burkina Faso, meaning "the country of men of integrity". The man who abolished ministers' official cars and replaced them with Renault 5s, worked for the emancipation of women, and sought food self-sufficiency for his country to free it from dependence on food, as well as economic and financial dependence. The "African Che" stood up to President Mitterrand during his visit to Ouagadougou, in a bitter-sweet verbal exchange concerning the official visit to France of South African President Pier Willem Botha, the proud champion of apartheid. He succumbed to the return of Jacques Chirac's "Monsieur Françafrique", Jacques Foccart, during the 1986 cohabitation.

Houphouët-Boigny, happy to regain his hold on this neighboring country from which all his immigrant labor comes, will do what it takes, hand in hand with Foccart and his spiritual son Blaise Compaoré, to whom he even introduces the woman who will become his wife.

As soon as he came to power, Compaoré eliminated potential opponents Henri Zongo and Jean-Baptiste Boukari Lingani, who were accused of plotting. Or a journalist, Norbert Zongo, murdered by the presidential guard. Despite the complaint lodged by Sankara's widow, Mariam, and the injunctions of the international community, Compaoré has always refused to investigate the death of his predecessor. In doing so, he has been condemned in principle by the United Nations Human Rights Committee, and given a free hand by the Western powers. Contradiction and paradox are only apparent. His accession to power brought relations between France and Houphouët's Côte d'Ivoire more into line with the wishes of Paris and Abidjan, to the great satisfaction of the West, still in a struggle for influence with the East on the African continent, two years before the fall of the Berlin Wall.

Endorsed by his prestigious sponsors, the President of Burkina has acquired a new stature as a mediator in regional conflicts. In 2006, he led the dialogue between the Togolese government and its opponents, and in 2007, he sponsored the Ouagadougou peace accords between

Laurent Gbagbo and Guillaume Soro. His role in the Ivorian conflict raises burning questions.

Starting with those concerning another assassination, that of Dr. Balla Keita, a brilliant Ivorian minister in Houphouët-Boigny's time, who remains unpunished to this day. A criminal case that is still the talk of Abidjan. The secrecy surrounding the identity of the perpetrators and sponsors is only due to the congenital absence of investigation on the continent. And the fear of speaking out.

In 1987, Dr. Balla Keita - he was a veterinarian - had been asked by Houphouët, France's man in Africa, to help Compaoré overthrow Thomas Sankara, who was considered too Marxist. Balla Keita continued to visit Ouagadougou regularly. In the summer of 2002, when he was informed of the coup d'état being prepared to topple Gbagbo, he learned that the operation was being staged for Alassane Ouattara, a friend of Compaoré, and not for Robert Guéï, his friend, which displeased him. What he disliked even more was Dominique Ouattara, Ado's French wife, whom he had known intimately under Houphouët-Boigny. He considered that this couple had no place at the highest level of the State, and made no secret of it. Former Houphouët caciques remember this, and have told me so. They confide very precise opinions on Balla Keita's disappearance. Or they may hint at what they could reveal about the past of the current holders of power in interviews that are subtly coded for those to whom they are indirectly addressed, when someone is out to get them...

The hard facts: Balla Keita was on his way back to Abidjan to make a splash. He was murdered on August 1, 2002 in a villa in "Ouaga 2000", a private area of the capital of Burkina Faso, guarded 24 hours a day by men-at-arms, with no official details of how the killers got in.

What we do know is that on the following September 19, a military attack launched from Burkina Faso by rebels who had found shelter, training bases and logistics there, swept through Côte d'Ivoire, while President Gbagbo was on an official trip to Rome, killing over 300 people in Abidjan, including Interior Minister Émile Boga Doudou, assassinated by rebels as he tried to flee his home under siege. General Robert Guéï and his wife Rose were also killed in mysterious circumstances.

What do these tragic meanders of African history matter to the venerable academicians gathered around Alassane Ouattara, in this month of November 2013, for his induction among them. Are we not, far from these savage turpitudes, in a very chic 16th arrondissement of Paris, among people of good company? Wasn't Blaise Compaoré re-elected to a fourth term at the head of his country on November 25, 2010, with over 80% of the vote?

Why wasn't I elected with 80% too, after having staged a coup d'état? That's apparently more credible for you in Africa than a democratic score! By the time he'd achieved one of those Soviet scores, in 2003, and while I was scrambling to get out of the Élysée's clutches, Blaise was already threatening me with the ICC. I found it delicious. It's true that he was expressing the secret wishes of his French masters.

Didn't Compaoré receive Ségolène Royal on a visit to Ouagadougou in November 2011, on the occasion of the General Assembly of the International Association of Francophone Regions? *"Mr. Compaoré, a former military coup leader, is not the most reliable man… to advocate democracy and favor civilian power,"* said Louise Arbour, President of the NGO International Crisis. We may not want to trust the judgment of an idealistic woman, allergic to the harsh realities of new countries, where power is snatched away more than it is won, and quite simply of politics, which is, in the words of Stendhal, *"a pistol shot in the middle of a concert"*. More realistically, Charles Pasqua, a connoisseur of the Françafrique of which he was a player, told me over a whisky in his RPF office on November 23, 2012: *"In the Houphouët era, obviously, everything went well. The ones who messed things up were Konan Bédié, out of stupidity, and Compaoré, who always had his eye on Côte d'Ivoire, where many of his compatriots were going to settle. This country has always been envied by its neighbors, and coveted by everyone: and now the Americans are getting in on the act. I think France could have played its card differently. But back home, there aren't any men left to invent a new African policy… and there are new generations of Ivorians, different from those we've known, and that's the Africa we'll have to deal with."* This is how he sums up the origins of the Ivorian tragedy, and the role he attributes to Blaise Compaoré in destabilizing the country of the elephants. After the end of Senegalese President Abdou Diouf's third and final term in office, there is talk of making him the next president of the OIF, the Office international de la francophonie. The ultimate Franco-African prize. Stronger than their dictator's foreign allies, the people of Burkina Faso will exercise their "right of veto" by ousting Compaoré from power on October 31, 2014.

In his speech to the Académie des Sciences d'Outre-Mer, Alassane Ouattara cynically points out that *"… Africa's economic performance coincides with the progression of democracy on the continent, and with the adoption by the African Union… of norms relating to the rejection of coups d'état and any illegal form of seizure of power"*.

This art of ellipsis is characteristic of Ouattara: *"I owe nothing to anyone, except the Ivorians, who elected me"*, he declares with a straight face in the May 29, 2011 edition of *Jeune Afrique*, during his first major interview in his presidential robes. I can still hear Jean-Marc Simon saying to me a year later, although it's not exactly a revelation: *"It's quite simple, we were carrying him at arm's length."*

Yamina Benguigui, then in charge of the French abroad and Francophonie at the Élysée Palace, represents François Hollande at the "pince-fesses" on rue de La Pérouse, headquarters of the Académie des Sciences d'Outre-Mer. Why this minimum service? Her friend, the Franco-Togolese Kofi Yamgnane, former Secretary of State for Integration under François Mitterrand, had, among other things, alerted François Hollande to the realities and risks of the Gbagbo case. He wrote him a note. As did Jean-Pierre Mignard, one of Ouattara's advisors in The Hague, a prominent member of the Socialist Party and close to President François Hollande: he is the godfather of his sons. Jean-Paul Benoit, the other lawyer for the current Ivorian government at the ICC, who is also close to Hollande, keeps the President informed of the case. An observer mandated by the French embassy attended the confirmation of charges hearing in February 2013, as well as all the important hearings. Nicolas Sarkozy wove the fabric of this story, and François Hollande probably didn't want to add a knot to it. At this stage of the trial, Gbagbo is not dreaming:

I'm not one of Hollande's priorities; I'm sure he was perfectly informed about the dossier. It was up to him to judge.

A cautious François Hollande delayed his visit to Côte d'Ivoire. In a sign of destiny, his first trip to Abidjan, scheduled for February 28, 2013, was cancelled due to Alassane Ouattara's surgery at the Percy hospital in Clamart, on the outskirts of Paris. A military establishment where Palestinian leader Yasser Arafat, but also former Prime Minister Pierre Mauroy, underwent surgery, received treatment and died. He is well aware that a favorable outcome for Gbagbo in the Hague court case would put France in an awkward position, as the international community's lead nation in this affair.

29

"AN OPERATION LIKE THIS ONE CANNOT BE IMPROVISES"

The Prosecutor's team's defeat came as a surprise to Laurent Gbagbo's opponents, who had come to believe in the Court's infallibility and professionalism, and in the message that the Prosecutor was circulating, via the media, about the damning evidence he claimed to possess.

The charges were narrowly overturned. This would have meant the immediate release of Laurent Gbagbo, in the spring of 2013. The French Foreign Minister's office closely followed the proceedings in The Hague. Laurent Fabius even went there just after the confirmation of charges hearing, to discuss with the ambassador - on the pretext that the French embassy was moving - the progress of the case. According to our sources, in the final days before the judges deliver their verdict, the Minister's office is busy trying to work out what the decision might be. The effect on French diplomats produced by the defense's demonstrations has been such that they are now convinced of the victory of Emmanuel Altit's team and the imminent exit of President Gbagbo.

French diplomats feared the judges' decision. On June 3, their fears were confirmed: the judges were divided. On one side, the German judge and the Belgian judge; on the other, the Argentine judge, who was Moreno Ocampo's right-hand man for three years and who, as a result, might have a favorable bias towards the prosecutor. Even so, the fate of the Court's most important defendant is at stake. The Court's credibility is at stake here. So anything is possible.

To release President Gbagbo is to admit that the prosecutor was wrong.

On June 3, 2013, while the judges attempted to "save" the prosecutor, they nevertheless acknowledged his defeat and his inability to present any evidence in support of his charges. As these charges are exactly the same as those brought against President Gbagbo by the pro-Ouattara side at the time of the post-election crisis, it is interesting to return to the four main incidents alleged against President Gbagbo by the prosecutor, who claims that it is possible to see crimes against Humanity in them. On June 3, 2013, the judges ruled that the prosecutor had not provided any evidence to support his account of these four incidents. For the judges, therefore, there were no crimes against humanity. Better still, the defense's deconstruction of the prosecutor's narrative allowed the truth about the four incidents to emerge. And what do they reveal? Repeated attempts over ten years by the Ouattara camp, backed by the French authorities, to seize power by force, and the fabrication of evidence designed to build a discourse that could be sold to the international media. An illustration of the large-scale manipulation of recent conflicts.

1) The march on RTI

The prosecutor alleges that, on December 16, 2010, a few days after the second round of the presidential elections, the security forces, supported by militiamen and mercenaries, suppressed a peaceful demonstration organized by pro-Ouattara supporters, in order to prevent the demonstrators from reaching the RTI by using violence. The defense demonstrated that, far from being a peaceful march, the demonstration itself was organized as follows: in the front row were women and children; at the heart of the demonstration were men armed with Kalashnikovs and RPGs. President Gbagbo's lawyers have released images that leave no room for doubt. The pro-Ouattara fighters taking part in the demonstration belonged, according to the Defense Department, to groups that had infiltrated Abidjan before the presidential elections. During the December 16 demonstration, they were accompanied and supported by groups of "militants", often thugs, armed with machetes and other edged weapons. The Defense showed *"that the so-called peaceful demonstration of December 16, 2010 was in reality a carefully planned violent attempt to seize power. On December 16, 2010, armed groups simultaneously attacked surprised police officers in Abobo, a powerful attack was launched from the Hôtel du Golf by rebel soldiers, and armed fighters attacked security forces within the general demonstration."* The defense has backed up its case with irrefutable evidence, including videos showing pro-Ouattara leaders, foremost among them Soro, on December 15, 2010, preparing for the following day's assault by exhorting the courage of rebel soldiers armed to the teeth.

First observation: during the proceedings, the prosecutor refrained from discussing the evidence presented by the defense. In its pleadings, the Defense stressed that this evidence *"radically challenges the Prosecutor's theory, which he repeats in his DCC, that 'the demonstration of December 16, 2010 was organized to take place peacefully and the demonstrators were not armed'. This lack of questioning on the part of the prosecutor is all the more surprising as it reveals not only a total absence of investigation into this specific event, contrary to the Chamber's instructions, but also a refusal to take reality into account, preferring instead a purely political narrative. It is worth noting here the prosecutor's reiterated refusal to investigate on his own behalf, or even to consider exculpatory evidence."*

Secondly, the attacks carried out by rebel forces on December 16, 2010 were clearly an attempt by the Ouattara camp to seize power violently. The aim was to attack not only the RTI, but also the primature and the presidency. Even more interesting is the *modus operandi:* the initiators of the offensive are going to disguise the attack as a peaceful march, and use the incidents they instigate to their advantage to denounce the brutality of the forces of law and order. And that's easy. The police and gendarmerie do not expect such brutal attacks from such professional and well-armed groups. The dead are numerous in the ranks of the forces of order. They retaliate. But the rebels involved are dressed in civilian clothes. The Ouattara camp's communicators had no problem claiming that the forces of law and order had attacked civilians. The communicators even seem to "recuperate" the civilians killed by the rebels during these days to transform them into victims of the forces of order.

2) Women's demonstration in Abobo on March 3, 2011

According to the prosecutor, "*on March 3, 2011, security forces loyal to Mr. Gbagbo used heavy weapons against a group of around 3,000 women who were peacefully demonstrating in Abobo against human rights violations and demanding Mr. Gbagbo's departure. As a result of this attack, seven women were killed and several others seriously injured*".

Firstly, the defense has shown that the prosecutor's information was probably false. At the time, there were no longer any law enforcement forces in the area; the presence of armored vehicles that would have reached the precise location of the demonstration is unlikely; not only did the heads of the security forces have no knowledge of any demonstration that was about to take place or was in the process of taking place, but they were only informed of the alleged incidents *after the fact*, following communiqués from the rebels.

Secondly, the Defense Department highlighted the fact that the demonstration was not spontaneous, but had, on the contrary, been carefully prepared, since cameramen had been positioned at the scene by the rebels. On the other hand, the rebels had been careful not to warn Western journalists. There was no reason for the demonstration to be held at this location, i.e. close to the main road running from east to west through Abobo, over which, once every two or three days, two or three vehicles rushed to supply police officers or soldiers besieged by the rebels a few kilometers away. The idea of staging then emerged, reinforced by the fact that the evidence presented by the prosecutor in support of his accusations was suspect. First of all, there are the videos, which turn out to have been edited. They even show a supposedly dead woman getting up again. Secondly, the videos do not appear to show an actual attack. Above all, the defense has demonstrated that none of the elements presented by the prosecutor to support the theory that people were killed on this occasion were credible. They even appear to have been fabricated.

3) The bombing of the Abobo market

"*According to the prosecutor, on March 17, 2011, several mortar shells were purposely fired from the Commando Camp, aimed at civilian targets in a densely populated area of Abobo.*"

Firstly, the defense has demonstrated that the prosecutor was unable to identify the areas affected, to prove mortar bombardment, and to determine its origin and reasons. Here again, it seems that government military officials had no knowledge of any such bombardment.

Secondly, the prosecutor relies on witnesses *"recruited by the Ouattara camp"*. In addition, the defense has also demonstrated that the evidence of deaths appears to have been fabricated.

4) On the events in Yopougon on April 12, 2011

"The prosecutor claims that on April 12, 2011, 'pro-Gbagbo forces' attacked people from the north of the country in the Yopougon district. Nevertheless, it is striking to note that the prosecutor is now much more vague than in his previous DCC, since he no longer speaks of April 12, 2011 precisely, but now indicates 'on or around April 12, 2011'."

First observation: the defense has pointed out that the prosecutor is incapable of specifying the date, place and perpetrators of the incidents he claims to have occurred. Not only has the Prosecutor been unable to provide these basic details for two years, but, according to the Defense, he has also accentuated the vagueness of his accusations.

Secondly, it seems clear that the accusations here are far too vague to be sustained, especially as President Gbagbo was arrested by French forces on April 11. So what's the point? Probably to conceal the fact that, at the same time in the Yopougon district, rebel soldiers, some from Abobo and others from the north of the country with the help of French forces, were attacking civilians. Hundreds were reported missing. Men, women and children were terrorized.

Some of the events put forward by the prosecution may even have been set up during the post-electoral crisis as traps to expose Gbagbo to sanctions. On December 16, 2010, the day of the demonstration, ICC Prosecutor Luis Moreno Ocampo warned that he would prosecute anyone responsible for deadly violence in Côte d'Ivoire. Two days earlier, on December 14, while rebel leaders were in the midst of preparations for the attack scheduled for December 16, Ouattara sent a letter to the ICC judges and prosecutor via his lawyers, in which he acknowledged the Court's jurisdiction over possible incidents. What incidents? The *"incidents"* referred to in the letter are logically those that the rebels know will occur on December 16, during the attacks they are about to launch. In this way, the premeditation is signed and the guilt of those behind the incidents is recognized in advance. Isn't this a Machiavellian scenario? Everyone believed, or acted as if they believed, that President Gbagbo was behind the incidents. On the evening of December 16, 2010, the Security Council warned those responsible for attacks against civilians that they would be held accountable for their actions and "brought to justice". The Council is targeting President Gbagbo's government. From that moment on, the government was outlawed.

In the same spirit, the alleged bombardment of civilian populations by government military officials, even though it appeared extremely dubious - even at the time - was immediately blown out of proportion by the French authorities to convince the members of the Security Council to vote in favor of resolution 1975 authorizing the use of force. The ink had not yet dried on this resolution when the rebel armies, made up - as Defense has shown - of foreign mercenaries, notably from Burkina Faso, poured into the south of the country. They had been waiting impatiently, equipped and organized by the French army, which took matters into its own hands and paved the way for the rebel groups. Problem: on their way to Abidjan, these rebels were guilty of numerous massacres and serious human rights violations.

A final word on the usefulness of damning President Gbagbo and his government. It is widely acknowledged that the rebels have committed numerous massacres. So, evoking the alleged massacres on the other side of the conflict certainly helps to conceal this reality, which is highly embarrassing for those who supported and armed the rebels, first and foremost France. But it also serves to conceal the fact that the French military intervention was brutal, with French helicopters attacking Ivorian security forces' bases and support points, and destroying their weapons. These attacks probably led to the deaths of many Ivorian soldiers, as well as civilians. And the attacks carried out by French forces in recent days against President Gbagbo's residence have resulted in numerous civilian deaths. The more we accuse President Gbagbo, the more we hope to conceal this other reality, which could give rise to proceedings against the

French military and a debate in the French Parliament. If justice were to fulfill the mission assigned to it by the Constitution.

Who, on the French side, gave the order to launch the attack from north to south in March 2011? Rebel troops and thousands of Dozos, traditional hunters imbued with magical beliefs, who are particularly cruel to the population, were on the move along the demarcation line between the north and south of the country. Their general and final assault on Abidjan was obviously premeditated and carefully planned. Gbagbo comments:

> **Such an operation cannot be improvised. It was carried out throughout by Burkina Faso's Régiment pour la Sécurité Présidentielle, attached to its then president, Blaise Compaoré. Its leader, General Djengélé, directed the maneuver, following the route of the railroad from Burkina Faso to southern Côte d'Ivoire. All along this route, in every town and village, there were caches of weapons.**

Who gave the order to launch the attack? What is certain is that the operation was prepared months beforehand: the appointment of General Emmanuel Beth as ambassador to Burkina Faso is a clear sign of this. His brother, Frédéric Beth, was head of the Special Operations Command Center. And it was the men of the COS who found themselves on the front line at every stage of the offensive. As for the rebel troops, they were made up of mercenaries recruited and armed in Burkina Faso, then sent to Côte d'Ivoire. Who paid for their weapons? Who trained them? Who organized them? All this time, President Compaoré has been working tirelessly in the service of his "brother" Ouattara.

This dossier is not the fruit of a genuine investigation, explained Emmanuel Altit to the Court, but a collection of second-hand documents, communicated by the Ivorian authorities, press cuttings and NGO reports, without any formal proof. During the post-electoral crisis, and even afterwards, Luis Moreno Ocampo never made contact with Gbagbo and his followers, and only worked with the prosecution, in constant contact with Alassane Ouattara's team. Some of Gbagbo's supporters may see no merit in the Altit team's reversal of the balance of power, so convinced are they that the reasons for their hero's appearance before the ICC judges are not criminal, but merely political. A fitting counterpart to Gbagbo's enemies, who had condemned him in advance. For diametrically opposed reasons, both sides paid little heed to the Hague trial. In a way, critical opponents and supporters of the ICC have taken the same shortcut: they minimize the importance of the battle being waged there. Whatever the inanity, for the former, or the merits for the latter, of what was conceived by the international community as a great sacrificial ceremony, celebrated by the high priestess Bensouda. However, the miscreants of the Defense had to put up their shields, confront and foil the traps, and fight this unequal battle.

30.
THE ABIDJANESE

Laurent Gbagbo's release has been the order of the day, since the confirmation of charges hearing held in February 2013 and especially since the Defense filed its observations on the Prosecution's evidence in April 2014, which totally destroy the Prosecution's case. In legal terms, the Defense has gained the upper hand over the prosecution. It confirmed this advantage with the filing of its final submissions in April 2014, proving once again that Laurent Gbagbo is guilty only of having continued to exercise power even though the Constitutional Council had proclaimed him President of the Republic. The judges undoubtedly foresaw for the prosecutor the risk of a formal trial: that of a rout, proportional to the symbolic dimension of the Gbagbo case, dragging the entire institution down with it. Health reasons could also provide the ICC with an opportunity to release Laurent Gbagbo without denying itself.

A trial would be all the more risky given that Emmanuel Altit's team made full use of the preliminary phase of the confirmation of charges, prior to the trial proper, to destroy the prosecutor's evidence without revealing their own trump cards. Fatou Bensouda has shown not only the poverty of her game, but also her mediocrity in strategy. The defense lawyers are now in a position of strength and can look to the future with equanimity. In these conditions, many believe that the institution would have everything to lose from a trial. A trial that would give the defense the opportunity to continue to play its cards close to the vest and reveal a truth that no one wants to hear, especially not the supporters of

Francafrique. Not only would the prosecutor risk being discredited, but the Court itself would be weakened.

Does this mean that no one is giving the prosecutor in The Hague any more credit? And that the prisoner is expected to be released? In Abidjan, but also throughout France and the rest of the world, Gbagbo's supporters took the plunge a long time ago. They believe in the innocence and inevitable release of Mama's Woody. Sometimes naively, they have rushed to the Netherlands, almost hoping to bring back their hero, freed at last! Norias of buses, private cars, groups coming by plane or train, flock to The Hague for each important hearing, without faltering over the months, and now, years. In December 2011, on the outskirts of the court's white concrete and glass building, they sang the Ivorian anthem, "L'Abidjanaise", at the end of Gbagbo's speech. In February 2013, during the confirmation of charges hearing, hundreds of them stood transfixed as their President appeared on a touch-screen tablet, wearing small round glasses and a blue suit. They had not seen him since his incarceration in the Netherlands, except once on the Internet, on December 5, 2011, when he was presented to his judges. One of Gbagbo's relatives, admitted to the courtroom, managed to send the images from his cell phone. Immediate delirium across the street, around the magic screen. Chants, tamtam, with the only slogan: *"Free Gbagbo"*.

In Côte d'Ivoire too, this popular incantation has become the watchword of Laurent Gbagbo's FPI party, and the core of its program.

Even if the release of the 800 or so political prisoners still being held in Ivorian jails for their opinions is their daily demand, expressed collectively by many Ivorian intellectuals - *Le Monde* of December 25 and 26, 2013 published one of their appeals - it's the release and return of the leader that the FPI caciques are hanging their hat on. Pascal Affi N'Guessan, who leads the FPI in its battle on the ground, is mobilizing crowds around this theme, with impressive popular success. The people are there, present, communing all over the country. The FPI leader's recent tour in February 2014 demonstrated by its success that the Ivorians who voted Gbagbo out in 2010 are still very much behind him. For them, his return is the only remedy for the collective humiliation suffered in 2010. Like a first revenge on fate, since the fall, imprisonment and deportation to The Hague of their President. It's a sentimental posture that suits the current government, which has yet to come up with a program for change and recovery. Some, such as Mamadou Koulibaly, author of *La guerre de la France contre la Côte d'Ivoire (France's war against Côte d'Ivoire)*, are worried. On the outs with the FPI, from which he was expelled, he is a staunch opponent of the Ouattara regime, to the point of calling for him and Guillaume Soro to be brought before the ICC, since he accepted the defeat of his own camp, that of Gbagbo: *"I've always supported Laurent Gbagbo, even if I didn't think it was necessary to go through the Marcoussis and Kléber forks in 2003: we entered a tunnel prepared to take us to where we are now. We have to look to the future. I was in favor of Laurent Gbagbo accepting the objective failure of our strategy, which would have enabled us to regain power in the next legislative elections. This would have enabled us to regain power in the next legislative elections, to put democracy on a permanent footing."*

It's not certain that a regime armed with men in arms would have respected such rules of the game: the 2010 elections proved the point. Mamadou Koulibaly has set up his own party, LIDER (Liberté et Démocratie pour la République), with a view to standing in the 2015 presidential election. He believes that the policy of the empty chair, or one occupied only by the shadow cast by the great absentee, is absurd, and that it opens up complicit opportunities for easy electoral success for Ouattara and his ilk. This is one of the reasons why he and his former FPI friends disagree.

Some are relying on the miracle of a return - one journalist wrote that it would be a greater popular event than if Didier Drogba brought the Football World Cup back to Abidjan - others remain paralyzed by the wait. Mamadou Koulibaly is regularly attacked and even insulted by his former political friends. The Scheveningen detainee's political clout is such that it condemns his supporters to find an answer to the dilemma between a strategy that reconciles magical thinking, mixed with nostalgia and sentiment, and dynamic action. Even if the latter must also take into account the uncertainties and possible surprises linked to the forthcoming decisions of the ICC, or Ouattara's health.

31

"THE AMBASSADOR WAS MORE OF A BEARD THAN A DIPLOMAT"

"Exactly 13 hours and 8 minutes." I owe this chronometric precision to the care taken by the French ambassador to record this historic moment: the brutal assault by French special forces on Laurent Gbagbo's residence. Jean-Marc Simon gives me this indication as proof of his mastery of maneuvers. It has to be said that he had an unobstructed view of the Ivorian presidential residence, adjacent to his own, and next door to those of the President of the National Assembly and the Apostolic Nuncio. Wasn't the fall of Gbagbo also, for the man who ordered it, his personal consecration?

Ambassador Simon was more of a barbouze than a diplomat. The Hôtel du Golf was regularly visited by French military and political advisors, Ouattara's French communicators in charge of manipulating the international press, and the chief organizer of these maneuvers, Jean-Marc Simon, the French ambassador.

Elevated a year later, for services rendered, to the rare and envied rank of French ambassador for life, Jean-Marc Simon gained not only the honors of the French Republic, but also the assurance of a golden life. The zealous diplomat, who had already distinguished himself in the Central African Republic by working to overthrow President Ange-Félix Patassé in favor of François Bozizé between 2001 and 2003, was gratified by the recognition of the new Ivorian power in the form of contracts through his company "Eurafrique Stratégies", created just after the events, at the time of his retirement. Alassane Ouattara gives him an arm's length *"mon ami Jean-Marc"*, in public, on all occasions. It's the least we can do to thank the man who, with his ear glued to his cell phone, permanently connected to Nicolas Sarkozy at the Élysée Palace, and to Alassane Ouattara and Guillaume Soro in Abidjan, managed the ultimate end of the battle around Gbagbo's residence in April 2011. Désiré Tagro, Secretary General of the Ivorian Presidency and former Minister of the Interior, is no longer with us to recount what the French diplomat said to him on the phone just before Tagro was killed by the rebels. Others have heard his last exchanges. Gbagbo's advisor, to whom Jean-Marc Simon was the last to speak, had in any case been sufficiently reassured by the ambassador to go out, white flag in hand, to organize the surrender of those who had taken refuge in the residence. The rebels immediately seized him and shot him in the mouth, pulverizing his jaw. He died a few hours after his capture, at the Hôtel du Golf, the political and military headquarters of Ouattara and his men. He would have been finished off there.

Yes, Jean-Marc Simon led the assault on Gbagbo's besieged residence, which the rebel army failed to bring down. He told me about it as a career highlight, between a glass of white Sancerre and a bite of salmon at Berkeley, the trendy restaurant where he has his napkin ring, in the Champs-Élysées district. A former den of spies, it seems. Michou has often been seen there with his court over a bottle of champagne. It's always full of businessmen, celebrities and beautiful women.

"It was like a hunt… a bullfight. First we tired the beast out, with political, economic and then military pressure, before the kill… the estocade," he says. *"I spent my time on the phone with com'zone Koné Zakaria, with Guillaume Soro, with Ouattara, and with the Élysée Palace, directing operations."* He continues ironically: *"While we were bombing them, you could hear bursts of Alleluias, songs and prayers. They probably thought the heavens were coming to save them… when in fact they were falling on their heads."*

The unanimity of Western opinion on the legitimacy of the action against Gbagbo, and the certainty of holding a monopoly on information, has long made it possible to say anything, and above all anything at all, without risk. Starting with Nicolas Sarkozy's solemn speech in Saint-Dizier affirming France's non-interference in Côte d'Ivoire. An astonishing assertion. Firstly, because the French army has been weighing heavily on the political affairs of Côte d'Ivoire for decades (the Licorne contingent will increase from 900 men to almost double that number in 2011), and secondly, because the decision to mobilize it against Gbagbo had apparently already been taken by then, if we are to believe Robert Bourgi and the authorized sources I revealed earlier. The words of politicians carry no weight: they blow in the wind like dead leaves. In Pretoria on February 28, 2008, Sarkozy announced that the withdrawal of the French army from the African continent could be envisaged. Two years later, he was preparing a military assault on President Gbagbo's government forces; three years later, he launched the Licorne force to attack government positions.

Invited to speak on Radio France International on April 11, 2012, Jean-Marc Simon also safely contradicted the promise he had made in confidence to a French woman in Abidjan during a private interview in his embassy office.

Firstly, in response to the question about the role of the French army in the final hours of the battle for Abidjan, he persists in a diplomatic tongue-in-cheek approach which, in the light of the facts, images and eyewitness accounts, rings hollow: *"French tanks enabled the FRCI to advance and penetrate Laurent Gbagbo's residence"*, he says. He denies that the Licorne force itself entered the compound. Video images show that the first attackers were white soldiers. Probably special forces. Sidiki Bakaba, filmmaker, director, actor, director of the Palais de la Culture in Abidjan, and author of the documentary *"La victoire aux mains nues" (Victory with Bare Hands)* celebrating Ivorian resistance to rebel and French aggression, told me he saw French Special Forces soldiers all around him inside the residence after the assault on April 11, 2011. Sidiki Bakaba had been wounded the day before by a rocket fired from a French helicopter as he filmed it firing on the defenders and civilians inside the residence. On April 11, in the rubble of the residence, he had been beaten and stabbed by the rebels who had entered the premises following the French commandos. Sidiki was a great artist, a Muslim from the North, like many of those who were with President Gbagbo in his final moments. But that doesn't stop Ouattara's French communicators from claiming that this was an ethnic and religious war. His account is all the more reliable in that Sidiki owes his life to other French soldiers who, just as the rebels were about to slit his throat, intervened and exfiltrated him to hospital. *"That's why I never wanted to go to trial,"* he says. Other civilians arrested in the presidential residence were summarily executed a little further on by the rebels.

"But couldn't the pro-Gbagbo forces overlooking the Plateau hill have fired on the French tanks?" the RFI journalist asks the diplomat.

"Of course they could have. They didn't," concedes the diplomat. *"The column was able to advance without difficulty."*

What Jean-Marc Simon is careful not to mention is that President Gbagbo had given the order to cease all fighting for several days, in order to spare human lives. At no time were government forces given instructions to attack or counter-attack. At no time were they authorized to fire on French and UN soldiers. Their instructions were clear: to protect the civilian population.

"Eye to eye, I can swear to you that a French bullet will never hit an Ivorian, unless of course, we are attacked", the ambassador told Liliana Lombardo, a French resident and Simone Gbagbo's rock. This was in March 2011, barely a month before the French army stormed Gbagbo's residence, under the pretext of *"destroying heavy weapons that threatened the civilian population [...] a decision taken at the highest level, naturally, by Nicolas Sarkozy himself"*, Simon finally confided to his interlocutor.

There were no heavy weapons at the residence.

"There were hundreds of people, civilians, especially young people, who had come to take refuge on the lawns of the residence, and on the road leading to it, to protect Gbagbo. When I was arrested and taken away on April 11, I saw hundreds of bodies of these people lying dead, killed by French bombing, or after their arrest, by the rebels, after Gbagbo's surrender", explains Sidiki Bakaba, who now lives in France... We'll never know the number.

32

WHEN ROLAND DUMAS
FORCED VERGÈS

Two old political stars from the Paris Bar, Roland Dumas and Jacques Vergès, may have landed in Abidjan to offer Laurent Gbagbo support that was more spectacular than effective, but on the eve of 2011, public opinion saw it as nothing more than a media operation. The result was two well-paid old lawyers. Roland Dumas imposes Vergès.

He had fallen out of favor with Laurent Gbagbo after visiting Guitrozon and Petit Duékoué in 2005, at the government's request, where massacres took place between May 31st and June 1st. A butchery: huts and houses burnt down with their inhabitants, heads split open with machetes, women raped and disemboweled, children shot at point-blank range or killed with knives. An identical repetition of the extermination that was to take place in the same village in March 2011, during the rebel advance. Just 500 meters from a camp belonging to the French Licorne contingent, and the UNOCI troop camp.

Not enough horrors, no doubt... or is it the unconscious ulterior motive that the mass death of human beings in certain regions is a matter of custom? Is it a seasonal fatality? Insufficient to achieve, by our standards, the exemplarity that elevates it to the rank of universal drama?

In the Kivu province of Congo, for example, hundreds of thousands of people have died since 1999, and more are still dying. Nearly 1.5 million refugees have been forced into exile, without making much of a fuss...

Have the famines of Biafra and the massacres of Rwanda exhausted our capacity for interest and compassion for Africa? Have they acclimatized us to the fate that dictates that people there die like flies rather than here? Or would a scrupulous examination of the reasons that created the favorable context for the fatalities of this African hell, after more than a century of overt colonialism, then total dependence, send us back to our own share of responsibility?

Vergès had approached the Ivorians through Captain B., who had introduced him to Désiré Tagro, former Minister of the Interior, at the Brussels Hilton. They had discussed the case of the families of the murdered victims with an Ivorian lawyer, Micheline Bamba. Vergès was tasked with defending the families in collaboration with the government's legal department. He was to work with Maître Bamba. The fact that Vergès had been in Ouattara's entourage a few years earlier does not seem to have bothered the Ivorian leaders.

Jacques Vergès received a deposit of 150,000 euros and Roland Dumas 67,200 euros from the Ivorian government. When, as agreed, Maître Micheline Bamba asked Vergès for an advance of 3 million CFA francs (less than 5,000 euros) to start work on site, Vergès refused outright. He never followed through. As a result, he was dismissed by a simple letter on July 22.

Gbagbo was astonished by the attitude of the French lawyer who had let him down en route, but did not object to his return to Abidjan at the end of 2010, in the midst of the post-election earthquake. Roland Dumas vouched for his colleague. Is he aware that, in 2005, Dumas and Vergès had asked for a substantial provision when what they had proposed to do was simply to assess the situation at the time and raise media awareness? But Laurent Gbagbo is like that. He was too lenient, people around him say. Indulgent with Vergès and Dumas, as with many French politicians who benefited from his generous hospitality but never returned the favor, indulgent with some of those around him. President Gbagbo is an intellectual and a statesman. Someone who outlines political action, explains its ins and outs, but doesn't indulge in backroom contingencies. The President delegates, trusts and relies on the competence and integrity of government and administrative officials. Unlike his peers, he never meddles in the day-to-day intrigues of the court, nor does he play into the hands of factions. But that's where the dirty tricks come from…

The only fruit of the operation to publicize the tragic events at Duékoué in 2005 was a small book published by Editions Pharos, *Crimes contre l'Humanité*, co-written by Roland Dumas and Jacques Vergès… who didn't write a single line. The company Mondio-Phonie-Médias, also commissioned to communicate the massacres abroad and archive the evidence, wrote the book for them.

In 2011, the action of the two "old-timers" will have had no effect at all, and will even have run counter to the objectives pursued. A few television appearances on their return to Paris will not have made the expedition of the two old lawyers any more useful to the cause defended. At least they had the merit of challenging the one-size-fits-all discourse propagated by official circles.

Roland Dumas, in particular, tried to stem the tide as former President of the French Constitutional Council and Minister of Foreign Affairs. His sincerity is indisputable. As early as 2002, he lent his support to Laurent Gbagbo. Along with Henri Emmanuelli, he was one of the first and only people at the time to express his solidarity with the President.

He congratulated Mamadou Koulibaly in January 2003, when the latter slammed the door on the Marcoussis conference to mark his disagreement with the trusteeship of Côte d'Ivoire's future. Through the same Koulibaly, Dumas advised Gbagbo before the Marcoussis Round Table not to come to Paris to sign agreements imposed on him. The two men used the same phrase to tell me: *"By coming, Gbagbo was entering a tunnel. He was never able to get out."*

At the start of 2011, Roland Dumas will deploy his experience and oratory talents. Vergès will play the provocateur, that's what he's there for. But he'll overdo it. It will be his last stunt. The two old pals seem to be having a bit too much fun *"making a mess"*, as they put it, in one last big show of strength… They will co-sign and publish a *White Paper*. All for naught. The anti-Gbagbo machine was launched, and has been rolling at high speed ever since… Jacques Vergès, that fierce anti-colonialist, will have realized this before he died, in August 2013.

33

"YESTERDAY IS NOT SO FAR BACK"

Côte d'Ivoire disappeared from view as if nothing had happened there. As if everything had been said. As if the media had written the story. Madame Ouattara charters expensive planes full of VIPs invited to charity galas in Abidjan, Ado nurses his health problems, Interior Minister Hamed Bakayoko, once known in Paris thanks to a nightclub called "L'Alizée" in the 15th arrondissement, and Guillaume Soro, the regime's No.2, stare at each other, finger on the trigger.

After the tragedy, life goes on in the land of elephants, where none of the issues that divide Ivorians have yet been resolved. Many of Gbagbo's supporters are in prison, others in exile, and those who fled the country are now afraid to return. Their homes and possessions have been seized by rebels.

As a result, Washington is critical of and cautious about the regime of Alassane Ouattara, its former champion. This despite a growth rate announced at over 8%[48], due to the return of investors after ten years of war and partition of the country in two. Impoverishing growth: *"money works but doesn't circulate"*, Ouattara ironizes. In truth, as Ahoua Don Mello explains, this is a fictitious growth rate: *"Côte d'Ivoire is an agricultural country. However, this sector has only grown by 0.2% of the announced GDP, and the rural population has increased, hence the rise in rural poverty. Growth is concentrated solely in the construction sector, and artificially at*

---

48. Growth rate of 9.8% according to Mamadou Koulibaly at May 31, 2014.

that. The 3rd bridge project in Abidjan cost 60 million euros under Laurent Gbagbo, but 180 million euros under Ouattara. The real economy is in free-fall: cocoa production fell by 10% in 2012, oil and gas plummeted by 22%. Why is this? Not because there's less cocoa, or less oil and gas. Only because all these raw materials are stolen, diverted and sold 'on the black market'."

In any case, the officially stated growth does not avoid borrowing 75 billion CFA francs (114 million euros) from the European Union, asking France to cancel its debt and, even more surprisingly, borrowing 100 billion CFA francs (152 million euros) from Congo-Brazzaville, as revealed by *Jeune Afrique* on October 27, 2013. France has urgently released over 400 million euros to cover civil servants' salaries and the running of the state. Since his arrival, Ado has been looking for 15 billion, and spends more time in Paris, at his Mougins residence, or on his plane than in Côte d'Ivoire. The sheer cost of these trips, with all the accompanying state support, in difficult times, seems ill-suited to the situation, when the population is tightening its belt. To ensure that the country's wealth is not squandered by others, Alassane Ouattara has taken care to place the Ministry of Mines under his control: the nerve of war, the vault of power.

For the past three years, Laurent Gbagbo has been deprived of public speaking engagements since his arrest in Abidjan on April 11, 2011, and his detention in Korhogo, in the north of the country. He has confided in no one, except his lawyers and two or three friends admitted to see him in The Hague prison after his transfer to the ICC. Some thought they could take advantage of his absence from the public scene, and his inability to communicate, to claim to have received a few confidences from him - even though they have never seen or spoken to him - and to add to this or that book. Indirect statements, spread by intermediaries, or outright fabrications. Côte d'Ivoire deserves better than this kind of mishmash of charlatanism and journalistic onanism. It was therefore necessary to know how Laurent Gbagbo, who has become the hero of African emancipation, speaks and spoke. In Paris, people in high places now know that things are going "badly" in The Hague, and, according to Jean-Christophe Notin, who is still in touch with some of his eminent informants, that everything could "blow up again", in the event of Alassane Ouattara's sudden disappearance or obliteration. The recent announcement of his illness and operation has sent his supporters into a tizzy. Requests for visas flooded in, foreshadowing a massive flight abroad in the event of misfortune. The death of Alassane Ouattara would put the tragic struggle for power back in Abidjan, where it began with the death of Houphouët-Boigny in 1993. An unfortunate prognosis, given that each of the protagonists still has his own armed militia. The importation of tens of thousands of people to the North, to ensure victory in the forthcoming 2015 presidential elections and reverse the balance of power with the South, is viewed with concern by specialists. Barely two years after the "victory of democracy" with missiles, Côte d'Ivoire has once again become what Nicolas Sarkozy and the international community made of it: a time bomb.

Laurent Gbagbo, the president who relied on his own strength, did not see this conjunction of powers united against him coming. His traditional tête-à-tête with France was skilfully transformed by President Sarkozy and his cohorts into a face-off between the African president and the international community in 2010. Faced with the political, diplomatic, financial and military war machine mobilized by the French authorities, he found himself almost alone, and virtually unarmed, until the fatal outcome… The great African voices of the last fifty years are no more: Nasser, Sékou Touré, Thomas Sankara, Patrice Lumumba and Nelson Mandela are all gone. The West fought them all. Or scorned them, like Senegalese President Léopold Senghor, poet and servant of the French language, buried in the absence of French President Jacques Chirac and Prime Minister Lionel Jospin in December 2001. A former adviser to Mitterrand, Erik Orsenna wrote an article on the subject in *Le Monde* on January 5, 2002, entitled "J'ai honte" ("I'm ashamed").

Throughout his life, Laurent Gbagbo has made his voice heard beyond the prison walls in which he has often been confined. In 1972, already incarcerated for political reasons in a military camp in the north of Côte d'Ivoire, he wrote in a play, *Le Lion du Manding*[49], these verses which are still ringing in the ears of Africans today:

---

49. Quoted by Guy Labertit, *Abidjan-sur-Seine, op. cit.* according to griot Mamadou Kouyaté, "passer de légende".

"The world is unhappy
But yesterday is not far off
And tomorrow is deep
Of hopeful depth
Listen to my word: it only knows how to move forward
Listen to my word: history is truth."

ODDS AND ENDS

Speaking in May 2018 about the International Criminal Court, of which he is one of the eighteen judges, in charge in particular of the trial of Laurent Gbagbo and Charles Blé Goudé, Cuno Tarfusser didn't mince his words when the magazine of the Bar Association near the ICC asked him for his opinion of the institution. While deeming it a "fantastic instrument", he stated bluntly: "*The Court certainly cannot continue on the same path because, as has been said, its credibility is very low, both internally in relation to staff whose morale is at an all-time low, and externally in relation to informed observers.*" As for the fairness of the procedures used at the ICC, the Italian judge is no more tender: "*If we now look at our procedures over years and years, in the absence of statutory time limits that could simplify the procedure, if we take into account the fact that even the maximum time limits linked to the different phases of the procedure are not fixed for detention, I have doubts as to whether the procedure can be defined as fair overall.*" In the mouth of an eminent member of the institution, the diagnosis is implacable. It reflects the doubts and criticisms that have marred the image of this court, which is supposed to deliver irreproachable international justice. The U.S. government itself got involved to deny the ICC any legitimacy, as soon as there was talk of an investigation into certain actions by the U.S. army in Afghanistan.

Presumed innocent, Laurent Gbagbo will have been detained for more than seven years awaiting trial!

His trial and its collateral effects will have done much to crack the facade of an institution that sought to be above political influence and suspicion.

Proceeding through a system of successive deadlocks, first prosecutors Luis Moreno Ocampo and then Fatou Bensouda blithely twisted the principles of law to their own liking. The decision to transfer Laurent Gbagbo to The Hague was taken firstly in violation of Ivorian law, as it was not validated by the Abidjan Court of Appeal, but rather by the Korhogo Court, and secondly in total disregard of international law.

It should be remembered that the International Criminal Court is based on the Rome Statute: no national of a country that has not signed the Statute can be brought before the ICC, as is explicitly specified in the founding texts. However, at the end of November 2011, when Gbagbo was transferred to The Hague, Côte d'Ivoire had not signed the Rome Statute. Alassane Ouattara would only sign it in 2013, illegally, as the Ivorian Constitution did not allow him to do so! He amended it in 2015 to erase the problem.

As this book recounts, arrangements had been made on the bangs of all legality between Luis Moreno Ocampo, Nicolas Sarkozy and Alassane Ouattara, in a secret meeting in Paris on November 26, 2011, to ship Gbagbo to the Netherlands. This was done just three days later. These diplomatic connivances have since been documented, and proven, by the publication of indisputable email exchanges between the Quai d'Orsay and the ICC prosecutor, in early October 2017. The International Consortium of Investigative Journalists, which published them in Mediapart in France, and *Le Soir*, in Belgium. The emails detail Moreno Ocampo's pressing requests to Paris from April 11, 2011, the day Gbagbo was arrested, to detain and transfer him to the ICC. This despite the fact that, at that point in the case, no indictment proceedings had been launched against him, and that the legal framework did not exist - as we saw above - to allow the ICC to issue such a request.

Jerry Rawlings, President of Ghana from 1992 to 2000, and a widely respected figure in Africa, described Gbagbo's arrest and transfer, outside the rule of law, as a "kidnapping".

It's true that Moreno Ocampo didn't pull any punches: he unashamedly developed relations with Alassane Ouattara, even before the fall of Laurent Gbagbo, to the detriment of the most elementary impartiality.

When Fatou Bensouda succeeded him as Prosecutor, she disregarded her commitments and proceeded in the same way. She fed her case against Laurent Gbagbo to the Ivorian authorities in place, i.e. the victors supported by France and the UN, and failed to examine the crimes - numerous and proven though they were - of the Ouattara camp. A one-way investigation.

The course of the Gbagbo trial, from its preliminary phase designed to establish the charges against the accused, turned to the prosecution's disadvantage. For example, a videotape intended to show the repression of an anti-Gabgbo demonstration in Abidjan turned out to have been shot in Kenya, during post-election unrest in Nairobi...

Laurent Gbagbo's defense dismantled one by one the prosecutor's arguments and the four main grounds of the accusation. So much so that in June 2013, as the charges were not sufficient to go to trial, it would have been fair and logical to release the defendant. Fatou Bensouda was therefore exceptionally given another year to improve her copy. A year later, she submitted a near-fac-simile of her first case. This time, on the basis of unchanged arguments, two out of three judges validated Madame Bensouda's wish to go to trial.

One detail, however, may cast doubt on the modus operandi that led to the trial: it was the voice of the German judge who swung the decision. A judge who left the ICC a week later for health reasons, and died a month later. Was he able and fit to vote during the examination of the Gbagbo case, and was his vote available? No one knows. Laurent Gbagbo's defense requested an inquiry, which was refused.

The big trial thus opened on January 28, 2016, and turned out to be a confusion for the prosecution: not only did it fail at any point to establish the slightest proof of Laurent Gbagbo's guilt, but it actually helped to clear him of the charges against him. Of the eighty-two witnesses called by the prosecution to "charge Gbagbo", not one did so. A few timid attempts, quickly nullified by blatant lies derived from memorized speeches, were dashed by a few key witnesses, including the heads of the army and gendarmerie, now at the service of the state headed by Alassane Ouattara. No, they asserted, there had been no criminal plan or order of any kind from those in power under Laurent Gbagbo. There were even ardent defenders of the deposed president among those whom the Court had summoned to hear the accused's case… Fatou Bensouda therefore gave up hearing the one hundred and thirty-eight witnesses cited, and stopped at the eighty-second, without having proved anything other than the emptiness of her case.

Faced with this setback, the ICC had to react, if only to save its own credibility - and break the final deadlock to which the tactical impasses of the Prosecutor's office had led it. Presiding Judge Cuno Tarfusser and his two deputies have all the facts in hand.

Laurent Gbagbo's lawyers were therefore granted a hearing for an outright acquittal, without even hearing his defense witnesses. Who's afraid of a released Laurent Gbagbo?

The death on November 3 of Abdouramane Sangaré, his long-standing companion whom Simone Gbagbo called "the friend of all days", cast a shadow over the final days of Laurent Gbagbo's stay in The Hague. Sangaré, whom Gbagbo met at Abidjan University in 1970, a former minister who was arrested with his friend in 2011 and detained for two years, held at arm's length back home the loyal followers of the FPI, whose motto is a frank "Gbagbo or nothing". He said publicly, like Gbagbo: *"If I die, step over my body to continue the struggle. Moses didn't enter the Promised Land. I don't know if I'm going to enter the Promised Land. If I don't, keep up the fight"*. This is the cry from the heart, and the vocation, shared by Laurent Gbagbo and his family for half a century in Côte d'Ivoire.

BIBLIOGRAPHY

AGBOHOU Nicolas, *Le Franc CFA et l'euro contre l'Afrique*, Solidarité Mondiale, 2000.

ADLER Laure, *L'Année des adieux*, Flammarion, 1995.

DELTOMBE Thomas, DOMERGUE Manuel, TATSITSA Jacob, *Kamerun! Une guerre cachée aux origines de la Françafrique, 1948-1971*, La Découverte, 2011. Guillaume, *Pourquoi je suis devenu un rebelle*, Hachette, 2005.

YAMGNANE Kofi, *Afrique, introuvable démocratie*, Éditions Dialogues, 2013.

KESSIE Raymond, *Laurent Ghagbo, au center d'un complot*, L'Harmattan, 2013.

KOULIBALY Mamadou, *La Guerre de la France contre la Côte d'Ivoire*, L'Harmattan, 2003.

LABERTIT Guy, *Adieu, Abidjan-sur-Seine! Behind the scenes of the Ivorian conflict*, Autres Temps Éditions, 2008.

NEYRAC Georges, *Ivoire Nue*, Éditions Jacob-Duvernet, 2005.

DUVAL Philippe, *Fantômes d'Ivoire*, Éditions du Rocher, 2003.

GLASER Antoine and SMITH Stephen, *Comment la France a perdu l'Afrique*, Éditions Calmann-Lévy, 2005.

GUISNEL Jean (dir.), FALIGOT Roger (dir.), *Histoire secrète de la Ve République*, La Découverte, 2007.

HUGEUX Vincent, *Reines d'Afrique: le roman vrai des premières dames*, Perrin, 2014.

KAHN Jean-François, *L'Horreur médiatique*, Plon, 2014.

KONAN BÉDIÉ Henri, *Les Chemins de ma vie*, Plon, 1999.

KOUDOU Christophe, *Le Crocodile et le Scorpion: la France et la Côte d'Ivoire (1999-2013)*, Éditions du Rocher, 2013.

NOTIN Jean-Christophe, Le Crocodile et le Scorpion, Le Rocher, 2013.

PÉAN Pierre, *La République des mallettes*, Fayard, 2011.

SEHOUÉ Germain, *Le Commandant Invisible raconte la bataille d'Abidjan*, L'Harmattan, 2012.

TABLE OF CONTENTS

Best sellers Max Milo Editions

Hitler's banker, Jean-François Bouchard

Confessions of a forger, Éric Piedoie Le Tiec

The Koran and the flesh, Ludovic-Mohamed Zahed

Governing by fake news, Jacques Baud

Governing by chaos, Collectif

A political history of food, Paul Ariès

Mad in U.S.A.: The ravages of the "American model",
Michel Desmurget

Mondial soccer club geopolitics, Kévin Veyssière

Putin: Game master?, Jacques Braud

Treatise on the three impostors: Moses, Jesus, Muhammad,
The Spirit of Spinoza

TV Lobotomy, Michel Desmurget